WHAT THEY ARE SAYING ABOUT

MAN IN THE GAP

"Brette Simmons masterfully presents an insightful look at the life of Swansea, South Carolina Hall of Fame high school coach, Doug Bennett, in *Man in the Gap*. He features several players and assistant coaches, provides intriguing anecdotes and highlights thrilling championship moments. Skillfully written, enjoyable read, a real winner.

A.J. Carr
Award-winning Sportswriter
Raleigh News & Observer
North Carolina Sports Hall of Fame

"Brette Simmons has captured both the nuances and details of how one man's life, character, and example can influence others in a positive and lasting way. Coach Bennett's story is an inspiration to inspire others."

Dick Sheridan
College Football Hall of Fame, 2020
Head Coach, Furman University 1978-1985
Head Coach, N.C. State University 1986-1993

"A treasure of a read about a Palmetto State treasure. Doug Bennett was a distinguished high school coach in South Carolina and ordinarily that would be impressive enough by itself. But what resonates more is the humanity and courage he showed in standing up for public-school integration when so many in his community and his state were profoundly – and even violently – opposed to it. By not staying quiet, by going against the segregationist grain, Bennett showed true servant leadership. Instead of ignoring the history that happened away from the Xs and Os, Brette Simmons digs deeply into it and provides a rich sense of place in chronicling the life of a remarkable man."

Larry Williams
Author, *Dabo's Dynasty: Clemson's Rise to College Football Supremacy*

"With depth and skill, Brette Simmons presents a moving tribute to his high school football coach, Doug Bennett, a man of unwavering faith and integrity, who, during his 36 years as a teacher, coach, and mentor in Swansea, South Carolina, touched and influenced the lives of an entire community."

Mike O'Cain
Head Coach, N.C State University, 1993-1999

"Way to go Coach! I loved it! It reminded me of so many instances and coaches in my own life. What a treasure!"

Bob D. Winstead
Founder, National Youth Football Organization

"A great read, not only for football fans, but for anyone who appreciates a well-detailed reminder – told through the lives of real people – of how the greatest generation directly impacted the culture of a nation."

Abe Hardesty
Former Sportswriter, The Greenville News

"Throughout the years, high school coaches have so richly impacted a tremendous number of young people across our country. Brette Simmons captures how Coach Doug Bennett, his high school coach, was such a positive difference maker in his own life, and that of so many young football players in the community of Swansea, South Carolina. In *Man in the Gap*, he richly illustrates the amazing legacy Coach Bennett has left behind. For anyone who has played sports, this book will resonate.

Eric Hyman
Collegiate Athletics Consultant
Former Athletics Director: Texas A & M University, University of South Carolina, Texas Christian University, Miami of Ohio University, and Virginia Military Institute

MAN IN THE GAP

MAN IN THE GAP

THE LIFE, LEADERSHIP, AND LEGACY
OF DOUG BENNETT:

WWII VETERAN, DEDICATED EDUCATOR,
AND HALL-OF-FAME COACH

BY BRETTE SIMMONS

Charleston, SC
www.PalmettoPublishing.com

Man in the Gap

First Edition

Paperback ISBN: 978-1-64990-053-1
Hardcover ISBN: 978-1-64111-681-7
eBook ISBN: 978-1-64990-901-5

I searched for someone to stand in the gap…
but I found no one.

Ezekiel 22:30

ACKNOWLEDGMENTS

When the idea to write a book about Doug Bennett was in its infancy, I had a conversation with Dr. Robert Maddox, superintendent of Lexington County District Four schools, during which he told me that there had been six Bennett brothers who had served in World War II and, further, that all had returned home. As we discussed how few people knew about them, I was incredulous. "Someone has to tell their story," I declared. Robert replied, "Brette, I think you're the person who needs to tell this story." I accepted the challenge, but what I thought would be a daunting task turned into a labor of love. For Dr. Maddox's support I am truly grateful.

I owe a debt of gratitude to Beverly Bennett Olson, who shared with me treasured stories she had recorded for posterity on her laptop during conversations with her dad about his childhood, his high school years, his service in World War II, his college days, and the beginning of his career as a high school teacher and coach. Without these accounts, writing this book would have been an arduous task. Additionally, her fact-checking done in collaboration with Coach Bennett uncovered some errors in the sequence and timing of events. This scrutiny, along with some suggestions about phrasing, resulted in improved and accurate accounts.

I am grateful to Swansea High School media specialists, Emily Taylor and Melissa Broadway, who provided access to yearbooks from 1954-1955 through 1989-1990 as well as a copy machine. Lee Heinrich offered valuable guidance in the early stages of this project. Amber Stokes and Perry Simmons did some significant editing of the early chapters.

Several people granted me interviews. All were patient and generous with their time. Their completed profiles were submitted to them for their approval to ensure accuracy and the intended representation of the thoughts and sentiments each had expressed. In these profiles you will learn a great deal about the individual, but each will also reveal much about the character and professionalism of Doug Bennett.

The game accounts and feature articles by several sports journalists made a significant contribution to this book. Among these were Mac McGrew, Bill Mitchell, Neil White, Mary Henry, David Shelton, Jeff Staser, and Skylar Rolstad. Dave Pickren's excellent website, *schighschoolfootballhistory.com*, was an invaluable resource.

My sincere thanks to my college football teammate and fellow author David Middleton. Our weekly two-hour writing and brainstorming sessions kept our projects moving forward. David's insights and encouragement were instructive and motivational. Colonel Lee Flake, US Army, (retired,) my high school quarterback, called me on a biweekly basis to encourage me and hold me accountable. It motivated me to know that I had to answer not only to "The Colonel," but to a true friend.

Dr. Steve O'Neil, professor of history at Furman University and a college teammate, offered a paper he delivered on the desegregation of Greenville (SC) schools as well as a bibliography of related works that proved to be valuable resources. These sources formed the framework for my chapter on the court-ordered desegregation of Lexington County District Four schools in 1968.

Special thanks to a friend from my college days, Amy Grant, whose recommendation of a book, *The War of Art,* provided the information and impetus to help me persevere through a period of staunch resistance during the creative process.

Later in the project, when I got a bit ahead of myself and started to speculate about the cinematic potential of the Doug Bennett story - a children's circus during the Great Depression, six brothers in World War II, racial unrest in the Jim Crow South in 1968, and the excitement of Friday night football - retired FBI agent Vic Holdren, a friend, proved to be the voice of reason when he wryly suggested to me, "It might be a good idea to finish the book first."

Throughout this project, at different junctures, dear friends offered encouragement and insight: Rick Lovett, Shawna Mills, Richard Bielat, Dee Markantes, Kim Ledford, Manny Garcia, Chris Wilson, Terry Southard, and Gayle Middleton. Several people, too numerous to mention here, stepped up and contributed to a gofundme.com fundraiser to help cover publishing, publicity, and marketing costs. Their generous donations helped make this tribute to Doug Bennett a reality.

Finally, no endeavor in life is ultimately worthwhile without family with whom to share both the highs and the lows. My two sons, Perry and Landon, have been in my corner throughout this process. Their love and support are a gift from above. My brother, Kevin Simmons, an aspiring writer in his own right, was inquisitive and supportive. As the last family member on my dad's side living in Swansea, he had a particular interest in the life story of Doug Bennett and his impact on that community.

My extended family offered encouraging morale support and substantial financial backing for this project: Sue and Henry Stanford, Susan and Marty Escoe, Anna and Ryan Chavis, Emily Escoe, Margie and David White, Spencer and Lisa White, Kay and Tim Hiott, Katie and Tim Whitson, Marci and Mary Stanford, and Ty and Brooke Stanford.

FOREWORD

The year was 1956, and Doug Bennett was in his third year as a young teacher and coach in Swansea, South Carolina. On his way home one afternoon, he noticed two young children attempting to play baseball with a stick for a bat and a crumpled condensed milk carton for a makeshift ball. Struck by their undaunted spirit and their ingenuity despite their want, Coach Bennett resolved to do something. He spoke with the boys for a few minutes, and then he set out to do what he thought was the right thing. From a bag of the used baseball equipment at the high school, Coach Bennett selected a bat and a baseball and went back and gave them to the boys.

For decades, few people would know anything about this - except the children and their families and friends. Then, on the evening of June 2, 1990, in Doug Bennett Stadium during "Doug Bennett Appreciation Day," a celebration to honor him for his thirty-nine -year career in high school teaching and athletics upon his retirement, the story of his quiet and powerful kindness to two young men was retold. After the reading of a joint resolution from the South Carolina General Assembly, State Senator Joe Wilson presented to Coach Bennett the Order of the Palmetto, the highest recognition awarded by the governor to a private citizen in the state of South Carolina.

Prior to Bennett receiving this honor, Andy Smith, a 1966 graduate of Monroe Pinkney High School and a member of the Lexington County District Four School board in Swansea, strode to the podium as a speaker on the docket with other community leaders and invited dignitaries. Mr. Smith explained how he had never had the opportunity to be taught by or to play for Coach Bennett but that he had been impacted by the man: "When I was eight years old and two or three of us were trying to practice baseball, this man stopped his car and spoke with us for a couple of minutes. Then about thirty or forty-five minutes later he came back - with a baseball and a bat and he gave them to us."

Andy and his friend were African American children growing up in the racially divided Jim Crow South. Astounded that a white man "from the other side of town" would behave with such generosity, young Andy pondered on that day for years to come: "Why would he have done that?" Over thirty years after Doug Bennett's drive home, his actions still resonated in Andy's life and in Swansea's black community at large.

In what may have been the most eloquent words spoken from the podium that day, Andy encapsulated Doug Bennett's life of unselfish service to others: "He gave us something for nothing."

Athletes don't remember techniques, drills, or coaching philosophies. They remember coaches. They remember how those coaches made them feel as a person and the impact they had on their lives.

Allistair McCaw

PROLOGUE

"WHAT WE DO IN LIFE ECHOES IN ETERNITY."
ROMAN GENERAL MAXIMUS, IN *GLADIATOR*

This book is more than a tribute to one of the most remarkable men of what journalist Tom Brokaw has called "the Greatest Generation": Douglas McDowell Bennett. This book is a memoir that lends itself as a testimony to the power of the profound influence of one man who decided early in life to serve his country and later to serve his community by being a high school teacher and coach.

One of six brothers in a family from York, South Carolina (all of whom served in World War II), Doug Bennett joined his brothers when he enlisted in 1944 and was assigned to the Philippines. He was the only Bennett brother who was purposefully held out of combat, and though some of his brothers repeatedly faced dangerous situations in a war where 416,800 American servicemen were killed, all six brothers returned home safely.

After the war, Doug enrolled in Erskine College in the quiet town of Due West. Doug joined three of his older brothers Charlie, Bill, and Stanley, at Erskine after he was released from duty. Though diminutive in stature, Bennett became a starting halfback for a Flying Fleet football squad that defeated college football power Florida State fourteen to six in 1948 (albeit in the Seminoles' inaugural season after the school converted to coeducational from a women's college.) He played halfback on offense and defense from 1947-1950.

Bennett's first job in coaching and teaching was as an assistant coach at Fort Mill, South Carolina. After serving there for two years, he accepted the head coaching position at Sharon High School. It was here that he experienced his first win as a head coach, a victory that he calls his "most thrilling" to this day. The next summer, through a series of serendipitous events and circumstances, Doug Bennett came to Swansea, South Carolina, a sleepy, working-class community, twenty-one miles from the state capital of Columbia. He was at Swansea High School for thirty-six years.

Doug Bennett's influence interweaves throughout the fabric of my family. In 1965, as a nine-year-old fourth grader, I moved to Swansea, where my dad had grown up and missed, by a few years, being coached by Doug Bennett. His sister, Sue Simmons, played on Coach Bennett's girls' basketball team in his first year in Swansea, 1954. Just two years prior to Doug Bennett's arrival, my mom, Shirley Yvonne Jeffcoat, a cheerleader for football, elected by her peers as "Most Studious" and "Most Likely to Succeed," had served as manager for the girls' basketball team in Sue's freshman year. In 1955, Henry Stanford, a young clerk in Sessions' department store in downtown Swansea, served as Doug Bennett's first unofficial manager / assistant coach who offered to "do whatever Coach Bennett needed me to do." He later married Sue Simmons. My mom's younger brother, Reginald, would become a starting right tackle on Coach Bennett's 1954 and 1955 Tiger offensive line opposite his bosom buddy, left tackle W. B. Adkins, one of the greatest players in Tiger history.

Coach Bennett had been in Swansea thirteen years when I met him in 1967. As a sixth grader, I played on the Swansea "midget" football team coached by "Red" Smith. I enthusiastically embraced the sport, and I would often linger after the "midget" practices to watch Coach Bennett and the high school team run through drills. I was intrigued by Coach Bennett, this man who, though short in stature, seemed to stand so tall with a quiet confidence and an air of dignity and class. For reasons unbeknownst to me, Coach Bennett took notice of me as well and invited me to serve as a manager for the varsity football program for the next season. Life, for me, would never be the same.

My sports idol as a young teenager was the Louisiana State University basketball superstar "Pistol Pete" Maravich: floppy socks, forty-four points per game. As a sixth grader, I could be seen throughout town dribbling a basketball almost everywhere I went, just as Pete had as a kid. But football is king in South Carolina, and by encouraging my interest in football and then recruiting me to become a team manager for the Swansea Tigers, Doug Bennett helped convert another devotee to our state's favorite pastime. As he had done with countless young men before and after me, he included me when he did not have to and gave me an opportunity to hang around the players that I had admired since coming to Swansea. I was hooked!

As a manager for Coach Bennett's 1968 and 1969 Tiger football teams, I never tired of the Saturday mornings when we washed the uniforms from the previous night's game while devouring Coach Bennett's stories about hilarious moments in bygone seasons. I remember watching him pause in near awe and wonder at the skill and toughness of former players like Benny Shivers, Kit Jackson, and W. B. Adkins, and I remember him shouting "dadgummit" well before the legendary college coach Bobby Bowden popularized this folksy exclamation in the eighties. In fact, Coach Bennett even coined a few expressions of his own: "golly buck" and "by cracky" being the most familiar, remembered with fondness by his players to this day.

During my elementary school years in Swansea before I met Coach Bennett, I had faithfully watched broadcasts of Atlantic Coast Conference basketball. I loved to watch the UNC Tar Heels like Rusty Clark, Larry Miller, Dick Grubar, Mitch Kupchak, and countless others. My absolute favorite player was Charlie Scott, the first African American scholarship basketball signee at UNC and in the ACC. In recruiting Mr. Scott to UNC in 1966, Dean Smith had taken a great risk that created a paradigm shift that shook the South.

Many other courageous, principled men would follow his example, standing for what was right and just. To be sure, it was a risk that was rewarded - UNC made three consecutive Final Four appearances in '67, '68, and '69, with Scott playing a major role in the Tar Heels' success. But Coach Smith had ignored - even defied - his critics. In his mind, it was time for change.

On February 7, 2015, basketball fans in the Raleigh-Durham-Chapel Hill area and across the nation lost a coaching icon and a national treasure when Dean Smith passed from this life into the hereafter. Said Michael Jordan, UNC great and NBA superstar, "Other than my parents, no one had more influence on my life than Coach Smith. He was more than a coach - he was my mentor, my teacher, my second father."

Coach Smith's innovations, such as a team huddle prior to a free throw, the "run and jump" defense, and the infamous "four corners" offense, set him apart from his peers as a master tactician. Other effective practices such as having a scorer point to the teammate whose assist set up the basket, freshmen carrying the team's luggage on road trips, and Coach Smith's "Thought for the Day" were wisely implemented to encourage team unity and to keep eager, uber-talented "hotshots" grounded and humble.

Not only his coaching genius but also his insistence upon team play became the gold standard for aspiring young coaches. Roy Williams, who followed in Coach Smith's footsteps when he became the head coach at UNC in 2004, said of his mentor's passing: "As sad as I am, I also feel very blessed because he was a great influence on me. I cannot imagine anyone being a better influence than Dean Smith."

Eight miles east of Chapel Hill, Duke University, home of the "Cameron Crazies," has hosted its share of intense rivalry games between Coach Smith's Tar Heels and the Blue Devil squads of a Bobby Knight disciple, the fiery Mike Krzyzewski. Despite obvious tension between these two headstrong competitors in early face-to-face contests, they came to respect and admire one another with each passing year in this bitter rivalry. Coach K noted with sadness, "We lost a man who cannot be replaced. He was one of a kind, and the sport of basketball lost one of its true pillars."

Krzyzewski further praised his worthy adversary who was "clearly ahead of his time in dealing with social issues. However, his greatest gift was his unique ability to teach what it takes to be a good man. That was easy for him because he was a great man himself." ESPN commentator Bomani Jones, who made his bones as a local sports radio host in The Triangle, added via Twitter, "Dean, basically, unilaterally decided to integrate ACC basketball, dared someone to say no. No one did."

Innovator, brilliant strategist, social activist, husband, and father, Dean Smith modeled for others what a well-rounded, balanced man who happened to be a basketball coach looked like, and he was loved for it. Former UNC and LA Lakers power forward James Worthy from Gastonia, North Carolina, spoke for many others when he said, "There are so many things I could say about Coach Smith but simply put, he was the greatest man I've ever known."

Just over forty years after I had graduated from Swansea High School, the death of this basketball giant caused me to reflect on the profound impact that the coaching giant in my life, Doug Bennett, had upon me and the community where I grew up. As a long procession of Coach Smith's former players (224 senior players in thirty-six seasons), opposing coaches, educators, journalists, and fans expressed their love and admiration for this coaching giant, I slowly began to recall poignant moments from my youth when I, too, had experienced a similar relationship with a role-model coach. For the three weeks following Coach Smith's death, I listened to the testimonials about the man's coaching prowess and strength of character, and I could not help but think of my own privilege of playing for, and, more importantly, of knowing one of the finest human beings to ever grace this planet, Swansea High School's head football coach from 1954 to 1989, Douglas McDowell Bennett.

Many parallels can be drawn from the lives of these two men who each served their community for thirty-six years, but important distinctives set them apart. Doug Bennett conducted a more quietly distinguished career, serving in relative obscurity in a rural community. Doug Bennett may not have been the tactical innovator Dean Smith was for basketball, but Coach Bennett was a genius in doing more with less, with an unsurpassed talent for getting the most out of his players. And though Doug Bennett may not have "unilaterally decided to integrate ACC basketball," he did skillfully lead a team and community through the challenges of federally mandated desegregation at one of the first integrated high schools in a state that only a century before had seceded from the Union to perpetuate the institution of slavery. Doug Bennett proved a quiet and effective advocate for the cause for justice and racial equality in the sixties South.

One of Dean Smith's lasting principles was his insistence that the player who scored on any possession for the Tar Heels instantly acknowledge the value of team basketball by pointing to the player who had set up his basket with a deft and timely pass. Indeed, Coach Smith modeled this foundational building block of his basketball program by immediately deflecting praise from the media and fans to his players and assistant coaches. In view of Coach Smith's habit of acknowledging the excellence in others, I believe that if Dean Smith had known Doug Bennett, Coach Smith would be pointing his index finger at the football coach/teacher/principal from South Carolina, deferring to him in humble admiration of a life well-lived in the service of others.

THE WONDER YEARS 1926-1944

"IF YOU WANT YOUR CHILDREN TO TURN OUT WELL,
SPEND TWICE AS MUCH TIME WITH THEM
AND HALF AS MUCH MONEY ON THEM."
AUTHOR UNKNOWN

Born on August 26, 1926, Douglas McDowell Bennett was the youngest boy of the eight children born to Olive McDaniel and Charles Pinkney Bennett, who raised their six boys and two girls in the bustling town of York, South Carolina. Charles served for twenty-five years with the police force in York after leaving farming as a young man to move into the town of York to work in the textile industry with Cannon Mills. Olive, after marrying "C.P." when he was twenty-six and she was nineteen, worked full-time as a stay-at-home mom with eight children, seven of whom were born two years apart.

On October 27, 1929, two months after Doug Bennett had turned three and on a day that came to be known as Black Thursday, the American stock market hit rock bottom. The intoxicating prosperity and delirious optimism of the

Roaring Twenties came to a crashing halt when, in less than two hours, over thirty billion dollars in stocks - much of it purchased in speculative investments with borrowed money - were sold off during a panic. British Prime Minister Winston Churchill, who had invested heavily in the American market, lost a fortune that day, the same day that, ironically, he had paid a visit to Wall Street. Millions of Americans lost everything.

The shock waves from this unprecedented financial catastrophe rippled throughout the nation - and the world. Within two years of the crash, three thousand American banks had closed their doors as American consumer confidence was shaken to the core and fearful customers withdrew their money. Companies, to stop their own financial bleeding, laid off workers in droves. Unemployment soared.

And no one - certainly not the Wall Street bankers and brokers whose greed and cavalier financing of wildly speculative investing had led to the crash - felt the painful after-effects more than the average American family. In many cases, dad, the family bread winner, lost his job. American farmers - even before the market crash - had begun to declare bankruptcy or experience the humiliating loss of farmland that had been in their families for generations. Poverty was pervasive and insidious. Bread and soup lines were on every other street corner in major metropolitan areas, or so it seemed.

Raising a family with eight children during the Great Depression, which lasted until the onset of World War II in 1939, became a daunting task. Olive Bennett more than answered the bell. To stretch her food budget, Mama created "egg gravy." She fried up fatback to be served for breakfast and then took the grease and mixed it with flour. She then broke an egg and mixed it all together to serve over mush made from cornmeal and cooked like grits, which were more expensive.

The Bennetts had a cow for milking, and they raised two or three hogs each year and butchered them for sausage and other pork cuts. A garden supplied fresh vegetables. But no matter what was served at the Bennett family table, there was an understanding that if you were late, you might miss out.

To help keep her boys as well-dressed as possible, Olive made "Sunday best" clothing from the blue serge wool of her husband's older police uniforms to supplement a wardrobe that included, for the younger boys, hand-me-downs. Each year every Bennett child was given one pair of shoes, which was to last them for the entire year. And so, to help to preserve their footwear for the cold months of winter, the children went barefoot throughout the summers. One year, Bill decided to push going barefooted to the limit. He went without shoes until Thanksgiving!

It was during the fall of 1929 - when the children were wearing their shoes - that "the circus came to town." In September, when the Barnett Brothers Circus - created in 1927 in Canada and the first motorized circus to enter the United States from Canada - finished its American tour in Easley, South Carolina, organizer and show businessman William Hamilton leased a lot in downtown York as the circus's winter quarters. Arriving with a fleet of thirty-five Chevrolet trucks, seven trailers, five passenger cars, and 130 personnel, Hamilton chose a lot that had water and electricity located near a railroad in case he might later decide to travel the show by train.[1]

Nancy Sambets, archivist for the Yorkville Historical Society and Cultural and Heritage Museums, has chronicled the history of the Barnett Brothers Circus's annual wintering in York and its growing relationship with the townspeople over the years from 1929 through World War II. According to Sambets, the show first occupied a stone livery stable on 6 East Jefferson Street and soon after acquired two lots across from the livery stable on which Rogers eventually built a metal-clad building and other buildings to house a cookhouse, dining room, sleeping quarters equipped with showers for men, and a lumber shed.

The circus elephants occupied a "bull building" located behind Trinity Methodist Church and spent time tethered to a "bull line" in the northwest corner of the lot. Many locals would turn out to see the elephants walked along East Jefferson Street for exercise. They also visited the lot to look at the elephants and other circus animals. For years, in December, the circus animals, and especially the elephants, were popular features in the York Christmas parade with Santa arriving on an elephant.[2]

Soon after the circus arrived in York, the sons of C.P. and Olive Bennett were inspired to start their own children's circus. When the Bennett family moved from their home located next door to the York School on Lincoln Street, the boys practiced and performed on a lot across from their new home. Ray Rogers, the owner of the Barnett Brothers Circus, enthusiastically supported the children by allowing them to use a big tent and seats for their shows. The Bennett Brothers Circus shows featured trapeze work, acrobatic tumbling, handsprings, wire walking, rope spinning, juggling, and clowns. Allowed by Rogers to use some of the animals from his circus, the Bennett Brothers Circus included bareback riding, dancing dogs, and a trick pony named Billy Sunday. There was even a Wild West show with roping and wrestling matches.[3]

The second-oldest Bennett brother, Joe, organized the circus in 1930 when he was twelve. He served as the manager and ringmaster while his younger brothers, Charles, Bill, Stanley, and Doug, were performers. Joe's ability as a promoter and hustler was captured by someone in the family who declared that "Joe could sell a two-dollar bill for five dollars." Bill, who Doug viewed as the most athletic of all the brothers, was proficient on a trampoline and could walk on his hands, including climbing steps. Bill could also jump rope while standing up on the back of a horse as it circled the ring. He and Doug had a tumbling routine that they performed when Doug was four years old. Charlie was skilled on the trapeze and also with wire walking.

In 1937, the oldest Bennett child, Orin, joined his siblings in the circus. It soon became a family joke that Orin waited to join the family circus until it "got famous." Orin formed a jazz band known as the Dinah-mites, and the two Bennett sisters, Vera and Bonnie, were musicians. An announcer used a loudspeaker to introduce each of the acts performed in a standard circus ring. By 1938, there were thirty child performers.[4]

The Bennett Brothers Circus performed each year from April to August in York and traveled to Rock Hill, Sharon, Clover, and Chester, always opening with a parade with horseback riders, bicycles, a band, and performers. On circus days, a late afternoon performance was held around 4:00 pm with admission charges of ten cents for children and twenty-five cents for adults. The circus also offered concessions with ice cream, peanuts, and soft drinks. According to newspaper accounts, their shows routinely drew crowds of about three hundred. The Bennett Brothers Circus ran for nine years, ending in 1938 when most of the children had grown older, gone to college, taken jobs, or joined the armed services.[5]

To this day, Doug Bennett celebrates the fact that their children's circus was integrated. Of the thirty children, three were black: John and Hazel Gore, "around ten to twelve years old," and Sam Powell, who was "fifteen or sixteen." The Gore brothers worked in circus operations. Sam was a buck dancer.

One incident set Hazel apart from even the adults in the Barnett Brothers Circus. It seems that the circus bison, which the children had borrowed from the main circus, escaped. When it came time for the circus to start, the entire crew was outside trying to corral the animal. To control the bison, a ring had been embedded in its nose. Young Hazel was the one person who was finally able to ease up to the animal, catch him, and keep him under control.

According to Doug Bennett, Sam Powell was a fantastic buck dancer who would "...dance awhile then stop to tell a joke - dance some more then stop to tell another joke." He remembers one particular joke that always drew a laugh from the crowd: Said Sam, "When my girl said, 'Sam, how are you?' I said, 'Like a barrel of molasses,' So she asked, 'How's that?' And I said, 'Black and sticky and sweet, oh Lord!"

Buck dancing is similar to a folk dance, clogging, only faster and involving more advanced levels of skill. Bennett's two oldest daughters, Susan and Beverly, were participants in a dance competition in Cherokee, North Carolina, which featured clogging and buck dancing. Beverly describes the buck dancing: "Some young kids from the hills, maybe ages four or five, were doing it. (Their) feet moved faster than anything I had ever seen. I'm not sure, but it's got to be a regional thing, obviously passed down and learned at a very early age. Having seen these kids buck dance, I'm sure Sam Powell would have been a tough act to follow. I would love that segment of the circus show!"

Raised for part of their childhood next door to the York School which housed grades one through eleven (there was no twelfth grade in American schools at that time), the Bennett children had no excuse for ever being tardy. And, according to Doug, tardiness was a punishable offense - at least with his first-grade teachers who he called "the meanest thing you saw." According to Doug and the older Bennett children, when this classroom tyrant got extremely frustrated with her students, she slapped them with an open palm. This act of retribution went unchecked by any administrator for years until the district superintendent walked into her classroom unannounced and caught her "red-handed," (perhaps from too many sequential slaps.) Doug said that even though she only slapped him once "up-side my head," he was upset that his classmates were being treated that way.

Doug's strong desire for justice, developed at a tender age, was an integral part of the moral compass that would help Doug navigate his way through youth and into adulthood. He once witnessed the teacher purposely taking a pencil from the desk of one of his friends, throwing it to the floor, and saying to the boy, "Go get it!" Doug winced when next he heard his friend say, "I ain't gonna do it!" As expected, the merciless teacher commenced hitting the poor boy repeatedly on his head, from side to side with the six-year-old ducking with each swat.

Doug Bennett was twelve years old when the Bennett Brothers Circus disbanded as the older Bennett boys - Orin, Joe, Charlie, and Bill - began their individual journeys to find their place in the world. Rarely invited to tag along with their older brothers, Stanley and Duddy, as the two youngest and closest in age, spent a lot of time together, especially after their older brothers left home. And the two of them had a penchant for adventure and mischief.

It seems that Stanley enjoyed doing things to aggravate his younger brother, and Doug would often end up chasing Stanley after one of his annoying antics. Once, when being chased by his kid brother, Stanley turned and punched Duddy in the mouth, dislodging one of his teeth. Unaware that this was one of his permanent teeth, Doug pulled the loose tooth out. Doug did not get the tooth replaced until years later after returning home from a stint in the service. A dentist in York, Dr. Douglas, made a false tooth that he glued in. That same tooth got kicked out when Doug was playing football at Erskine after the war. Doug was able to stick the tooth back in, but it was no longer cemented in. Later, when the Erskine team was traveling to a game at East Tennessee State and stopped at a restaurant, his tooth fell out and shattered on the sidewalk.

Once, while on a visit with their cousins in Patterson, a small community outside of Lenior, North Carolina, Stanley and Doug were inspired by the creativity of their cousins who had taken pieces of a tree trunk and made wheels for a little car. Upon their return to York, the duo cut down a tree and dragged a four-foot piece of the felled tree's trunk about a half mile back home. From a piece of the trunk, they fashioned wheels and a steering wheel for a small car in which they were able to ride.

The concept that "it takes a village to raise a child" was no more true than on East Jefferson Street, and Mrs. Marie Correlle, who lived across the street from the Bennetts, time and again played a significant role in the rearing of the Bennett children. It was in Mrs. Correlle's home that Doug met Anne Harriet, a former slave who by that time was an elderly lady. Early in life Duddy and the other Bennett children had many opportunities to meet and spend time with black children and adults. For years the boys went fishing in a pond near the home of a black couple in town. The Bennett boys would regularly ask the couple's children to go fishing with them. Raised in a home where their parents and neighbors taught them to treat all people with respect and dignity, the Bennett children thought nothing of the color difference.

One teachable moment for the mischievous pair came when Stanley and Doug teamed up to pilfer apples from Mrs. Correlle's prized backyard apple tree. Doug climbed onto a branch of the tree and was dropping apples down to Stanley when Mrs. Correlle came outside and caught them. She promptly took them inside her home and instructed them to sit down at the dining room table where they awaited, in their minds, certain doom, as their parents would soon learn of the incident. Mama Bennett, as a stay-at-home mom, took care of most of the discipline. It was her practice to have the Bennett children pick their own hickory branch with which to be switched. Sometimes the Bennett child in violation had to wait nearly all day for the administering of justice.

However, instead of scolding or threatening them, Mrs. Correlle brought out a beautiful bowl full of red apples and set it down in front of them. She told them, "Eat as many as you want - Those out there aren't very good and probably have worm holes." Stanley, who later in life - after his service as a P47 fighter pilot in World War II - entered the ministry, recalls this surprising reversal of fortune as "the first time I learned what grace was."

When Doug was fifteen, a young circus performer, Jack Heinsohn, came to live with the Bennett family. To make some extra money for the family during the Depression Era, Olive Bennett started taking on boarders in their home, which was located on Main Street by this time. And because she had already taken in Jerry Moskovitz, who was staying in the same room as Doug, Mama Bennett had some concerns - that Jack and Doug would get along - because Jack and Doug were already living in the same room. Specifically, she was afraid that adding another boy might adversely impact the dynamics of the household and possibly increase the squabbling among the teenage boys.

Jack, who soon became like another son to Olive, years later became an ordained Presbyterian minister. At Mama Bennett's funeral, Jack retold the story of coming to live with the Bennett family: "It was easy to see that she really didn't want to keep me. But she agreed to keep me for six weeks until the circus came in. Years later I heard her tell the story and she said, "I was afraid to take in the 'poor little boy' for besides Duddy I was keeping Jerry Moskovitz, and you know how little boys fight. But in a little while, Duddy and Jerry came in, and they began to laugh and pound each other on the back...and I realized they were friends already and everything would be all right. So this poor little boy moved in for six months' which gradually stretched into forty-two years."

Jack's father was a well-known slack rope walker in the Barnett Brothers Circus that wintered each year in York. Jack's parents had split up, and since the circus began to tour in April and did not finish until late in the fall, Jack's dad wanted him to stay with another family in York. When this arrangement did not work out, Jack came to stay with the Bennetts as Olive Bennett was running the York Tourist Home out of the family dwelling.

Doug, Jack, and Jerry Moskovitz all roomed together. Doug and Jack slept in one bed, and Jerry, since he had epileptic seizures, was given his own bed. Ever the pranksters, Doug and Jack delighted in inviting unsuspecting friends to sleep over - since their overnight guest would have to sleep in the same bed with Jerry. Counting on the possibility that Jerry might have a seizure and likely frighten their unaware friend, Doug or Jack would usually say to the other, "I sure hope he has a big seizure!"

It was during this time that Doug began to get involved in high school sports. Nicknamed "Duddy" because that's how his brother Stanley, just two years older, pronounced his name when he was born, Doug played every sport at York High School. At that time there were only three - football, basketball, and baseball. Prior to his high school days, Doug played "midget" football, and the sport became his first love in high school. He played football all four years in high school and basketball and baseball for three years. York had no gymnasium or basketball court, so practices and games were held on the big stage in the auditorium. Doug recalls having to put one foot on the back wall to go up for a layup. Baseball games were played on the football field. Duddy was a shortstop on what he now looks back on as "mediocre" teams. One of the most vivid memories from his baseball days is that of hitting a line drive to right field on what he thought would be an inside-the-park homerun - only to be thrown out at home plate.

While Doug was a very skilled athlete overall, he excelled in football. In a day when sportswriters referred to a football as "the oval" and the goal-line as the "pay line," the fortunes of the York High School Green Dragons rose as he matured as a player - especially during his junior and senior seasons. Bennett played every position in the offensive backfield - quarterback, halfback, and fullback, while backing up the line as a linebacker and also serving as his team's punter and placekicker.

On offense, Doug was lining up in various backfield positions, the origin of whose names may be unfamiliar to fans of modern American football. Logically, the quarterback began each play a quarter of the way back from the ball. The two halfbacks aligned side-by-side halfway back. And the fullback began each play the farthest back. From the 1870s when American football evolved from the game of rugby, the halfback position was both an offensive and a defensive position. On defense, Doug played linebacker. Before the prominence of the T formation, all four backfield positions were legitimate threats to run or pass the ball. Like the York Green Dragons, most teams used four backs on every play.

Prior to 1930, the shape of the football was a somewhat oval shape called a prolate spheroid. Gradually balls were elongated from the melon shape twenty-eight to twenty-two inches in circumference to the modern football measure of twenty-one inches. This reduction made streamlined passes with a spiral possible. During his high school days, Doug became quite adept as a passer from the tailback and fullback positions. As the tailback, Doug called the plays, essentially making him the equivalent of the modern-day quarterback.

Bennett's position in the huddle varied depending upon which position he was playing on a particular play. The huddle, initially a circle in which all players faced inward, was invented by a quarterback at Gallaudet University to prevent opposing teams from seeing the signing he was doing to "call" plays to his deaf teammates. The huddle also served as a form of insulation when the level of noise on the field or in a stadium as such that the normal on-field communication was difficult. During Duddy's playing days at York, a typical crowd was a one hundred to two hundred spectators, with larger crowds when they traveled to away games at larger schools.

For much of the history of football, coaches were not allowed to call plays from the sideline[6] Doug Bennett was the tailback for York his senior year, and since the tailback was tasked with the play calling, Doug called the plays. During his junior and senior seasons, Doug Bennett emerged as a star for the Green Dragons. In a nineteen to zero win over Winnsboro, Duddy Bennett gave his usual good performance. Dubbed by *The Charlotte Observer* as "York's star fullback," Duddy scored three touchdowns against Fort Mill as a junior. Years later - perhaps remembering his outstanding performance in this game - the Fort Mill administration would hire Doug Bennett as an assistant football coach and teacher where he served the first two years of a thirty-nine-year career.

In a few of his more outstanding games, Duddy Bennett was "...practically a one-man show" in a loss to Tech High School in Charlotte. He was "the loser's standout both offensively and defensively." In his final home game as a senior, Duddy, playing with an injured shoulder, scored his team's only touchdown in the second half. The defense added a safety for the winning nine to zero score.

The Green Dragons held on for a six to zero win over Kershaw. The next week, after a week of publicity and buildup leading up to the game, Duddy and his teammates defeated Chester High School for the first time in twenty-five years, fourteen to six at the Chester Fairgrounds: "Bennett spearheaded the York offensive play by scoring both touchdowns and one extra point," that is, thirteen of his team's fourteen points.

Bennett's touchdowns came in the first and the last quarters of the game. Coach P.W. Aycock asserted that the game was won at the line of scrimmage as his line "played the best game of the season," despite playing with two substitutes for their two starting guards. To Coach Aycock's delight, the Green Dragons piled up "between fifteen and twenty first downs, the most scored against any team this season."

This historic win for the York program provided momentum as the Green Dragons prepared for a Thanksgiving Day contest against Gaffney, the first time in several years that these two teams had faced one another: "It is reported that the Gaffney eleven are plenty capable of pushing the pigskin across the pay line, and ranks close to the top in the state this year, but despite those reports the Dragons are in a position to give keen competition."

Seniors remember their last game for a variety of reasons. What Doug Bennett remembers most about his final game with Gaffney is that he played with injuries to both shoulders. During practice the week before the Chester game, he tore the rotator cuff in his left shoulder. Then, in the game against Chester, he had the same injury to his right shoulder.

Against Gaffney he was unable to "wrap up" while attempting to tackle ball carriers. "I had to butt them with my head," Duddy remembers. Bennett was also unable to pass the ball because of his shoulder injuries, so Dusty Oates, the Green Dragons' fullback, had to do the passing. Unfortunately for Doug, his last game in high school would go down as a loss.

BAND OF BROTHERS

"THOSE WHO DO NOT BATTLE FOR THEIR COUNTRY DO NOT KNOW WITH WHAT EASE THEY ACCEPT THEIR CITIZENSHIP IN AMERICA."
DEAN BRELIS

In the 1998 Steven Spielberg film *Saving Private Ryan*, there is a scene in which a black sedan winds its way uphill on an Iowa farm road leading up to the Ryan family home. Standing at the kitchen window watching the car deliberately making its way up the hill, Mrs. Ryan, the mother of four sons, all serving in WWII, is washing dishes. Just before the car reaches the summit, the filmmaker shows a banner gently wafting in the breeze on a beautiful sunny day, a field of red cloth with four blue stars, one for each Ryan son deployed in the war effort.

The sedan stops in front of the Ryan home, a cloud of dust in its wake as Mrs. Ryan opens the screen door to greet the visitors. But when a car door opens and a priest, dressed in his black cleric vestments gets out, the mother of four sons falls to her knees in grief as she knows he has come to comfort her in the loss of a son. Tragically, she is about to be told that not one, but *three* of her four boys have lost their lives in the war. Her greatest fear - that all her precious boys would not return from the war - has come true, but her immense grief is compounded by with the dreadful news that only one child is still alive.

Now imagine, for a moment, the anxiety and fear that may have gripped the hearts of Charles and Olive Bennett, who proudly displayed a banner with not four, but *six* blue stars. During the final year of a war that lasted for 2,174 days and claimed an average of 27,600 lives every day, 1,150 every hour, or nineteen a minute or one death every three seconds,[1] their six sons were deployed in Europe and the Pacific. Remarkably, all six Bennett boys returned home safely.

This little-known story of the six Bennett brothers was recounted to me by Dr. Robert Maddox, superintendent of Lexington District Four schools. When Dr. Maddox told me the story, I was incredulous. We know much about the five O'Sullivan brothers who all died when their ship, *The Juneau*, was struck by a torpedo from a Japanese submarine. Their tragic deaths moved the U.S. War Department to implement the "Sole Survivor Policy." This directive, years later, became the premise for the film *Saving Private Ryan* about a special WWII mission to safely extract from combat the last survivor of the four Ryan brothers.

Yet virtually no one knows about the six Bennett brothers of York. Obviously, the fact that all six brothers returned home safely from the war is not as dramatic as the ultimate sacrifices made by all five O'Sullivans and the three fictional Ryans. But in a day when reality shows generate wealth and fame for (often) people of questionable character who become famous for being famous, why do we know so little about this patriotic family? The inequity and injustice of this historical omission, especially in an age of the proliferation of so much useless information, troubled me.

As the youngest Bennett son who was not of age and had to wait to enlist, Doug was nonetheless the first to learn of the circumstances that brought the United States into WWII. On a Sunday afternoon in early December 1941, Doug went to the Sherer's Drug Store in downtown York after church to buy a Coke at the soda fountain. As he waited, he heard the shocking news on the store's radio that the Japanese had attacked the U.S. naval base at Pearl Harbor. The next morning his entire school assembled and listened to the radio broadcast of President Franklin Delano Roosevelt's "date which will live in infamy" address to Congress. The president urged Congress to declare a state of war against the Japanese Empire.

Orin Bennett, the oldest of the six brothers, was passed over initially in the draft because he was married with two young children. Teased unmercifully by his siblings for waiting to join the Bennett Brothers Circus until after it was successful, Orin was again late to enter the war effort when he was drafted into the infantry and served as a medic in Paris.

Joe Bennett, the second oldest, was drafted first and served with an antiaircraft artillery battalion. Charlie, the third oldest, served in the Army Air Corps as chief mechanic for P47 fighter planes. Joe's unit was a part of the invasion of Nazi-occupied North Africa that chased Field General Rommell's Afrika Korps across North Africa to Sicily and Italy, then France, and finally into Germany in an arduous three-year campaign. In the middle of the North Africa campaign, Joe and Charlie were briefly re-united in Sicily.

Bill, fourth in the birth order of the Bennett boys, enlisted and was assigned to the Army Air Corps, the precursor to the U.S. Air Force.[2] He became a B29 bomber pilot while assigned to Maxwell Air Force Base in Alabama before being shipped out to Guam. The B29 was one of the largest operational aircraft in WWII. At over $3 billion and with state-of-the-art equipment, the B29 was the most expensive weapons project in WWII - using the value of dollars in 1945. Oddly, Bill flew only one bombing mission while in Guam, as most of the missions in that area initiated on another base. He later served several tours as a flight instructor.

Stanley, the fifth brother, attended Clemson for a year and then enlisted. He was assigned to the Army Air Corps, where he became a P47 fighter pilot. The first piston-driven fighter, the P47 Thunderbolt, was built in greater quantities than any other U.S. fighter and could exceed 500 mph. Stanley's missions were flown out of Europe.

The Bennett family did their best to keep up with any news of the war - mainly by radio - and by letters home from the boys. However, the letters their sons sent home were censored for security reasons. "V mail" was reduced from the original size of the letters after being censored. With anything taken out that might aid the enemy, there was little news. But the Bennetts cherished the letters nonetheless.

In February of 1945, Charles and Olive said goodbye to their youngest son, Doug, who had enlisted in the Army Air Corps. As the youngest, Duddy had waited impatiently to join his five older brothers when he would graduate from high school and soon afterward reach the age for enlistment - his eighteenth birthday. Shortly after graduation Doug enlisted in July of 1944 at seventeen without permission from his parents since he was not quite eighteen. He was not called up, however, until February 9, 1945, - about seven months before the end of the war (September 2, 1945).

As a gift for her youngest of eight children, on the day he was called into duty, Olive gave Doug a New Testament of the Bible with the following words inscribed:

Presented to Duddy Bennett by Mama
Feb.9th 1945
Dear boy,
Read your bible daily and say your prayers every night. Trust in the Lord and he will give you strength and protect you from harm.
Mother

Although he had to wait three years to enlist, Doug had been receiving excellent preparation to go into the service by his participation in sports at York, especially football. As Wallace Wade, head football coach at Duke University (1931-1941, 1946-1950) stated:

> "I know of nothing that is a better preparation for a young man who is going into the army than football. The greatest benefits that football gives to a young man is that it teaches him to be a competitor, to never give up, to get back up after you're knocked down. Success in both football and war depends on morale, loyalty, and sound fundamentals."[3]

When Doug entered the Army Air Corps, Bill and Stanley offered him advice: "Don't ever volunteer for anything." When Doug got to Fort Bragg, he didn't volunteer for anything. When he and two other new recruits were the only recruits who had not volunteered for anything, they were taken to the officers' quarters to clean ashes out of the furnaces.

Doug was processed for two weeks at Fort Bragg, (whose population swelled from 5,400 in 1940 to over 70,000 in 1941) before he was sent by train to Biloxi, Mississippi, and assigned to duty at Kessler Field.[4] While Doug was stationed at Keesler, Bill Bennett was at Maxwell Field in Alabama where he was serving as a B29 flight instructor. With his youngest brother stationed so close, Bill went to Biloxi to visit Doug. When Bill arrived at the barracks, he questioned a young private about the whereabouts of his brother and was told that Doug was in the hospital. "You lie," Bill asserted. "Oh, no sir," replied the private. Later Bill found Doug in the hospital where he had had his appendix removed. During their visit, Doug had to repeatedly ask Bill to stop saying things that made him laugh as he was still in pain from the surgery.

While he was training in Biloxi, Doug was sleep-deprived. When he went to see a friend from York, Billy K. Moore who was stationed in Gulfport, Mississippi, Doug experienced the effects of his loss of sleep. Billy K. Moore was the crew chief for a B29 and thus responsible for performing the routine preflight inspection. While Billy went about his duties prepping the plane, Doug was so sleepy that he crawled into the space over one of the bomb bays, which was padded, and fell asleep. The next morning he was awakened by Billy, who told him, "You better get outta here if you don't want to go up with them."

When Doug completed B24 training at Keesler Field, the war had ended, and he was sent to Amarillo, Texas, for B29 training. However, the normal three-month training was cut short when Doug was pulled out of training and assigned to Las Vegas, where he would be processed and trained for an overseas assignment in the Philippines. Doug was first sent by ship to Manilla aboard the *Marine Shark* and spent a couple of days before being sent by train to Clark Field in Luzon. His second or third night there, the "bomb dump" (where all bombs and ammunition were stored) went off as shells and bombs exploded for most of the night.

After being processed at Clark Field, Doug's unit was transported by C46 cargo plane to Palawan, where Doug would spend the next year. When he arrived in the Palawan for his assignment as an aircraft mechanic, most of the fighting in the Pacific Theater had ceased, so Doug served in the "Army of Occupation" after the war had ended. In Palawan, Doug was assigned to supervise a group of Filipino teenagers who were picked up daily from a labor camp. Their assignment was to clean up the area from which the previous labor camp had been moved. Doug's interaction with these young people was cooperative, as they enjoyed teaching him expressions in their native language and having Doug communicate with them using these expressions. This experience made it apparent that Doug Bennett had the right demeanor and gifts for working with young people.

When this detail was completed, Doug was assigned to the motor pool as a mechanic working on jeeps and trucks. Try as he might, Doug could not convince his lieutenant that his training as an airplane mechanic was totally different. "If you can work on planes, you can work on anything," Lieutenant McNair reasoned. Thus, Doug Bennett spent the remainder of his time - about a year - in the Philippines assigned to the motor pool.

The odds of six brothers returning from World War II were, unfortunately, not that good. Yet Orin, Joe, Charlie, Bill, Stanley, and Doug all made it home safely. Mama Bennett prayed for her six boys each night and wrote each one a letter once a week. Her diligence in prayer perhaps explains what appear to be providential acts involving her sons and their friends.

During the pursuit of Rommell's Afrika Korps, Joe and Charlie and their respective units progressed through Sicily and invaded and occupied the Italian coast at the Anzio beachhead. Because Anzio was not under heavy fire from the Germans when Allied troops arrived, many of the soldiers did not dig new foxholes the first night. Joe Bennett did. That night the Germans pummeled the Americans with a barrage of 88-mm artillery. Those who had failed to dig a foxhole had to scramble for cover, and several took shelter in Joe's foxhole. Unfortunately, many died that night. Joe recounted that the sound of the digging of foxholes could be heard the rest of the night.

War correspondent Ernie Pyle described the importance of the foxholes or "dugouts" to the troops in Anzio:

> "Around the outside perimeter line, where the nfantry faced the Germans a few hundred yards away, the soldiers lay in open foxholes devoid of all comfort. On that beachhead there must have been tens of thousands of dugouts housing from two to half a dozen men. As a result of digging in, our losses from shelling and bombing were small. It was only the first shell after a lull that got many casualties. After the first one all the men were in their dugouts and you should have seen how fast they got there when the first shell whined."[5]

After his unit had been in Anzio for a while, Joe's foxhole had gotten worn down. He determined that he needed to dig a new foxhole for better protection. The soldiers were instructed to dig L-shaped foxholes so that depending on the direction the shells might be incoming from, they could move away from the shells and into the safest leg of the foxhole. After Joe completed his, he could not get comfortable. "It didn't feel like it was right," he concluded. And so he left his new foxhole and went back to his former one. That night his new foxhole took a direct hit from a German 88-mm artillery shell.

* * * * * *

In Germany, shortly after the war had ended, Stanley Bennett and his childhood friend from York, Bruce Youngblood, were riding in a jeep with one other soldier who was driving. Joe Bennett was in Germany, and they were taking an opportunity to visit with him. As they were driving back to their unit after dark, the driver did not see a bomb crater in the road. When the jeep hit that crater, the vehicle flipped upside down and skidded with sparks flying everywhere, leaving the driver and passengers under the weight of the inverted jeep.

Stanley's best friend Bruce and the driver were killed. Stanley would later point to his survival of their tragic accident as pivotal in his calling into the ministry as he wondered, "Why was I spared?" From time to time he experienced "survivor's guilt." A few years later he decided to serve the needs of others in ministry.

* * * * * *

Olive Bennett told of a particular time after the war ended, but before any of her boys had returned home, when she was traveling by car and felt a sudden need to pray for them. "Pull the car over now," she instructed the driver. As soon as the driver was able to pull over and stop the car, Olive Bennett got out of the car and knelt beside the road to pray for her boys. In subsequent conversation with Stanley, it was learned that the same day and nearly the precise moment that Stanley survived the jeep accident that took the lives of two of his comrades including his best friend, Mama Bennett was praying for him, kneeling on the side of a road.

* * * * * *

Tom Cartwright, one of Stanley Bennett's closest friends from York, was a B24 pilot in the Pacific Theater. He and his crew were shot down over Hiroshima and taken prisoner. Because he was the captain of the aircraft, Cartwright was moved to Tokyo to be interrogated. After he was moved, the atomic bomb was dropped on Hiroshima, killing the other men in his crew.

After the bombings of Hiroshima and Nagasaki, the instrument of the Japanese surrender was signed onboard the USS *Missouri*. Bill Bennett was one of the pilots who flew a B29 bomber in a massive show of force along the thirty-eighth parallel during the signing ceremony.

* * * * * *

After the Bennett brothers all returned home from the war, the six brothers followed career paths that took most of them away from their hometown of York. Orin, the oldest sibling, went into the furniture business, opening a store in York. Joe married Ethel Rogers from Lancaster, and the couple settled in her hometown, where Joe became a tire salesman. Charlie, Bill, Stanley, and Doug all left home for college.

UNINTENDED CONSEQUENCES

"A COACH WILL INFLUENCE MORE PEOPLE IN ONE YEAR THAN THE AVERAGE PERSON WILL IN AN ENTIRE LIFETIME."
REVEREND BILLY GRAHAM

While he was stationed in the Philippines, Doug received a letter from a childhood friend, Harold Parrot, who was serving in the Navy. Harold proposed that after the war was over, Doug, along with two of his older brothers, Bill and Stanley, and a "number of the fellows from York," should join him in enrolling in Erskine College situated in the small South Carolina community of Due West. And after the war was over, the three Bennett brothers, as well as other young men from York, did, in fact, join Harold Parrot at Erskine.

When Doug Bennett was considering enrolling at Erskine College in 1947, he and his brothers Bill and Stanley were in downtown York where they got into a conversation with the owner of the menswear store. The owner asked Bill what he was interested in studying. "Business administration," replied Bill. Stanley, who had spent a year at Clemson before the war, replied that he had plans to major in premed. When the store owner posed the same question to Doug Bennett, before he could reply about his own interests, Bill answered for him: "Oh, he's going to be a teacher and a coach."

Afterward, Doug asked Bill, "Why did you tell him I was going to be a coach?", Bill replied, " Because I've always known you were going to be a coach." Upon reflection, Doug admitted that he had not yet given much thought to what he would do. He had decided to go to college because the G.I. Bill enabled him to go for free. It made sense, though, that Doug would pursue a career in athletics in view of the success and enjoyment he had experienced as a high school athlete while playing all the sports that York High School offered.

Not long after their arrival at Erskine in the fall of 1946, Stanley Bennett and some of the other fellows became curious about what had become of their childhood friend, Jack Heinsohn, who had lived with the Bennetts for a time. When Stanley went home one weekend, he opened the front door of the Bennett home and found Jack standing in the kitchen talking to his mother. On a break from touring with the circus, Jack had decided to return to York for the weekend to visit the Bennetts.

Stanley told Jack that everyone was at Erskine, and he convinced Jack that he should rejoin the whole gang by enrolling. Jack decided to visit the school. He bought a 1934 Ford coupe, and with $150 in his pocket, he drove the ninety miles to visit his friends in Due West.

While on his visit to Erskine, Jack decided that he wanted to enroll. Stanley took him to see Dr. Browning, who advised Jack to exchange his money for larger bills to impress the admissions staff. Jack did, and he was admitted.

Doug arrived at Erskine one semester later than Bill and Stanley after being released from active duty later than his older brothers. Charlie had enrolled at Erskine in the fall with Bill and Stanley, but he dropped out after the first semester to marry Martha Mitchell.

Although Bill was the best athlete of all the Bennett brothers (by Doug's own admission), he chose not to play football at Erskine. Instead, he chose to employ his athletic and acrobatic skills as a cheerleader. Orin, the oldest Bennett boy, enrolled in Erskine immediately after high school and played freshman football. Doug played all four years. As the oldest, Orin had left Erskine before his brothers enrolled.

When coaches John McMillan and Gene Alexander arrived at Erskine in the fall of 1947, Doug Bennett was one of the few outstanding football players already enrolled. Bennett was one of several World War II veterans around whom the new coaching staff would build Erskine's postwar football teams. Doug played halfback on both offense and defense. He backed up "Rabbit" Lowry on offense his first two seasons and became the starter for his last two years. Bennett was on the Erskine team that went 7-3 including a 14-6 win over Florida State in 1948. The 1949 squad posted a six and four record. His years on the team, 1947-1950, were the last four years that Erskine fielded a football team until the school restarted the program in 2018.

Although it was not quite as funny to him at the time, Doug recalls with a laugh a preseason scrimmage when they traveled to Duke. When Doug and his teammates saw a rather large group of Duke football players - large in size and number - moving in unison toward them, they assumed that the scrimmage would be starting soon. But the group just kept jogging past them. Evidently, it was the junior varsity heading to practice.

What came out of the Duke locker room next was an even larger team of more experienced players. And they were ready to scrimmage. Led by All-American defensive tackle Al DeRogatis, the Duke defense was tough and stingy. Although they employed the Split-T formation that the Duke team had not seen before, Erskine had such difficulty gaining the ten yards necessary for a first down that the Duke coaches offered Erskine first-and-five series so that the Duke coaches could get their defensive players more work.

In a game against East Tennessee State, near the end of the first half, Bennett was rolled up on after a tackle, and he lay on the ground injured for several minutes. "I was laying on the ground with the wind knocked out of me, saying, 'Send somebody; send coach.'" With halftime approaching someone said to Coach McMillan, "You better go see Bennett." Coach Bennett recalls, "I'm sitting there on the sideline, and they're going in for the half. And he said, 'Oh, he's just tuckered (out).' I was bashed in is what I was."[1]

Bennett's education was financed by the GI Bill his first three years before he was awarded a scholarship for his final year.[2] According to Dick Haldeman, Erskine public relations director from 1961-1995, Doug was a true student athlete at Erskine, combining participation in athletics with numerous musical activities and a membership in the Philomatheon Literary Society. On the field, he was a good student of the game, with an ability to observe and understand, to get along with others, and to communicate his knowledge to others - all qualities that would serve him well in a career as a teacher and coach.

While Doug was growing accustomed to the idea of becoming a teacher and coach with the required physical education curriculum, his older brother Stanley, with whom he had spent so much time during their childhood, began to have some doubts about his own career plans. At some point during his premed studies, Stanley was advised, "Unless you love medicine, don't go into medicine." Not long afterward, while attending a Presbyterian conference in Montreat, North Carolina, Stanley began to have strong reservations about medical school, and he decided to pursue a career in the ministry. A couple of incidents in Stanley's life further convinced him that he was being "called."

While students at Erskine, Bill and Stanley Bennett (both former pilots in WWII) and their friend Fuzz Curence acquired an old Army L2 observation plane, which they flew back and forth between Due West and York, often flying home on weekends. One Sunday afternoon they left York too late in the day, and during their trip back to Due West it got dark well before they were near Erskine. Aware that it would be too dark to land in the cow pasture in Due West where they routinely landed, they remembered that there was an old airstrip near Laurens, about thirty miles from Due West. It was, in fact, too dark to locate the airstrip. But the caretaker of this old airstrip happened to choose this night to test the lights for the runway - a test performed only one night out of the entire year. And so, by what these fliers came to view as an act of providence, they were able to land safely.

From time-to-time, when Stanley thought about being spared in the horrific jeep accident that took the lives of the other two passengers just after the war had ended, he felt a deepening conviction that he had been spared "for a reason."

The incident of an improbable, safe landing on an airstrip where they tested their landing lights just one night a year likewise strengthened a growing resolve to make himself available to serve others through the ministry.

Soon after graduation from Erskine, Stanley accepted a call to become the pastor of Craig Avenue ARP Church in Charlotte. After four years of service to that congregation, Stanley was called to pastor a congregation in Montreat, North Carolina, a small town near Asheville. Among the congregation he served there were evangelist Reverend Billy Graham and his family. During his pastorate there, Stanley baptized two of Billy and Ruth Graham's children, Bonnie and Anne. After five years at Montreat, Stanley gave up the pastorate and became a missionary in Brazil, where he was called upon to use his flight experience as a P47 fighter pilot in Europe to fly a Cessna to travel to various small villages to preach and to encourage members of the church plants.

When Stanley and his wife, Jo Ella, finished their assignment in Brazil, they spent a year in Richmond, Virginia, before leaving to start a church in the college town of Cullowee, North Carolina, home of Western Carolina University. While in Cullowee, Stanley led a ministry to college students. While they were there, Doug came to Cullowee during the spring semester and first session of summer school for three years to work on a master of education degree, which he received in 1967.

After their time in Cullowee, Stanley joined his Erskine classmate and former circus performer Jack Heison, who was now senior pastor at Immanuel Presbyterian on Wilshire Boulevard in Los Angeles. As the largest Presbyterian church in Los Angeles, Immanuel had a large and diverse congregation in this cosmopolitan city. Stanley was called on to employ his skill as a counselor within this diverse group. Stanley and Jack served together for ten years before Stanley accepted a call to become the pastor of a small congregation in the mountains of North Carolina, in Spruce Pine, where he served until his retirement.

After graduation from Erskine, Bill Bennett went to work for the Cellonese Corporation in Rock Hill. Although he served as a B29 flight instructor in the Pacific campaign and returned stateside with no injuries, Bill was involved in a serious car accident and lost the use of his right leg. This condition worsened, and eventually the leg had to be amputated. Bill would later enter the insurance business, where he worked until his retirement.

Soon after he received his bachelor's degree in physical education in January of 1951, Doug Bennett soon was offered and accepted a job as history teacher and assistant football coach at Fort Mill (SC) High School. Bennett served the youth in Fort Mill for two years before being offered a job as the head coach at Sharon High School.

Transitioning from being a college student to a first-year high school teacher and coach with all the responsibilities of preparing lesson plans for five or six classes per day before he shifted gears to coach whatever team happened to be in-season at the time was quite challenging for Doug. He experienced the normal learning curve of being prepared to meet his students each day prepared with knowledge to impart as well as the demands of challenging high school students to excel as athletes. "Free time" was hard to come by. But as a single man without family responsibilities, Doug was not without some semblance of a social life.

With two years of this routine coming to an end at Fort Mill, Doug Bennett took on a new challenge when he accepted a position as the head football coach at Sharon High School. Now he had the responsibility for directing the football program with the requisite planning for a season, scheduling opponents, preparing and maintaining the practice and game fields, preparing practice schedules, purchasing and maintaining equipment, travel logistics, mentoring of coaches and players, and laundering of the practice and game uniforms. Whatever free time Doug had enjoyed as an assistant quickly evaporated with his new hectic schedule.

One lovely summer evening after his first year at Sharon, his movie date with a young nursing student was abruptly canceled when she told Doug, "I can't go out with you anymore." Having been out on a few dates with the attractive future nurse, Doug was taken aback by her sudden lack of interest and countered her declining of his invitation to a movie in Charlotte with a direct query: "Why not?" Without a trace of irritation, his potential girlfriend told Doug bluntly: "Because I'm engaged!" Evidently Doug's busy schedule as a teacher and coach - with the added duties and responsibilities of being the head coach - had prevented him from keeping pace with another suitor of this lovely young woman, and now she was "taken!"

Thrown a bit off center by this sudden change in his world, Doug meandered down the streets of uptown Charlotte and decided to go see the movie anyway. As he waited in line to attend the second showing of the evening, Doug recognized a coaching acquaintance who was coming out of the theater. After they greeted one another and exchanged the usual pleasantries, Ralph Gahegin, head football coach at Winthrop Training School, informed Doug that a Class B school located in a small, rural community just south of Columbia was advertising a position for a physical education teacher, athletic director, and head football coach.

This opportunity came unusually late in the summer, well after most coaching positions had been filled. Administrators at Swansea High School in Swansea, South Carolina, a sleepy, working-class community located twenty-one miles from the state capital, Columbia, had hired a recent graduate of Newberry College for the job. Although he was not a college football player, he had served the Indians' program as a student manager and, apparently, had displayed to the hiring committee that he had enough football knowledge to coach the sport. However, neither the committee nor the recent graduate about to embark on a career in teaching and coaching had anticipated that he would be drafted by Uncle Sam!

Reflecting on the fortuitous events of a broken movie date with a nursing student, his decision to see the film anyway and bumping into a coaching acquaintance who happened to know about the Swansea teaching and coaching position that had just been vacated and then his own decision to pursue the job at Swansea, Doug Bennett concluded, "The Lord had him drafted!" After an interview with Superintendent Herbert E. Taylor, Doug Bennett was offered the job of athletic director, football coach, and coach of every other sport offered by the school with teaching duties in physical education and history.

After renting a room in the home of Thad and Mary Haigler situated next door to the parsonage for Good Shepard Lutheran Church in August of 1954, the newest bachelor in town began what would become a thirty-six-year tenure at Swansea High School. Serving as a physical education and history teacher - and an "interim" principal for five and a half years - as well as the athletic director and head football coach (each position for his entire tenure at Swansea), Doug Bennett taught, coached, mentored, and, most importantly, served and loved hundreds of students. Among the 352 senior football players he coached were young men who would go on to become solid citizens and husbands and fathers, some achieving remarkable feats. Most, however, lived relatively quiet lives of service to others like the splendid man who made an indelible stamp upon their very souls. In many cases, they did not fully realize Coach Bennett's impact in their lives until years later.

A MAN FOR ALL SEASONS

"GREAT LEADERS DON'T SET OUT TO BE A LEADER. THEY SET OUT TO MAKE A DIFFERENCE."
LISA HAIRSHA

According to the townsfolk, Swansea High School had been playing football since around 1925. There had been success, like the undefeated team in the thirties, but overall participation had been limited. Football was the town's first love. Years later, Sherrie Martin Manuel, a former Swansea cheerleader and the wife of former player Tommy Manuel, would describe what football means to the people of this small South Carolina town: "Everyone in Swansea has a pride that is connected to the uniform and those young men who wear them."

The arrival of Doug Bennett in 1954 improved the fortunes of Swansea football rather quickly. But as the school's athletic director, Bennett was responsible for student participation in all the sports offered. He also taught physical education and history classes.

Coach Bennett began his inaugural football preseason with six players, three of them seniors. They practiced for three weeks with only six. "We started school on Monday, and we had a game that Friday. Six more boys came out that week. I had some real green players. I had an eighth grader who had never played that I put at center and another player who had never seen a game of football. In fact, the first game he saw he was playing in. I guess by the end of the season we had about twenty players." Bennett declared, "That's the only time I ever tried to recruit anybody. I was just trying to get enough to play a game." His first and only "recruited" team went 5-5.

Bennett's second team at Swansea had only three seniors again. The team went 5-5. But in his third year in Swansea, with seniors who had been playing since they were sophomores, Bennett molded his first undefeated squad that many viewed as capable of winning a state championship were it not for a scheduling mistake.

Bennett was responsible for scheduling of games as well as transportation to away games. In 1955, Olympia High School changed classification during the school year. Following conference procedures, Doug Bennett had dropped them from the football schedule for 1956 after they moved down. However, Olympia had an enrollment change and moved back into the same classification and conference as Swansea - after Bennett had already set the ten-game schedule. Unable to schedule Olympia as a conference opponent, Swansea was disqualified from playing in the state playoffs, despite posting a 10-0 record, since they had not played enough conference games. The scheduling snafu proved costly. "I have no doubt that the 1956 team would have won the state championship," Bennett said later. Swansea would compile a 60-30 record during the fifties, making the Tigers the decade's dominant program in Class B.

During his early years at Swansea, Bennett also coached girls' and boys' basketball, and baseball. "If they played it, you coached it." In his second year there, Melva Hoover served as the girls' basketball coach for one year. After this one-year hiatus, Bennett directed the girls' basketball program through the 1961-1962 season. At that point, school superintendent Arthur L. Goff coached the girls' team from the 1963 season until the 1968 season when Coach Bennett directed the team for one more year.

Bennett coached the boys' basketball team during his first three years at the school. For his first three years at Swansea, Bennett coached all four sports without an assistant. Ed Rast, his first assistant for football in 1957, coached the boys' team that winter. School principal Jimmy Jenkins coached boys' basketball from 1960-1962 before Coach Bennett reassumed the job in 1963 and 1964.

Doug Bennett also coached the Swansea baseball teams from the spring of 1955 through 1961. Assistant football coach Elwyn Carter then coached boys' baseball for three seasons before Coach Bennett returned to the helm for four more seasons (1965-1968.)

During the second semester of the 1968-1969 academic year and after Lexington County District Four had gone through desegregation in the fall, Doug Bennett was asked to serve as the "interim" principal of the high school and the middle school when Jimmy Jenkins resigned. With Bennett still serving as the school's athletic director and head football coach, it would become even more critical to hire good coaches since his coaching duties would, out of necessity, be curtailed. English teacher Jim Walton was asked to direct the girls' basketball team, and he served for five seasons. Football Assistant Wayne Cole and Don Woolsey, Sr. coached the boys' basketball team in the 1968-1969 season. Bobby Brock coached the boys in 1969-1970 before Cole resumed those duties in the 1970-1971 season. Coach Cole led the baseball squad from 1969 through 1971.

When Wayne Cole left, Swansea needed a coach for both its boys' basketball and baseball squads. Steve Carter was hired as a football assistant and as the head coach for both of these sports. Carter coached the boys' basketball team for six straight seasons (1972-1977) and again in 1979. He coached baseball three straight seasons before directing the newly formed golf team in the spring of 1975. In 1977, he coached the baseball team once again.

Doug Bennett served as the "interim" principal through the spring of 1974. That fall he had three new assistants for football. With Steve Carter, it was the largest football staff up to that point in his tenure in Swansea. With five coaches, including additions Rudy Cooper, Allen McNeil, and Ed Pauling, the players received far more individual attention and instruction than the years when Bennett had only one or two assistants.

The addition of football assistants enabled an expansion of Swansea's overall sports program as more assistants were available to be head coaches in other sports. Football offensive line coach Rudy Cooper became the head coach for a new wrestling team as Bennett launched a program that would go on to win ten state championships under the direction of a few different head coaches. Allen McNeil directed the track program. Up to this point, the school had not been able to field teams, including girls' track, on a consistent basis. Steve Carter directed a new golf program that started in the spring of 1975 while Ed Pauling led the baseball team.

Doug Bennett served as head football coach and athletic director from 1969 through 1980 with no other coaching responsibilities until he started a girls' softball program in 1980 and became its coach. In 1986, with his youngest daughter, Jane Ann, as his pitcher, Bennett led the Lady Tigers to the state championship game, where they lost by one run to Liberty.

Of all the new programs that he initiated as athletic director, the most dominant program was wrestling, which won ten state championships: 1979, 1980, 1981, 1985, 1986, 1989, 1990, 1992, 1995, and 2002, six during his tenure at Swansea. The Tigers were state runners-up another six times: 1978, 1982, 1991, 1993, 2001, and 2018, two of those with Bennett still serving as the athletic director.

W.B. ADKINS
PLAYER 1954-1956

"YOUR LIVING IS DETERMINED NOT SO MUCH BY WHAT LIFE BRINGS TO YOU AS BY THE ATTITUDE YOU BRING TO LIFE."
JOHN HOMER MILLER

Doug Bennett's first year at Swansea High School was W.B. Adkins's sophomore year. While it is customary for starting positions on high school football teams to be manned primarily by juniors and seniors, as a tenth grader W.B. was already one of the Tigers' better players. On the first day of preseason practice in August of 1954, he was called into the coaches' office to meet Swansea's new head football coach. Upon entering the office, W.B. looked around the room and then asked of the new Tiger coach, "Where is he?" while looking right over the head of the five foot six Doug Bennett. Though he stood nearly a foot taller than his new coach at six foot four, from that day forward, W.B. would never again "overlook" this man who would go on to impact his life in powerful ways over the next three years.

From his first practice with the 1954 Swansea team until his last in 1989, Doug Bennett modeled a quiet strength. That calm confidence impressed W. B. Adkins right away. "I never saw Coach lose his cool or get angry over anything the way our coach from the previous season, Robert Lannigan, would." A former Marine, who according to prevailing rumors had been a drill instructor at Marine training grounds on Paris Island, Lannigan was "ruthless and relentless" in driving the team to exhaustion in his quest for perfection. At one point, W. B. quit the team. But he returned, and, admits W.B., "He broke me from being a mama's boy."

But there was something about his new coach that motivated W.B. in a different way, to strive to be his very best: "Coach Bennett led and inspired us by his example. He was positive and never yelled and screamed." In fact, according to W. B., when Coach Bennett let out a "golly buck" or "golly ding," or when he squatted down and pulled up a piece of grass and started to chew on it, you knew he was not pleased with what he was witnessing.

As a single man during the fifties, Doug Bennett had time to pursue a variety of interests, including one of the true passions in his life - hunting. Although it might now be viewed as "inappropriate" in our present politically correct and litigious society, Doug Bennett would join W.B. and some of his teammates or W.B, and his dad on Saturdays to hunt rabbits or doves. It was an unusual opportunity for these players to spend time with their head coach in a more relaxed, social setting. W.B. relished the time.

Thinking back on one foray into the woods to hunt rabbits with W.B. and his dad, Doug Bennett recalls with a laugh that W.B. always had a "pack of dogs that were mixed breeds but fierce hunters." In fact, these dogs were such vicious hunters that "if you shot a rabbit you had to try your best to get to the rabbit as soon as possible before those dogs got there and tore the rabbit to pieces." It was during these adventures on weekends that W.B. saw another side of the young Swansea coach, a balance and serenity in his life, that left a lasting impression.

Coach Bennett, who had played halfback on the football team at Erskine College but - did not have the same passion for basketball as football, nevertheless took W.B. and his offensive lineman teammate C. L. Wise to some of the Flying Fleet's games, as Erskine had a formidable program in the fifties. Being at Swansea High during Coach Bennett's days as a single man afforded W.B and his teammates an opportunity to get to know their coach on a more personal level than is normally possible in high school athletics. In W.B.'s senior yearbook, Coach Bennett wrote: "It has been swell coaching you these last three years and hunting, etc. Congratulations on being selected to play in the North-South All-Star game. Continue to be a leader and not a follower."

Not only did W.B. appreciate the kind and challenging words from the young coach he had grown to respect and admire, he also found out, for the first time in Bennett's yearbook note, that he had been selected to play in the North-South All-Star game against other outstanding players from around the state of South Carolina. And, thought W.B., reflecting on this significant moment in his life as a young man, it was just like Coach Bennett with his fun-loving nature and great sense of timing, to surprise W.B. with news of his selection to this prestigious team with such a personal and creative touch.

At six foot four and 240 pounds - huge for a high school lineman in those days - W.B. was so fast for his size that he had to run wind sprints with the Swansea running backs in order to be challenged. In 1956, when the Tigers went undefeated, allowing only twenty-four points in ten games, W.B. anchored an offensive line that averaged 210 pounds per man, massive for that day. W.B. and his bosom buddy Reginald Jeffcoat were the right and left tackles respectively, Larry Wannamaker and C. L. Wise were the guards, and Gus Hydrick the center.

Normally, an undefeated regular season would yield a conference championship and an automatic playoff berth. But there would be no playoffs in W.B.'s senior season, the last opportunity to play football for most seniors in high school. Because of its marginal student enrollment, Olympia High School in Columbia, had been moving back and forth between classifications and in and out of the conference. When Doug Bennett, in his role as Swansea's athletic director, set the Tigers' schedule for the 1956 season, Olympia had moved out of the conference. The ten-game regular season schedule was set, and contracts were signed.

But before the 1956 season began, Olympia had been moved back into the conference once again. Doug Bennett, for reasons he now sees as perhaps foolish, decided not to break a contract with another school and try to schedule Olympia. Perhaps he did not expect his team to run through the ten-game season undefeated, yielding a total of twenty-four points for the season. Though many thought Swansea to be the best team in Class B, because Bennett had failed to schedule enough conference games for the Tigers, his team was declared ineligible for the state playoff despite their unblemished record. Today, this error could not be made as all teams in a conference or region play every other team.

W.B. and his Tiger teammates, nevertheless, were disqualified and denied the opportunity to pursue what many felt would surely be Swansea's first Class B State Championship. The heartbreak for these young men who had sacrificed much and worked so hard was painful and palpable.

Some of the pain from the disappointment of being undefeated with no playoff destination was abated six months later when W.B. and his senior teammates and other fellow students took their senior trip to Washington, D.C. Unaware that they were from a famous town, at least in the eyes of a certain group of consumers, W.B. and some classmates learned of their hometown's reputation from a hotel elevator operator. After the group of students boarded the elevator and greeted the operator, the hotel employee asked where they were from. "Swansea, South Carolina," they replied. "Hey, that's the town where you can get that real good 'shine," he enthusiastically replied.

In the forties, fifties, and sixties, apparently some enterprising businessmen and women in the Swansea area were unaware that Prohibition had been repealed. Purchases of grain corn and corn mash were so frequent and substantial that eyebrows were never raised, and these transactions were completed with knowing smiles. Production of moonshine in the area was so prosperous that farmers came to measure their corn crop yields not in the standard bushels-per-acre but in terms of *gallons-per-acre!* Thus, over five hundred miles away, and perhaps further, Swansea came to be viewed as a place to purchase "some of that real good 'shine." To hear a hotel elevator attendant reveal such familiarity with their hometown based upon an illegal activity was both surprising and amusing to W.B. and his classmates.

But without a doubt, Swansea was even better known for its high school football team. W.B. and his Swansea teammates, though extremely disappointed about this lost opportunity to possibly continue on their winning streak all the way to a state title, nonetheless made a significant contribution in establishing Swansea as the premier program in the state's Class B division. According to schighschoolfootballhistory.com, which has records beginning in 1960, Doug Bennett's Tiger squads won ninety games including the 1960 state championship (they were runners-up the next year) while competing in Class B and posted the best winning percentage (67 percent) of all teams in the classification. In the years prior to 1960 (1954-1959) Swansea teams were among the very best competitors in Class B. During W.B.'s three varsity seasons, the Tigers posted a twenty and ten record including the perfect ten and zero season cut short by unfortunate scheduling circumstances.

In addition to his selection to the North-South game, for his outstanding play and for his prospects as a football player at the college level, W.B. earned a full scholarship to Clemson University to play for the legendary Frank Howard. He was a starting offensive lineman on Clemson's freshman team, as first-year players were ineligible for varsity competition in those days. During spring practice of his freshman year, after he had gained forty pounds from hard work in the Tiger weight room and an equally impressive dedication for eight months at the Clemson training table, W.B. weighed in at 280 pounds. During the stretching period at the beginning of one of the spring workouts, Clemson Head Coach Frank Howard paused for a moment to visit personally with his massive freshman offensive lineman. "Damn, Adkins, if I was as big as you, I'd knock people down and shit in their face!" growled the colorful Clemson legend-in-the-making.

W.B.'s career at Clemson was cut short, however, when he, his brother Clark, a sophomore at Swansea High, and four other teammates were involved in a horrific automobile accident on August 18, 1958, on their way to go swimming in Sandy Run Creek. "I got a call that the boys had been in a bad wreck near the American Legion hut, and Ed Rast (Bennett's first paid assistant coach at Swansea) and I drove out to the scene," recalls Coach Bennett. He and Coach Rast would later learn that when a front tire blew out, W.B. struggled to regain control of the '41 Ford coupe before crashing into a three-foot concrete culvert. Impact at sixty miles per hour and the car flipping end-over-end drove the car's motor into the front seat. W.B.'s brother, Clark, who was riding in the "suicide seat" on the front passenger seat next to the door, in a time before vehicles were equipped with seat belts, had broken a leg and would receive several hundred stitches for multiple lacerations.

Both of W.B.'s ankles were broken. Herbert Stabler suffered a severe kidney injury and a broken leg and missed the entire football season while Perry, the youngest of the three Adkins brothers, had multiple contusions but was able to play for the Tigers that fall. Wayne Jumper and Billy Rucker, seated in the back seat with Perry, were also severely bruised but were able to play that fall. And because enough ambulances were not available, some of these young men were transported to the hospital in a hearse provided by Thompson Funeral Home!

Clark would eventually fully recover to play for Doug Bennett's Tiger squads, including the 1960 Class B state champions. Like his older brother, Clark was awarded a full football scholarship to Clemson. W.B. was never quite the same. He missed the entire season of his sophomore year as he did not enroll for classes to concentrate on rehabilitation and recovery. In the spring semester of 1959, he attempted to participate in spring practice but was too limited, as he later concluded that he had attempted to come back too soon. Disillusioned by his bleak prospects for being the same player he had been, W.B. decided to move on with his life. On June 1, he took his last exam of the spring semester that would actually be his final academic term at Clemson. Four days later, on June 5, he was married to Carolyn Jumper, who has been his life partner for fifty-eight years. Later that summer W.B. began his career as an employee of Lybrand Supply Company, where he worked for four and a half years before launching an independent insurance agency, where he served the public for forty-one years.

W.B. was not only one of three brothers who had the privilege of playing for Doug Bennett (younger brother Perry signed a scholarship with Clemson's archrival, the University of South Carolina Gamecocks) as a dad he thoroughly enjoyed watching with immense pride as his own son, Bill, played in the offensive line for Coach Bennett's Tiger squads in 1977 and 1978. Former Swansea assistant coach Phil Williams said of Bill, "He's as fine a young man as I've ever coached - just like his daddy." After graduation from Swansea, Bill attended Presbyterian College, where he played football and baseball while he roomed with Tiger teammate, Robert Maddox, the young man who would eventually succeed Doug Bennett as Swansea's head football coach.

At Presbyterian, Bill took one course in computer science, which sparked a deep interest in information technology, and to pursue this interest, he transferred to Midlands Tech in Columbia. After completing an associate degree in computer science, Bill pursued a career in information technology. In October of 1999, while traveling throughout the United States troubleshooting information systems and helping companies prepare for "Y2K," Bill, at age thirty-eight, was diagnosed by local doctors with melanoma on one of his fair-skinned arms - most likely caused by repeated exposure to the sun during his days of hunting, fishing, baseball, and softball. He was quickly referred to the premier cancer hospital in the southeast and one of the best treatment centers in the country, Duke University Hospital. Cancer specialists there, sadly, had to break the news that Bill was expected to live no more than six months. By January, just four months later, he was gone.

Parents should not have to bury their children. And as anyone who knows Doug Bennett would expect, the coach attended the funeral of his former player Bill Adkins. And though that day is still somewhat of a blur in W.B.'s mind, he knew that Coach Bennett would tell him what a privilege it had been for him to coach Bill and that his thoughts and prayers would be with the entire Adkins family. Attending weddings and funerals of former players is both one of the joys and one of the sorrows of investing so much of one's life in others as a coach. Doug Bennett always did it with dignity and grace.

One of the qualities that W.B. most admired in Doug Bennett and one he tried to emulate in his own relationships with others was his coach's positive way of expressing a need for a change in a person's work habits or attitude. "Coach never said 'You need to [do this}' He never criticized his players. Coach's emphasis was always on 'We,' not 'You,' and definitely not 'I' or 'Me' He always said 'Let's do it this way. We need to try this,' etc. He was always seeking the best possible outcome for others." As W.B. was to learn from his coach's example, "A leader assumes responsibility. He does not blame others when (s)he is in charge." This positive approach to mentoring others became a core value for W.B in his own insurance business. He wanted employees and clients to understand that he was seeking solutions to their needs or problems from a team-oriented, "we/us" mindset.

Doug Bennett, early in his career, as a single man spending time hunting with some of his players, may have been, at least initially, more like an older brother in the minds of some of his players than the stereotypical authoritative, dictator-like coach that was in vogue in the fifties and sixties. But Coach Bennett deftly maintained his role as a mentor and role model to these young men, never compromising by trying to be "buddy-buddy." His players were able to see him as a single man with character who had goals and drive and yet a man who knew how to have fun while investing in others.

One of the chief benefactors of Doug Bennett's commitment to young people was W.B. Adkins. In the summer following his senior year as he prepared to enroll at Clemson University on a football scholarship, W.B. had the privilege of playing in the North-South All-Star game for another legendary South Carolina high school coach. John McKissick would, over the course of a sixty-two-year career, establish a high school dynasty at Summerville High School and set the national record for wins by at high school football coach with a 622-155-13 record.

W.B. counts it a privilege to have been around coaching greatness at such an early age. As he moved on in his career in the insurance business, he continued his commitment to the Swansea program as he watched his son Bill help lead the Tigers to back-to-back conference championships and playoff berths in his junior and senior season. W.B. has been a leader in the community's support of Swansea football, a central figure involved in the weekly Thursday "Burger Night" meals for the team during the season. He and others pushed for the construction and dedication of Doug Bennett Field, a new stadium and fieldhouse for Swansea football.

Yet, without a doubt, the most profound impact of Douglas M. Bennett upon the life of W.B. Adkins, not only as an impressionable young man but as an appreciative dad, and as a lifetime community supporter, was the quiet force of Coach Bennett's humility and servant heart as a man of faith: "Whenever I have an opportunity to share my Christian testimony, I inevitably talk about the effect that Coach Bennett's example had - and *still* has on me." In searching for a way to describe Coach's Bennett's impact on him and hundreds of others at Swansea High School, W.B. said simply, "Coach Bennett didn't make football players; he made citizens."

A COACH'S WIFE

"LET THE WIFE MAKE THE HUSBAND GLAD TO COME HOME AND LET HIM MAKE HER SORRY TO SEE HIM LEAVE."
MARTIN LUTHER

When Doug Bennett met Landis Sharpe, he had no idea about the opportunities his new friendship might afford him. Landis owned a TV repair business, but his knowledge of electronics and other technical areas made him the closest thing to an expert in cutting edge technology in small town America.

Landis Sharpe also owned an 8mm camera. Soon after their meeting, Landis and Coach Bennett started discussing how they might use the camera to film Bennett's teams' games. A six-foot platform was constructed on the visitors' side of the football field, and Landis began filming the games.

Soon after Doris Sharpe learned that her husband had befriended the town's most eligible bachelor, she set about arranging a meeting with Landis's sister, Jane Sharpe. Doug was invited to accompany Jane to the Valentine's Day dance at the community center. He accepted. A ten-month courtship followed.

Young people raised during the Great Depression and those who learned of the brutalities of World War II - even if not firsthand - were less inclined to postpone marriage and family for career. Many had endured the economic hardships of an unparalleled financial crisis and had come to believe it necessary to find a partner with whom to face economic reality. The high loss of American lives overseas made many young men more aware of the brevity of life and of their own mortality. For Doug and Jane, ten months was long enough.

On December 16, 1957, Beverly Jane Sharpe and Douglas McDowell Bennett were married in Resurrection Lutheran Church in Columbia. Jane received a quick introduction to life as a coach's wife when they did not have time to go on a honeymoon because Doug was in the middle of basketball season. The couple attempted to go on a honeymoon later, but they determined that the tires on their car were too worn to risk a trip. Purchasing new tires was not an option. They never got to go on a honeymoon. But during Coach Bennett's retirement ceremony, team physician William H. "Bud" Granger presented Doug and Jane with an all-expenses-paid cruise to Alaska, which they enjoyed immensely.

Doug Bennett was blessed with a wife who was enthusiastic about her husband's teams. In a feature article written by sportswriter Bertram Rantin in 1985 on her role as a coach's wife, Jane revealed that her love for football was not a result of her marrying Doug: "I was a football fan even before. I'm a dyed-in-the-wool fan. I think someone who married into coaching would have to be. Before we were married, my interest was more in college football. Now I'm more interested in high school football, but I still love college football."

Beverly, the couple's middle daughter, can remember her mother talking excitedly about a Friday night football game one morning before she left for work. Looking back on his wife's sports enthusiasm, Doug Bennett remarked, "My goodness, she was into it!" Oldest daughter Susan is convinced that "we had several diapers changed in the bleachers." Yet, in her enthusiasm for the Swansea program, she never spoke negatively of her husband or of the coaching profession. As Doug states it, "She never meddled."

While she considered herself a knowledgeable spectator, she said, "I leave it up to him. I know the rules - touchdowns, first downs - enough to follow the games. I'm not really into the plays and types of defense. I recognize some of them but not a lot." Because of her work schedule, attending home games required some coordination between meals and getting her girls ready. "It leaves a lot of family things for me to do, but I've gotten used to it," Jane told Rantin.

Susan and Beverly remember going to away games with their mom and family friend Wilma Davis. Some of those trips were taken on rural backroads, not the ideal route for two women and two girls in the event of car trouble. But most of these trips were without incident. When her sisters were older and on the cheerleading squad and traveling by bus, Jane Ann, seven years younger than Beverly, followed her sisters on the trips with her mom and Mrs. Davis.

"I'm just a loyal fan who's always there," said Jane. "Our whole family lives and breathes football." One of the most enjoyable aspects of high school football for Jane Bennett was getting to know many of the players and their families. "That, she said, "makes going to the games a little more special."

Over Doug Bennett's thirty-six-year tenure in Swansea, Jane missed very few games. She said that she enjoys her husband's games "when they're close, but more so when we're on the winning end." But she said that she was blessed to have a husband who was not temperamental win, lose, or draw. "He's always the same," she said. "He's pretty much easy going and doesn't show that much emotion."

Most high school teachers and coaches are not paid enough to support a family on their own salary, so a working spouse in coaching families is common. Jane Bennett worked for over fifty years, in part, to support her husband's passion for teaching and coaching high school students. After two years with the Swift Corporation, Jane worked forty-nine years with the March of Dimes in Columbia as an administrator.

Jane's sacrifice was for her entire family, not just for her husband's endeavors. "Mama went above and beyond to make sure we received what she felt was a good education," recalls Beverly. Because Swansea had no preschool or kindergarten programs at the time, Jane took the girls on her work commute and dropped them off at Timmerman Preschool and Kindergarten in Columbia. Since the school's program was a half-day format, Jane had to leave work every day on her lunch break to pick up the girls. She then drove them to her sister Sarah's home and left them in her care until she could pick them up after work and drive home to Swansea.

Piano lessons with Billie G. Jolley in Columbia were a part of Jane Bennett's ideal education for her three girls. On Monday evenings, Jane would drive home from work to pick up the girls to drive back to the Forest Acres section of Columbia, forty-five minutes away. When football season was over, Doug Bennett took over this weekly responsibility for his wife. The two oldest girls took lessons for five years together, and Susan continued for another five years. Jane Ann, who was born seven years after Beverly, took piano and organ lessons for ten years.

Many coaches hail football as the ultimate team sport. It has become a cliché, but it is nevertheless true that "there is no 'I' in team." As the wives of football coaches know and demonstrate on a day-to-day basis, for things to run smoothly within a coaching family, teamwork and cooperation are essential. Each member of the family has a role and a contribution to make. Jane Bennett was the consummate team player. By working full-time outside the home, she sacrificed much so that her family could have more.

To help Jane navigate her family life responsibilities as a full-time working mother, she and Doug decided to hire a housekeeper who would watch after the Bennett children during Jane's absence from home. Ineatha McBride stepped into that role. Lovingly known as "NeeNee" within the Bennett family, she served the Bennetts for twelve years.

Early on, NeeNee established her integrity with Jane and Doug Bennett. Doug had purchased a beautiful emerald cut diamond ring when he proposed to Jane. Shortly after hiring Ineatha, Jane noticed that the one-carat solitaire was missing from its setting. An urgent search commenced; however, it did not turn up. Several days later, while Doug and Jane were away at work, NeeNee spotted the diamond behind the toilet while she was cleaning. When Doug and Jane returned home from work, NeeNee excitedly presented the recovered diamond to them. From that point on, there was an unwavering trust between the Bennetts and NeeNee. For even more valuable than a diamond, was Ineatha's honesty and her heart of gold.

Out of sheer financial necessity, NeeNee sacrificed raising her own children to raise the Bennett children. She left her family five days a week to earn twenty-five dollars a week. In that day and time, twenty-five dollars a week was the difference, for NeeNee and her family, between eating and going hungry. Although NeeNee's help was far more valuable than such a wage might suggest, it was a fair wage for those times. Living off salaries as a football coach and a secretary, Doug and Jane paid all they could afford.

In Jane's absence throughout the weekdays, NeeNee became a beloved second mother to the Bennett children. Susan and Beverly claim, "NeeNee pretty much raised us. She taught us, disciplined us, cared for us, and loved us just as a mother would. She truly partnered with our parents in shaping us into God-fearing children; and still today she's an important part of who we are. We owe so much to her. No children anywhere could have been more blessed than we were for having her."

After working for the Bennett family, NeeNee became the director for the Swansea Elementary cafeteria. Says middle daughter Beverly, "It was the perfect job for her because she was a great cook! I remember thinking how lucky those school children were!"

Having been raised to prioritize faith, Jane was never absent from church. Just as she had grown up attending church on Sundays, she made sure that the Bennett children followed suit, and she was a stickler about it. Susan recalls that even when the family was about to leave for a week-long vacation, Jane made sure that they all attended church together on Sunday morning before they left for the trip. Similarly, if Christmas fell on a Sunday, there were no passes for missing church that day either. "I can remember going to church a time or two even when I was sick. It was easier to go than trying to explain to Mama that I didn't feel well and risk looking like I was trying to get out of church!" Susan adds, "Stressing the importance of consistent church attendance was one of Mama's ways of demonstrating the priority God should have in our lives."

APPLE TREES GROW APPLES

"THE ONE WHO LIVES WITH INTEGRITY IS RIGHTEOUS; HIS CHILDREN WHO COME AFTER HIM WILL BE HAPPY," PROVERBS 20:7

One of the occupational hazards of the coaching profession is a fractured marriage, a dysfunctional family. Time demands of the job, pressure to win, time spent away from home, and poor communication, all contribute to a family's demise if certain precautions are not taken and firm boundaries are not set.

Doug Bennett was able to avoid these pitfalls and achieve balance because he had a partner, Jane, his wife, who was not simply supportive but *enthusiastic* about her husband's job. Jane accepted her husband's extended hours with an in-season sport and found a way, while working a full-time job to keep things organized in the home and still make it to every game. She was especially fond of football, and she did not hide her enthusiasm.

To be sure that he had time to spend with his three daughters, Doug included the girls on many of his routine coaching duties, such as getting the film developed in the days of 16mm film, and making the film or video exchange with the next opposing coach on Saturday mornings. His third daughter, Jane Ann, when her older sisters were otherwise occupied, often accompanied her father to the fieldhouse when he had to do laundry or some other chore.

Of Susan's and Beverly's earlier times of accompanying their dad to the fieldhouse, Susan enthusiastically declared, "We loved going to the fieldhouse. It smelled like sweat and athletic tape. I loved the smell of the towels when they were coming hot out of the dryer." In addition to doing the team's laundry, their dad was responsible for mowing and watering the football field, and the girls found pleasure even in that mundane task. "We loved the smell of the grass," said Susan.

"We loved to be able to go to the field and just run around. We loved to go to practice. We wanted to play!" While some may have viewed a fieldhouse or a practice field as inappropriate places for young girls to be spending time, middle daughter Beverly notes, "He never put us off for anything or anyone. He always included us in that he was doing. Having full access to the football program made us feel special, not better than anyone, just special."

One of life's transitions occurred for Beverly one afternoon while attending a practice when she was twelve years old. During practice Doug Bennett noticed a rather large cloud of dust behind the bleachers at the same time he noticed that his Chevy II, in which he normally left his keys, was missing from his regular parking place. Upon closer examination, he realized that his daughter Beverly was driving in circles behind the bleachers and kicking up dust. Rather than get angry about it, he laughed about it since he knew she was safe. "After that, it became a routine thing, and I got pretty good at driving," says Beverly.

Having a dad who was the football coach and who immersed them in the game as much as they wanted, presented certain advantages to each of the Bennett girls when each became a cheerleader. "We knew the rules of the game, so we never suggested a cheer that was contradictory to what was happening on the field: We didn't select 'Push 'em back, push 'em back WAY back' or 'Take that ball away, hey, take that ball away' when Swansea was on offense," Susan points out with a laugh.

"We loved traveling to the away games. Friday and Friday night was like Christmas for us," recalls Beverly. Oldest daughter Susan adds, "It was exciting - we were so proud of our daddy. We felt that the Swansea football program was something special. It was a highlight of small town living in a tight-knit community."

Even when Coach Bennett had to be away for his job, the children experienced no void or sense of loss. Beverly observes: "We never felt his absence was significant. We always felt his presence. He more than made up for the time that he was away."

When Lexington County District Four desegregated in 1968, Susan Bennett was in the fourth grade and Beverly was in the second grade. Both have vivid memories of white parents picketing as part of the nine-day boycott. Susan attended during the nine-day boycott with a total of four students in her class: two were white, and two were black. Beverly was among three students who attended during the boycott: two white and one black. Even as the schools were going through integration, the girls remember that some restaurants required blacks to stand outside and order to receive food and that the town's two doctor's offices were segregated with separate patient waiting rooms.

One of the greatest life lessons for the Bennett girls occurred at home as they listened in on a conversation their father had with nanny/housekeeper, Ineatha McBride, or "NeeNee," as she was affectionately called by the Bennett family. NeeNee posed a question to Doug Bennett about the beliefs or decisions that had led to a boycott by white parents. His reply to her was simply, "People can be stupid, ignorant."

"Everyone in our household was on the same page. There was no doubt in our minds that Daddy was teaching us the right things with his words and deeds," asserts Beverly. While the Bennett girls may have heard an occasional criticism of their father from a disgruntled fan or parent, they were "very aware of the esteem and respect others had for our daddy. As a parent, Daddy had the X Factor - like a quarterback with both character and intangibles, beyond the measurables. He was beyond extraordinary in that way," declares Beverly.

As might be expected from three daughters who grew up in a sports environment and were themselves cheerleaders, each of the Bennett daughters married a man with an athletic background. And all three were married in Good Shephard Lutheran Church, the church that they had attended as they were growing up.

Susan Bennett met James Inman on a blind date arranged by her sister Beverly and James's best friend, Jody Truesdale. The group went bowling, and Susan beat James. "I think he liked that," says Susan, "that I was competitive." The two did not start dating immediately, but over time they saw each other more frequently. "About two years later" they were engaged and married.

James Inman played football and wrestled at Airport High School in West Columbia. He never got the opportunity to play baseball, his first love, in high school as he had to help support his family by working during the spring. James picked up a nickname when he lost twenty-six pounds to wrestle at the 112-pound weight class. His football coach, Don Richardson, did not like the idea of James losing that much weight to wrestle, so he began to call him "Skinny" to discourage him from making that sacrifice to participate in the sport. But James continued year after year to lose several pounds from his football playing weight to wrestle at a lower weight class. The nickname stuck.

After earning an academic scholarship and a partial scholarship for wrestling, he attended The Citadel. "Skinny's" plan after graduation was to become a pilot, but his career path was altered by medical issues that prevented him from completing flight school. In his junior year, he signed a contract with the Air Force after ranking in the top two of his class. A childhood injury on a playground had developed over time into a cyst that grew to within one-eighth of an inch of his lower spine. After experiencing pain in his lower back area during flight training, "Skinny" was diagnosed with this growth that would require surgery. After the cyst was removed, "Skinny" received a medical discharge from his Air Force contract.

"Skinny" graduated with a degree in business management, on May 13, 1981. He and Susan were married on May 30. "Skinny" has spent the past thirty-plus years in retail management. Susan parlayed her ten years of piano and music theory lessons into a thriving teaching business that she has maintained in every city to which their family has moved. The heyday of her teaching career was the seven years she spent with students in a studio with as many as sixty students and more than forty per year. She also taught piano at North Myrtle Beach Christian School for two of those years.

Susan's students and studio entered and dominated several competitions. She marveled at the way her students performed against players who had been taught by instructors with PhDs in music and music theory. After witnessing student after student from her studio winning these contests, Susan concluded, "I'm a better coach than I am a teacher. I got that from my daddy." For her excellence in working with her students, Susan won two "Best Teacher (Studio) Performance" awards.

Music, in fact, was a gift that her father gave Susan and her sisters. During the many times he drove them to piano and music theory lessons in Columbia, Doug Bennett taught his daughters how to sing melody and harmony, or "wildcat harmony," as he called it, in the car. Often the songs were words from the scriptures set to music, such as Matthew 6:33: "Seek ye first the kingdom of God / and His righteousness / and all these things will be added to you." This verse was, in the eyes of many in Doug Bennett's family, words that he has lived by his entire life, his life motto. These singing sessions were a highlight for his daughters who have, in turn, taught them to their own children. On the many occasions that Doug and his girls have been asked to sing, whether at local churches or at the annual Bennett family reunion, "Seek Ye First" is their song of choice, as it is a reminder of how to order one's priorities, how a Christian's life is to be lived.

Despite not taking organ lessons, Susan played the organ in Good Shepherd Lutheran Church as a twelve-year-old and in the Episcopal Church of Dublin, Georgia, as an adult. Susan and her entire family are musicians and singers, and they have been leaders in music ministry in each of the churches where they have worshipped. Music is one of the many gifts Doug Bennett imparted to his daughters that they, like Susan Inman and her gifted family, have employed in service to others.

The Inmans have three children: Skylar, Jamie, and Doug. Susan homeschooled Skylar and Jamie from the second grade through tenth grade and Doug from kindergarten through eighth grade. Skylar and Jamie got involved in competitive gymnastics in the fifth grade. Skylar was recruited and signed a full scholarship for gymnastics at the University of North Carolina. Jamie played volleyball and pitched and played shortstop for the softball team at North Myrtle Beach Christian School. Doug played Dixie Youth baseball from age five until high school, when he played all four years. He also played football a couple of seasons, but baseball was his passion. Doug went on to play baseball at Clearwater Christian College in Florida.

* * * * * *

In the fall of 1983, Beverly Bennett met Bruce Olson, who had been a three-sport athlete in high school, recruited in both football and baseball. He was a scholarship quarterback at the University of Minnesota from 1978-1982. When his football career ended, he joined the baseball team as a senior. After graduation, Bruce was hired as a sales representative for corrugated paper products with Champion International. That September, a group of sales trainees took a trip to visit Champion's top seedling producing nursery - in Swansea. After a day of touring the nursery, Bruce and some of his fellow trainees went out on the town in the Five Points area of Columbia near the University of South Carolina.

That night Bruce met Beverly, a coed at the university, who was entering her senior year. After an engaging conversation, the two exchanged phone numbers, and a whirlwind courtship commenced. Bruce returned to his home in Milwaukee, and a series of phone calls and letters between the two followed. After three weeks of phone calls and letters back and forth, Bruce purchased a plane ticket for Beverly to fly up to spend the Thanksgiving holiday with his family in Reedsburg, Wisconsin. Her visit was the first time the two had been together since their initial meeting.

Their long-distance relationship progressed quickly, and by February, Bruce, who had learned to make quick decisions as a college quarterback, purchased a diamond ring and a ticket to visit Beverly. She said yes. They were married August 18, 1984, at Good Shepherd Lutheran Church in Swansea. Including that night they had met in Columbia, Beverly and Bruce had only been in one another's presence a total of five times during their eleven-month courtship.

The couple had three sons and a daughter. After years of being mostly homeschooled, the boys attended Irmo High School in Columbia, South Carolina, where all three played football. Two earned major college football scholarships. The oldest son, Aram, came into the national spotlight his senior year in 2005, ranking number two in the country at the fullback position according to ESPN, while making the network's Top 150 overall prospects. After receiving full scholarship offers from Ohio State, Florida State, Texas A&M, Auburn, and Alabama, Aram was impressed by head coach Jim Tressel and signed with the 2006 Buckeyes' recruiting class.

David, the youngest son and a quarterback, received a full scholarship with Dabo Swinney and the Clemson Tigers as a fifth-year graduate student, following a four-year undergraduate career as a walk-on at Stanford University under Jim Harbaugh first and then David Shaw when Harbaugh left to become the head coach of the San Francisco 49ers. After his year at Clemson, David made a name for himself in the arena leagues for two years before being signed during training camp by the Baltimore Ravens in 2017.

The Olsons' middle son, Jacob, displayed prowess on the defensive side of the ball as a middle linebacker who, in his senior season, lead his team in nearly every defensive statistic. As a result, Jacob was named to the Division 4-A All-Region team, received local media and coaches' awards, and became the recipient of the Irmo Yellow Jacket Student-Athlete Scholarship. As a standout performer, Jacob drew the attention of college recruiters, but he decided to forego future playing opportunities and focus strictly on academics. He went on to earn a business degree from the University of South Carolina. Soon afterward, he heeded a new calling, and in keeping true to form with his grandfather's mantra of "God first," Jacob completed a master's degree in ministry leadership from Columbia International University.

By earning a master's degree himself and by devoting his life to teaching and coaching, Doug Bennett was an example and an inspiration to the Olson children, each of whom embraced his love of learning. With master's degrees in hand, both Aram and Jacob turned their interests to medicine: first Jacob became a vascular sonographer, and then Aram left the teaching profession after five years to attend medical school and become a doctor. David, having earned a degree in management science and engineering from Stanford, also continued his education in pursuit of an MBA as a football graduate assistant at Charleston Southern University coaching quarterbacks.

The Olsons' daughter Alyssa continued to grow her knowledge as a paralegal after graduating cum laude from the University of South Carolina and becoming a licensed real estate agent. As the youngest child, Alyssa gave notice to her older brothers early on that she would not be standing in anyone's shadow athletically when she rode a bicycle with no training wheels at the age of three! Not long afterward, she became a threat in the water as she took to the pool like a fish in competitive swimming, making her first marks in the sport around the state as an eight-year-old and taking first place in the butterfly at the annual Columbia citywide swim meet. Alyssa also played soccer during her primary years and into high school, but she never missed a football game in show of support to her older brothers - a devotion that inarguably was passed down to her from her mother and from her grandmother, Jane Bennett.

Beverly Olson's devotion to her children was displayed early on after marrying Bruce in 1984. With the birth of their first son in 1987, she left her job with a commercial real estate company in Milwaukee, Wisconsin, to begin her new career as a stay-at-home mom. Although she had earned a business education degree from the University of South Carolina, she felt no loss in not becoming a classroom teacher. Instead, she embraced what she considered to be her "true calling" - being at home to raise her children, which led to homeschooling over a span of thirteen years. As their children grew up, Bruce and Beverly served in various roles in the high school booster club and sports parents' organizations. Bruce was also very involved early on and through the children's pre-teen years as their baseball coach and in-line hockey coach.

******

Jane Ann Bennett attended the University of South Carolina with a plan to pursue a career in nursing. However, she began to have doubts about nursing and reasoned that she had always loved working with children. Jane Ann left the School of Nursing and chose to become a teacher like her father. After graduating with a degree in education, Jane Ann's first teaching job was at Swansea Elementary in 1991, where she taught a child development class for four-year-olds for one semester. Later that year she taught first grade at Francis Mack Elementary in Gaston and worked there for eight years. She then moved back to Swansea Elementary to teach first and second grades. In the 2010-2011 academic year, Swansea Elementary and Francis Mack Elementary in Gaston were merged and moved into a new facility, Sand Hills Primary/Elementary School, where Jane continues to teach first and second graders in a Montessori-based curriculum.

In 1991, when Jane was teaching the child development classes at Swansea Elementary School, she was called upon to conduct teacher-parent conferences with each of her students during visits to their homes at the outset of the program. She went to the home of Analese Meredith. Analese's parents, Brett and Mary, were present, but also her Uncle Chad. That evening Jane Ann and Chad Meredith were introduced. Chad was impressed, but both were busy professionals. A few months later, Chad wrote Jane Ann a letter expressing his desire to get to know her better. In October, they started spending time together regularly. In December, Jane Ann, who had been a pitcher for Swansea's 1986 state runner-up girls' softball team coached by her dad, received Chad's best pitch when she accepted his proposal. They were married August 1, 1992, at Good Shepherd Lutheran Church.

Chad Meredith played football and wrestled at Howland High School in Warren, Ohio. After graduation, Chad traveled and sang with his family's gospel group, The Merediths. He enrolled in the University of South Carolina in 1993, the summer after he and Jane Ann were married. During his college career, he worked several jobs to help provide for his bride while majoring in mathematics. In 1997 and 1998, as an undergraduate Chad helped to coach the Swansea High School wrestling team as a volunteer. Upon graduation from the university, Chad accepted a position as a mathematics teacher at Swansea and served as an assistant with the wrestling program for one year before directing the program as its head coach from 2000 to 2004. During his tenure, the Tigers won a state championship in 2002, their tenth.

In 2005, Chad became the coach of the girls' soccer team in the program's second year. In his inaugural season he sought to build a solid foundation for a program in which his three daughters would play. At the time, his oldest daughter, Haley, was a seventh grader, and he hoped to have the program up and running smoothly by the time she would join the team. The Lady Tigers won the region in their first season, and Chad was named the region's coach of the year.

Since its inception, the program has won nine region titles and appeared in the state semifinals three times. Coach Meredith has had numerous players named to the All-State and All-Region teams including his three daughters, Haley (two-time All-State), Hannah (two-time All-State), and Jane Ashley (three-time All-State). A dozen players have participated in the state's annual all-star game. Coach Meredith has sent forty-seven girls from his teams to play in college, including Jane Ashley and Haley, who signed scholarships with Erskine College, their grandfather's alma mater, and Hannah, who signed with the University of South Carolina-Aiken. In recognition of his coaching excellence, Coach Meredith has been named the region coach of the year in ten of his fifteen seasons at the helm.

Chad and Jane Ann also currently direct the music ministry at Swansea First Baptist Church. After serving briefly as the youth director in 1997, Chad was asked to accept the position of minister of music when the acting director resigned that same year. Jane Ann, who took piano and organ lessons from Billie G. Jolley during those years when her mother and father were driving her to and from Columbia, serves as the church organist.

Doug and Jane Bennett set a tremendous example of work ethic and character for their children over the years. What was most important to them, though, was that their daughters grew up with an awareness of the spiritual dimension of life. But more than that, Doug Bennett often told his daughters, "At some point in your life you have to make a decision whether or not you will serve Jesus Christ." Each daughter's journey was different, but all three reached this critical point in life and chose to follow and serve Christ. They view this spiritual influence of their father upon their lives as his greatest gift to them. Says Susan, "We are serving God today because of Daddy."

All three daughters married men of integrity who happened to be athletes. But before Doug Bennett would offer his blessing upon the union, he wanted to be sure that each man was a committed Christian. He also asked that these men not move his daughters out of the state of South Carolina! However, "Skinny" and Bruce both had career obligations that dictated out-of-state residency at the time of their marriages. Fortunately, both were eventually able to move their families back to South Carolina, and all three couples now reside within thirty minutes of Swansea.

By following the example of their parents, Susan, Beverly, and Jane Ann and their husbands have proven to be excellent parents to their own children. Each couple has incorporated the values of the Christian faith that they saw modeled by their own parents, and they are passing on those values to the ten grandchildren of Doug and Jane.

As J. W. Whitehead has said, "Children are the living messages we send to a time we will not see." Investing time in the lives of his children and in the lives of his children's children, this passing on of the faith from one generation to the next, is the most treasured part of the legacy of Doug Bennett.

Skylar Inman Apple, daughter of "Skinny" and Susan Inman, tells a story of how her grandfather's spiritual depth impacted her profoundly: "I remember visiting him one summer day when I was a girl. We were walking along in his garden, and he turned to me and said, 'Skylar, make sure you put God first in your life and everything else will fall into place.' I've never forgotten those words of advice."

She goes on, "If you were to come to my house and ask my children about their great grandaddy's advice for life, all three would say, word-for-word, 'Put God first in your life and everything else will fall into place.' Or you might hear them trying their best to get the harmonies right singing 'Seek ye first the kingdom of God and His righteousness' You see, we're trying to make it our motto too."

THE ASSISTANT COACHES

"YOU HAVE GOOD CORPORALS AND GOOD SERGEANTS AND SOME GOOD LIEUTENANTS AND CAPTAINS. AND THOSE ARE FAR MORE IMPORTANT THAN GOOD GENERALS."
UNION GENERAL WILLIAM TECUMSAH SHERMAN

One of the marks of a great coach is his or her ability to stay current. To be effective with the young people in his program, he must possess the wisdom to recognize when - as sixties musician and songwriter, Bob Dylan wrote - "the times they are a-changin" A good coach must be able to take the pulse of his or her team and adjust accordingly.

It takes a certain degree of humility to be able to make certain changes in your approach to a sport, anything from tweaking this or that to making major adjustments or even a complete overhaul of your system. Fortunately for Swansea High School and the coaches and players under his charge, Doug Bennett was such a coach.

By entrusting his coaches to do their job and not micromanaging them, Doug Bennett stood in stark contrast to some "control freak" head coaches who feel compelled to demonstrate how much football (or any other game they may be coaching) they know. As a result, they miss the opportunity to mentor younger coaches who could gain much from their expertise.

The story is told of a major college head coach who once pushed a young assistant out of the way and took over his drill with players in front of several other college and high school coaches who were visiting that university during a spring practice session, an annual ritual for coaches seeking to learn and grow as coaches. These visiting coaches had come to practice that day in a spirit of innovation and of being coachable and teachable themselves. And what a lesson they learned that day!

"Coach Bennett let his coaches coach," observes Bob Novinger, who served on the Swansea staff from 1979 to 1989, making him the longest-tenured assistant coach of the Bennett era. "He had a great feel for assigning assistant coaches to the position groups where they were most likely to be effective teachers. And he had the flexibility to do that because he could coach any and every position on offense or defense."

Novinger adds that Coach Bennett led his staff by his example: "Coach Bennett is a special coach and person. He's a class act, a true gentleman and truly a gentle man." Novinger points out, Bennett, though kind, was no pushover: "Coach was like a father to the kids. He knew how to dress them down when they needed it. Yet I never saw a player react in anger because of the way he corrected them because they knew he was right and they knew that he truly cared about them."

Rather than micromanage his assistants, Doug Bennett demonstrated and expressed confidence in them. Says Donnie Woolsey (the first former player to become a part of Doug Bennett's coaching staff):

> "During the two years I assisted him. I was amazed at the confidence he showed in me. He was there as a resource person, but he never dominated in an authoritative manner. Our transition from a player-coach relationship to a coach-coach relationship was a positive and seemingly easy one largely due to his personal capacities as a coach and teacher - he was still consistent, patient, and caring - but above all, loyal to his profession and to the people whose lives he touched."

In fact, as Phil Williams (1976-1980) points out, Doug Bennett was willing to allow his assistants to learn from their own mistakes - without him intervening - as they were growing and developing their own style as coaches:

> "Coach Bennett pulled me aside one day and told me he was going to send me Cecil Batson who had been working with the offense. He told me, 'I want you to train him up; he's going to be a good player for us.' Well, I think Cecil (known to his teammates as "Waterhead") was the worst looking defensive lineman I'd ever tried to work with – not only was he too fat but he couldn't run [fast]."

Coach Williams, convinced that Cecil was going to be a long-term project and that he quite possibly would be wasting a lot of good coaching on this "soft" player, decided to toughen Cecil up. He would drive him to the point that he would either get better or quit. But his cajoling and pushing did not seem to be getting through to this young guy, who Williams thought just might not be quite tough enough to make it in a program whose players had established and took pride in a reputation for their physical and mental toughness.

After about two weeks, Phil Williams saw little improvement in Cecil and decided to approach Coach Bennett to let him know that this experiment was not working out: "Coach, I'm just not sure that Cecil is a good fit for our defense - he's not getting better." Doug Bennett let his assistant give his evaluation and then calmly countered, "Well, Phil, you haven't coached him in two weeks. All you have done is criticize him. That's not coaching. He needs instruction with encouragement and positive feedback on the improvement he makes, even if it's just a small step."

From that point on Coach Williams changed his whole approach and found some positive attributes to encourage instead of criticizing what Cecil could not yet do. As it turned out, hidden beneath all the extra layers of fat was a storehouse of what Coach Williams came to call "Superman strength." Once he began to focus on how to help Cecil leverage his superior strength, "Waterhead" became for Coach Williams not just the "strongest fat boy I'd ever seen," but "the best defensive tackle I ever coached. People could not block him. He was so good that teams designed their game plans to run away from him."

And so, Coach Williams learned a valuable lesson in humility from "the most humble man I've ever known." It was not just a short, overweight player - who the new Swansea assistant had too quickly decided "would never play"- who needed coaching; Phil Williams needed some coaching as well.

Of his head coach who cared enough about developing his assistant coaches to take time to coach them as well as the Swansea players, Steve Carter adds: "Coach Bennett was so knowledgeable and yet so unassuming. He impressed me with the way he lived and with how he interacted with people. He is the most humble person I have ever met."

In fact, as Carter explains, because Doug Bennett was so unpretentious and so deferential in his coaching and teaching style, he demonstrated a wisdom that often went unrecognized until days, weeks, or even years later: "Coach Bennett always expressed ultimate confidence in his coaches. And because he did, he would often teach you something before you even realized he had done it."

Phil Williams adds, "Doug Bennett did not realize how great he was. He didn't know how much he influenced us as coaches through "osmosis," just being in his presence."

One of those lessons was learned by Steve Carter a little over four years after his initial August camp as a new member of Doug Bennett's staff. With preseason practices in his first year at Swansea winding down, Coach Carter asked his head coach, "When are we going to have cuts?" Coach Bennett paused and then replied, "Coach, we don't cut anybody." But Coach Carter brought up a tall, gangly ninth grader who was so uncoordinated that Coach Carter thought he was going to hurt himself. Carter thought that for this young player's own safety he should be cut and perhaps allowed to try out later. But Doug Bennett was committed to a principle of getting young men involved in football early and keeping them around and involved until they matured, and, in this young man's case, until his agility and coordination caught up with his physique. There would be no cuts.

Four seasons later in the semifinal round of the 1974 state playoffs against undefeated McColl, the Tiger coaches called four consecutive plays to run behind offensive tackle Buddy Harley, no longer the gangly, uncoordinated freshman who Coach Carter thought should have been cut from the team. Harley, an all-conference selection, was named the Class A Lineman of the Year as Swansea went on to claim the state title. In deference to the wisdom of his head coach, Carter can now laugh at himself: "Yeah, cutting Buddy Harley was a great idea, huh?"

Russian novelist, Leo Tolstoy, author of *War and Peace*, describes an attitude that Doug Bennett recognized early in his life as a potential character flaw: "Everyone thinks of changing the world, but no one thinks of changing himself." The primary reason that Doug Bennett was able to mentor his coaches and players so effectively was because he took the opposite approach to that tendency Tolstoy had observed in human nature - the young coach thought first of changing himself before attempting to change or influence others. He practiced the daily discipline of professional and personal growth - reading and observing and listening, looking for ways to grow and improve.

And though he was constantly looking for ways to improve his own leadership ability, he was keenly aware that any head coach is, in the truest sense, no better than the quality of his assistant coaches. He invested his efforts in teaching and mentoring these young coaches who, in turn, were investing themselves in the lives of the young men in his program. Doug Bennett's assistants, almost to a man, came to realize that they needed to be coachable and willing to learn new things because the man who was in authority over them and yet never led with a heavy hand, was himself a humble and willing lifelong learner.

Many former assistant coaches describe Doug Bennett as the consummate "coach's coach." Former Swansea Assistant Coach (1978-1987), Fred Orr, who over the years has developed a close personal friendship with Doug Bennett and who continues to spend time with his mentor on nearly a weekly basis, notes: "When I met Coach Bennett for the first time, I was not that impressed. Here was this short guy in rumpled up coaching shorts, with an old hat with a little *s* on it, chewing tobacco and I said to myself, 'This is a ball coach?'"

Orr, who was attending the South Carolina High School Coaches Association's summer clinic, had been offered a position at Richland Northeast High School as the head coach for cross country and as an assistant for track and field. But the school did not yet have an open teaching position for him. But Coach Bennett informed Orr that Swansea had an open teaching position, and "he asked me to come down the next day to look and around and talk about coaching."

Not long into the visit, Fred Orr began to realize that his initial impressions of Doug Bennett may have been wrong. As they walked around looking at the football facilities, Fred was impressed by Doug Bennett's calm demeanor, his sense of humor, and his obvious depth of character: "I thought to myself, 'This guy's a little different than what I (first) saw. If he offers me a job, I think I'll take it.'"

It is the conviction of several Bennett assistants that because Doug Bennett is a man of moral excellence and integrity, many have mistakenly undervalued his technical coaching ability and his knowledge of the game. Woolsey notes: "I have never heard him use profanity or say anything unkind about another person. Many young coaches and teachers have been the recipients of his kind words of encouragement."

But Woolsey is quick to point out that Coach Bennett's excellent character and concern for the overall physical, mental, emotional, and spiritual well-being of his players did not preclude him from stressing the basics of the game: "Coach Bennett was a coach who always taught fundamentals, re-taught, and then taught those basics again. He taught football techniques and approaches that I have personally used throughout my eighteen-year coaching career. Many coaches throughout South Carolina, benefitted from the tutelage of Coach Bennett."

And though Coach Bennett was "of the highest moral fiber and integrity," he was, according to Phil Williams, "the best halftime coach I've ever seen or heard about. He was a master at what has very nearly become a lost art - halftime adjustments." Because he was at Swansea for thirty-six years and had coached fathers and their sons, Coach Bennett had amazing recall and was, according to Williams, "an encyclopedia of football knowledge. "I remember one game during the 1978 season our opponent ran a completely different defense than they had run all season, and it was giving us fits. But there was no panic with Coach Bennett at the half." Drawing upon his vast experience, Coach Bennett turned to offensive lineman Bill Adkins and told him, in front of the team, "In 1956, Dentsville ran this same junk defense against us, and we hadn't seen it. Ask your daddy (W.B. Adkins) about it. Well, we got in at halftime and figured it out and then we went out for the second half and wore their butts out! So we're going to change our blocking just a little and trap the second linemen from the center instead of the first and we'll be fine. And I expect we'll do the same thing to them!"

Doug Bennett's strongest contribution to enhancing the careers of his assistants, was greater than allowing them to coach their position players without interference. He made his strongest impact in their lives upon by the force of his character.

Says Steve Carter, "Coach Bennett gave me an indelible impression as the consummate coach, father, husband, and, above all, a Christian. He always brought out the best in his coaches and players. It has been [several years] since I worked with him [but[the influence he has had on me still lives with me today."

Terry Pound, a senior player on Swansea's 1960 state championship team who became a professional photographer, may have captured the image that most clearly demonstrates the humility and "we"-ness of Doug Bennett. It is a shot from almost inside a sideline huddle in which Coach Bennett is admonishing and encouraging his players. On the front of his coaching shirt are not the words "Head Football Coach" or "Doug Bennett, Head Coach" but rather, to the surprise of no one who has ever been around him, simply the words "Swansea High Coaching Staff."

DONNIE WOOLSEY SWANSEA PLAYER 1968-1972 / ASSISTANT FOOTBALL COACH 1976-1977

"EXAMPLE IS NOT THE MAIN THING IN INFLUENCING OTHERS. IT IS THE ONLY THING."
ALBERT SCHWEITZER

When Donnie Woolsey was in the seventh grade, having recently moved to Swansea from Charleston, he noticed several young men "doing calisthenics" on a long field with tall posts on either end. Curious because he had never witnessed such activity, he asked the high school head football coach, Doug Bennett, "Is that football?" Donnie's dad, Don Sr., who had been a talented college basketball player at Newberry College and who would later serve as Swansea High's boys' basketball coach, had never exposed Donnie or his four brothers to football in any significant way. As a native of Indiana, whose long-standing love affair with basketball is captured in the 1986 movie *Hoosiers,* Don Sr. had little time between his job as vice-president of American Bank in Swansea and his responsibilities as a basketball coach to teach his five boys any sport other than "hoops." Basketball had become a way of life for Donnie, and he knew of little else in the world of athletics.

On what would turn out to be a pivotal day in the life of this young man, Doug Bennett clarified for Donnie that these young men were indeed football players, and he took some time to share with the naïve newcomer some of his own passion and enthusiasm for the game. Had he not, Donnie may have returned home that night to relay a version of this experience not unlike that described by Andy Griffith in "What It Was Was Football":

> "...I seen this pretty little green cow pasture... someone had took and drawed pretty little lines on it and drove postes in it...(where a contest was played where the objective was) ...to run from one end of that cow pasture to the other one without either getting' knocked down or steppin' in somethin'."

Donnie was hooked. Two years later, during the early stages of the white boycott of the newly desegregated Swansea schools, Don Woolsey, Sr. stated, in no uncertain terms, that his five sons would not be attending the newly proposed William Barrett Travis Academy. Even though he was a vice president of the local branch of American Bank, by no means could he afford to send five children to private school. Donnie was relieved and elated.

A five foot eleven 155-pound ninth grade starting center on Swansea High's JV football squad, Donnie was having the time of his life. Then he, along with other players in the Swansea program, including 105-pound quarterback Lee Flake, an eighth grader, were "called up" to start in a varsity game against Denmark-Olar. With its vaunted running back/linebacker, Willie Faust, who apparently was flourishing as a black student at a previously all-white school, the Vikings were not the team that the Tigers would prefer to face without several starters.

During the pregame "snap and step off" drill with the quarterbacks, Donnie slipped and fell to the turf, dislocating the thumb on his right (snapping) hand. Woolsey, now retired after a career in public education and athletics spanning thirty-nine years, relates that Dr. "Bud" Granger, the team physician was "pushing my thumb back to my index finger just after he had finished, (as I recall) calling me a dumbass."

"It hurt really bad - either my thumb or being called a dumbass - I'm not sure which hurt more." Now it is important to understand, now, that it is a cardinal sin in football to get injured in warm-ups, much less in the game, if you have been "called up" to a starting role from the JV squad because the player whom you are replacing is injured and cannot play!

As he resorted to the ability to adapt and adjust that would later serve him so well in his future as a teacher, guidance counselor, coach, and athletic director, Donnie learned, out of necessity that night, to snap with both hands - a technique he would use for the remainder of the 1968 season. After this one-game promotion to the varsity team, he would go on to make approximately four hundred two-handed snaps in competition for the JV squad while the injury-riddled Tiger varsity struggled to a 1-9 record, abysmal by Swansea standards.

When he thinks back on his career as a player for Swansea, Donnie recalls a crucial play in a heated contest with the rival North High School, just nine miles south of Swansea on Highway 321. In a near epiphany - if it's possible to have one in a high school football game - it became crystal clear to Woolsey just who this man Doug Bennett was. This impacting moment revealed a standard of excellence to which Donnie would later aspire as a coach:

> "That year North had a great team, and their head coach was a very physically imposing, hard-nosed leader who motivated his players to play with great physical intensity, even if it might border on 'playing dirty' I remember catching a pass on a buttonhook (route) and turning upfield to fight for extra yards. As I was being dragged out of bounds on the (opponent's) sideline, I heard their coach yell to his players, "Break his neck!"

Shocked by both the rage of this coach and the fury unleashed by his tacklers, Donnie, after picking himself up off the ground, was amazed by the stark contrast between this opposing "leader of young men" and Swansea's gentlemanly, but fierce competitor in his own right, Doug Bennett: "Until that moment, what I didn't realize was that all football coaches weren't like Coach Bennett. But not only was Coach Bennett an outstanding football coach, he was just a good man." This seemingly "just another play" moment in an inconsequential high school football game made a lasting impression.

When, as a young football coach, Donnie began to formulate his own coaching philosophy, he would look back on this play along the North sideline as a pivotal, life-changing eureka!: "I thought if I could just become half the man Coach Bennett is, I would be a heckuva coach. I would be a good one." Ironically, Donnie Woolsey's opportunity to enter the coaching profession came after he had decided to pursue other endeavors. And that opportunity was afforded him by a familiar figure from his past.

Upon graduation from Newberry College in 1976, Donnie accepted a job as an assistant manager at Mid-Carolina Country Club. As a senior physical education major, he had a very dissatisfying student teaching experience while on track toward a career in high school teaching and coaching, an unexpected "bad bounce of the ball" that led him to reevaluate his goals and reorient his career path. However, it did not take him long as a country club employee to feel, once more, the relentless tug of high school coaching and teaching.

While an undergraduate at Newberry, Donnie, a skilled high school basketball player, tried out for the Indian basketball team. However, a knee injury that had hindered his three-sport high school career, resurfaced when he tore the meniscus in the same right knee in a practice. Surprisingly, when he returned the sixty miles to Swansea to have his knee examined, Dr. Granger, a proud graduate of The Citadel in Charleston, after thoroughly examining Donnie's twice-injured knee, proved to be a kinder, gentler physician than before. In spite of his frustration that Donnie had probably tested this weakened joint beyond what wisdom would advise, the good doctor did not provide a deja vu moment by tagging him once more with one of his favorite monikers for Swansea players who sometimes committed acts of folly.

Undaunted by his injury, Donnie decided that if his playing career was over that he could at least become a mentor to young people in the classroom and a coach in the sanctuary of his first love, any gym with a varnished hardwood court. When his stint as an assistant manager at Mid-Carolina did not satisfy the longing of his heart to stay involved in sports, Donnie resolved to give coaching and teaching another try. Remembering the positive influence that Doug Bennett had on him from an early age, Donnie decided to consult his high school mentor for advice and to ask whether, as an athletic director, he might be aware of any high school basketball coaching jobs that might be attractive.

"No, Donnie, I'm not aware of any basketball coaching jobs out there," Doug Bennett responded. "But I do know about someone who's looking for a head B team football coach who can assist with the JV and varsity...me!" There was no deliberation on Donnie's part; he gladly accepted an offer from Doug Bennett to rejoin the Tiger program, this time as a fellow coach. The player whose view of what a high school coach should be was transformed by this man, a fierce, yet gentlemanly competitor, had now become a member of Doug Bennett's coaching staff.

As Head B Team Coach, Woolsey directed his eighth and ninth graders on game day and then coached in the second game of a double-header with the JV team. In those days, the B Team and JVs practiced with the varsity team during the week and played games on Thursdays. Some JV players dressed with the varsity squad on Friday nights and only on occasion saw action in varsity games that were blowouts. The opportunity to coach at all three levels of this perennially strong program proved invaluable to this young coach who was actually living the dream of many of Doug Bennett's former players: having a chance to coach football with the man who had such a profound impact on their lives.

The following year, Woolsey was offered a promotion to coach the offensive line on the varsity. Thankful for the opportunity to expand his coaching knowledge and expertise, he gladly accepted with one caveat - he wanted to remain the Head Coach of the B Team, which Coach Bennett granted. In 1978, Woolsey inherited four starters from the previous year: guard Robert Maddox, who would go on to enter the education and coaching profession and become Doug Bennett's successor at Swansea, center Bill Granger, son of team physician "Bud" Granger, Kurt Woodruff, younger brother of Donnie's wife Karen, a former head cheerleader at Swansea High, along with John Riley. Coach Woolsey's four returning starters were the latest members of a long line of outstanding offensive linemen that included, at that time, brothers W.B. Adkins (1956) and Clark Adkins from the 1960 state champions, Marshall Riley and Buddy Harley from the back-to-back state champions of 1974 and 1975, and Victor Riley, who followed his uncle Marshall to Auburn years later. What Donnie learned by being an offensive line coach would serve him well in the future.

Joining the Swansea staff in 1978 was Keith McAlister, who had starred as a fierce-hitting safety at Newberry College, where he was a senior when Donnie enrolled in 1972. After a brief stint with the Oakland Raiders in 1972, McAlister had entered the coaching profession three years ahead of Donnie on the football staff at Thomas Sumter Academy in Sumter, South Carolina. During Swansea's preseason camp that August, thrilled by the coaching staff's decision to train at Newberry

College, the former "stomping grounds" of the two newest Tiger coaches, Coach Woolsey was determined to make the most of this unforeseen, serendipitous opportunity.

Woolsey wistfully recalled this stroke of good fortune: "When the boys went down, I went out." With the Tiger squad safely tucked in their beds, Coach Woolsey, a young, energetic traveler on a nostalgic journey down memory lane, headed out for a college reunion on Main Street and, a few miles away, at the Newberry Inn. Accepting the challenge that presents itself to young coaches everywhere, Woolsey set out to prove that he could "fly with the owls at night, and soar with the eagles" the next day.

At around 3:30 am when Woolsey stumbled (not literally) into his head coach in the hallway in the team's dormitory, he fumbled for the proper words to explain why he obviously had not gone to bed yet and carried about his person the distinct odor of adult beverages. Before he uttered one syllable of what likely, considering his condition, would have been a string of slightly incoherent, self-incriminating words, Coach Bennett broke the awkward silence with a warm greeting. "Woolsey," he said, "A year ago, when I brought you on, I thought to myself, 'Bennett, you sure have hired yourself one fine, outstanding young man.' Now, come to find out, I hired myself a hoodlum!"

Delivered with his magnanimous, tongue-in-cheek playfulness Coach Bennett "coached up" his second-year assistant without leaving him feeling busted and condemned, or at least condemned. Before it registered with the young Woolsey just how graciously he was being guided (let's just say at this hour Woolsey's mental acuity was not razor-sharp), he experienced a flashback to his halcyon days as a Swansea Tiger when, on more than one occasion following a physical or mental mistake, he had heard Doug Bennett, in exasperation, exclaim, "Woolsey (excruciatingly long pause) Gol-ly buck!" But one thing he did not hear that fateful morning - nor did any other young man who played for Doug Bennett over his thirty-six-year stint in Swansea ever hear - was profanity or any demeaning put-down. Coach was too classy for that.

It might be useful at this point to take a moment to define and clarify a couple of entries in Doug Bennett's coaching vernacular: the ubiquitous "golly buck!" which should never be confused with the equally popular but distinct "by cracky!" As is evidenced by the mention of "golly buck" above as it pertained to Donnie Woolsey, this was one of Coach Bennett's expressions of his frustration, particularly with repeated errors. Few, if any of Doug Bennett's players ever received a "Golly buck" when a mistake, mental or physical, was made when the young man was putting forth good effort, demonstrating concentration, and showing a genuine desire to improve. Repeated mistakes were the problem, and in the mind of Doug Bennett, bone-headed errors would try the patience of Job.

"By cracky," on the other hand, was one of Coach Bennett's expressions of determination and resolve. Former Swansea assistant Fred Orr (1978-1987)is fond of telling the story of a halftime coaching meeting when a frustrated Swansea offensive staff was brainstorming ways to scratch and claw out a first down against the formidable defense of the Silver Bluff squad. As play after play was suggested with no resounding approval by the staff, Coach Bennett finally stepped forward and confidently declared, "Well…we can trap 'em, by cracky!" (A play where a quickly pulling offensive guard or tackle crushes an unsuspecting defensive lineman who is intentionally unblocked or only slightly nudged to influence him, thus usually creating a larger seam in the defensive front than normally possible using less deceptive techniques.) "By cracky" was most often a positive utterance, and as a player, you much preferred to hear "by cracky" than the dreaded "golly buck," especially when the "golly" was drawn out extra-long, as in "gawwwllllllleee (excruciatingly long pause) buck(your name here!)"

In describing the influence of Doug Bennett on his own approach to coaching, Woolsey is quick to point out that Coach Bennett, so often praised by players and coaches for his positive motivation and for his genuine spiritual presence as a man of integrity, was a tremendously effective teacher of the fundamentals of the game: "Coach put a very strong emphasis on fundamentals. That's one of the things about him as a coach that gets overlooked."

This emphasis on fundamentals became foundational for Woolsey as he began building his own coaching philosophy from the ground up: "I used a lot of his drills, including board drills, for offensive linemen when I got out on my own." And following in the steps of his mentor when he became a head coach, Woolsey trained his assistants to uncompromisingly teach the fundamentals of the game to their players.

In a forty-year career in education that included twenty-one years as a head football coach, Donnie Woolsey (and, he will tell you, his staff) was recognized by his coaching peers and the media by being named coach-of-the-year twelve times on the conference and state levels, including the state's Class AA Football Coach-of-the-Year in 1997, while compiling a 132-104 overall record. Woolsey also served his fellow coaches as President of the South Carolina Athletic Coaches Association 1998-1999.

But Coach Woolsey's passion for excellence and his resulting accomplishments as a servant to high school students were not limited to his coaching ability. After becoming an athletic director in 1984 and completing his master's degree in secondary counseling from South Carolina State University in 1988, Woolsey was selected to serve as a director on the board of the South Carolina Athletic Administrators Association, being elected as the association's president for 2002-2003 after being named the state's Class AA Athletic Director-of-the-Year for the association for 2001-2002. Woolsey also served as a member of the South Carolina High School League Executive Committee from 2000 through 2004. After the 2009-2010 academic year, Donnie Woolsey "retired" from coaching. However, he continued to serve young people as he saw a mentor in his life, Doug Bennett, do, but on a part-time basis as director of guidance at Strom Thurmond High School (where he served as head football coach 1990–1994 after previously coaching as a football assistant 1978-1982) until his full retirement in 2017. After his retirement, Woolsey was inducted into the South Carolina Athletic Administrators Association Hall of Fame in 2018. Not only has Donnie Woolsey proven to be more than "half the man" his mentor was, but a "heckuva coach" in his own right.

And as Coach Woolsey will tell you today, it was Doug Bennett's humility, witnessed by Donnie on several occasions, and his former coach's willingness to share his expertise and experience with younger coaches - even opposing coaches, that made a lasting impression:

> "When I took the head coach's job at North in 1984, I realized that I knew a lot about offensive football having played in the offensive line and coached the position as well as from my years as an offensive coordinator. But I didn't really know how

> to coach defense. And I especially did not know Coach's preferred "split six" defense even though I had been around it.

Although he never faced his mentor in head-to-head competition (Donnie refused to schedule Swansea in a nonconference game), he is sure that even if they had been scheduled to play in this bitter rivalry, "Coach would have taught me the split six."

Another lesser-known fact about Doug Bennett is that he is a "grass man" extraordinaire. In the same year that Woolsey accepted the head coaching job at North High School and called on Coach Bennett for help with his defensive approach, he felt compelled to ask for assistance with the discouragingly poor condition of his football game field. Not surprisingly, Doug Bennett's approach to turf building was a near replica of his commitment to building young men: straightforward, simple, fundamental, and consistent: "Donnie, you have to fertilize what grass you have and give it a proper watering. Then you just cut it and water it...and cut it and water it...and cut it and water it...."

Coach Woolsey relates that he had to move his Rainbird sprinkler an inestimable number of times just to complete one proper watering of 57,960 square feet of turf (dimensions of a standard football field: 120 yards including end zones by 53.3 yards.) And after following the regimen shared with him by the best "grass man" high school head football coach in South Carolina, Coach Woolsey proudly boasts that North High School had the best football playing surface in the history of the school.

And for anyone who would dispute Swansea's proud claim that during the tenure of Doug Bennett, it had the finest high school football field in South Carolina, Jimbo Raulerson, one of five brothers to play on that turf, puts forth an argument that Swansea, without question, had the most dedicated "grass man." According to the former defensive tackle, a 1979 graduate, Coach Bennett took a special pride in taking care of that field, but especially in preparing the turf on game day: "Most Fridays they would let some of us out of shop class to go down and help Coach Bennett with the field. He prepared that field with so much precision, taking special pride in cutting straight lines for the yard lines and hash marks and then coming back and pulling that string tight so that when he lined the field with chalk, everything was exactly straight and just right."

As further evidence of his coach's commitment to providing his players with the safest and plushest field possible, Jimbo, the third of the five Raulerson brothers adds, "There's many a day when I would look out the window of a classroom and see Doug Bennett down on all fours looking for armyworms," the dreaded and, in Coach Bennett's mind, the hated, grass-munchers. Perhaps Coach Bennett had added incentive to develop the best grass he possibly could. For decades, players and fans observed him on several occasions during a game as he bent down to pull a couple blades of grass to chew on as he watched his teams perform.

Funny how, in a twist of fate or in an unusual "coincidence," life sometimes returns us to old, familiar places, and we learn new lessons. In similar fashion to the stories Squire Rushnell tells in his 2006 book, *When God Winks at You,* in 1984, thirteen years after being viciously tackled by players whose coach had yelled for them to "break his neck!," Donnie Woolsey returned to that same sideline, this time as the North High School head coach himself. And because of the powerful influence of the man whom he mistakenly thought all coaches were like, he would model an entirely different set of values and morals, so foreign to those players who were on that sideline years ago. And the grass on that same field, from which he had picked himself up when he suddenly realized that Doug Bennett "was just a good man," coincidentally was, because of the most dedicated "grass man" head football coach in South Carolina, a much better playing surface!

DESEGREGATION OF SWANSEA HIGH SCHOOL AND LEXINGTON (SC) COUNTY DISTRICT IV

"DESEGREGATION IS DISTINGUISHED FROM INTEGRATION; DESEGREGATION IMPLIES MERE REMOVAL OF SEGREGATION BOUNDARIES. INTEGRATION IMPLIES A POSITIVE ACCEPTANCE BY WHITES OF BLACKS AS PERSONS INTO THE GROUP."[1]

At the beginning of the school year in 1963, no black student went to a white school in South Carolina.[2] In defiance of the landmark 1954 Supreme Court case, *Brown vs. The Board of Education*, the Palmetto State claimed the double distinction of being not only the first state to secede from the Union - providing a spark to a powder keg that helped start the Civil War in 1861 - but also, just a little more than one hundred years later, the last state in the Union to comply with the *Brown* decision. Two years after the court's ruling that declared segregated schools unconstitutional and mandated desegregation of all U.S. schools, Congressman Mendell Rivers proudly declared, "Regardless of the Court's decision, we will never see integration in South Carolina in our lifetime."[3] Governor George Bell Timmerman vowed that "segregation in South Carolina will not end for a thousand years.[4]" Thus, Timmerman echoed the sentiment of newly elected Alabama Governor George Wallace, who on January 14, 1963, in his inaugural address, said, "I say segregation now, segregation tomorrow, segregation forever."

The *Brown* decision met with strong and sometimes violent opposition in the Deep South. In September of 1957, nine black students who became known as "The Little Rock Nine," attempted to enroll at Central High School in Little Rock, Arkansas, and were denied admission. A National Guard squad called out by Governor Orval Faubus prevented the students from entering the school while a crowd of a whites, agitated by angry provocateurs sent to Little Rock from outside the state, began to yell, "Let's get those niggers outta here!" Three weeks later President Dwight Eisenhower federalized the Arkansas National Guard and sent members of the United States Army's 101st Airborne Division, the "Screaming Eagles," to Little Rock to ensure the safety of the students and to enforce this small step in the integration of Central High.

Congressman Rivers' and Governor Timmerman's bold assertions as South Carolina politicians - a little more than a year before the Little Rock incident - might nearly have been fulfilled were it not for the passage of the Civil Rights Bill of 1964. This landmark legislation most significantly tied the awarding of federal funding for education to compliance with the bill's Title VI guidelines for desegregation of school districts throughout the nation. Moved to action by the threat of loss of federal funding, Charleston County's Cooper River School District announced South Carolina's first completely voluntary public-school desegregation, ten years after the Brown decision, on June 10, 1964. However, indicative of the mood and sentiment of educational administrators and school boards throughout the state, North Charleston school officials refused to use the word "voluntary."[5]

The potential loss of federal funding proved to be an effective component of the Title VI section of the Civil Rights Act. By May of 1965, ninety-five of South Carolina's 108 school districts had submitted plans for desegregation: eighty-eight voluntary, five court-ordered, and two initiated by the federal Department of Health, Education, and Welfare. Yet, none of the plans of the local school boards had been approved, and seventy-two had been evaluated and issued notices that their plans were inadequate.[6] As might be expected, prior to passage of the Civil Rights Act and even afterward, South Carolina followed the approach to federally mandated desegregation by a mode of very public and total defiance of *Brown* on a sizable scale. "Massive Resistance" sought to mobilize the resources of the state and the private sector to prevent even one black child from entering a white school.[7]

Several strategies within the "Massive Resistance" movement were implemented, but all eventually proved ineffective. The most controversial of these resistance tactics took shape in an argument that ethnic differences between the races should be a factor in school placement. Prior to proposing the first "voluntary" school desegregation plan in the state, Charleston school board officials "attempted to prove by testimony of experts that wide intellectual differences between the races would cause a lowering of educational standards if desegregation were allowed."[8]

Incredibly, the argument for ethnic difference actually made it to the Supreme Court as a group of white parents were allowed to intervene as parties defendant in the action.[9] This group of parents appealed a decision by US District Judge J. Robert Martin, who heard the following arguments:

1. There were differences in brain weight and brain characteristics between whites and Negroes and that some scientists believe the Negro race is two hundred thousand years behind the white race in brain development.
2. Standardized tests showed intellectual differences between the races widened progressively to the point where a gap of three to four years was noted in the higher grades.
3. Forced contact of the two races in a hostile environment would tend to increase hostility.

In essence, these parents put forth an argument embraced by the Charleston school board a year earlier when they argued that wide intellectual differences between whites and blacks would cause a lowering of educational standards if desegregation were allowed.[10] The Supreme Court refused to rule on the matter.

A more long-lasting countermeasure to federally mandated desegregation was the advent of the segregated private school movement. In South Carolina, segregation leaders in the city of Orangeburg sought to create a private school system that would accommodate all the city's 3,500 white school-aged children. Leaders of the Orangeburg initiative sought to pattern their plan after one employed earlier in Prince Edward County,

Virginia. At the heart of this strategy was the desire of white parents to receive payment of tuition grants that they could use to pay for enrollment of their children in a newly formed private school to be named Wade Hampton Academy. Under the tuition grants law, school boards had to approve grant applications and forward them to the State Department of Education. If the private academy involved met established standards, the student would receive an amount equal to the per-pupil expense for public education from state and district sources. This meant that the public school would lose the money offered in the tuition grant and then be forced to supplement the school budget from local sources.

Previous Supreme Court decisions had cast doubt on the validity of state tuition grant programs as seen when the court banned tuition grants for a private academy in Surry County, Virginia. According to the court, the state would be providing funding that would enable white families to defy federal desegregation by enrolling their children in segregated private schools. White parents were marshaled into action when a federal judge ordered the Orangeburg city schools to admit twenty-eight black children. Soon after, the federal judge presiding over *Adams et al. v. Orangeburg School District Five*_ordered full integration of Orangeburg schools for September of 1964. In August of 1964, Wade Hampton Academy, named after Confederate General and eventual Governor of South Carolina Wade Hampton III (whose father was a wealthy planter and owner of the greatest number of slaves in the South prior to the Civil War,) opened its doors.

Four years later, in August of 1968, the drama of federally mandated desegregation unfolded in the sleepy, blue-collar South Carolina community of Swansea, thirty miles from

Orangeburg. Most of the white population embraced Massive Resistance and opposed the school board's decision to send black students from all-black Monroe Pinkney High School to its "separate but equal" counterpart, Swansea High School. Initially, the Lexington County District Four board approved a plan for desegregating schools from the elementary through high school. Opponents quickly let their voices be heard, and the board reversed itself in August with the opening of schools in the district imminent.

According to Attorney Matthew J. Perry, Jr., serving at that time as chief counsel for the South Carolina chapter of the National Association for the Advancement of Colored People (NAACP), "The board made its decision on the Wednesday before the Monday on which the school was to open. They sent letters to all of the parents of all the black kids saying, 'Your children will return to such and such formerly black school on the first day of school.'" Perry, who would go on to try over six thousand cases and almost every case in South Carolina involving the integration of public schools, hospitals, restaurants, golf courses, parks, playgrounds, and beaches, "...got the people to authorize me to bring the lawsuit...because of the action that had been taken (the school board's reversal.) I called Judge (J. Robert) Martin and stated that...I would need an immediate hearing on a motion for a restraining order."

Judge Martin, who had recently been appointed to preside over a case in West Virginia in which the governor was on trial for bribery, was leaving the state for an indefinite period of time, so he assigned the lawsuit to US District Court Judge Charles Earl Simons. Judge Martin asked Perry, "When will you have the suit ready?" and Perry responded, "I plan to have it ready later today." Then, according to Perry, Judge Martin

"...called me back to say Judge Simons was going to hear me, but that he would not be available until Saturday." (Swansea schools were slated to open on that Monday). Judge Simons, after hearing the lawsuit, ruled in favor of the plaintiffs and ordered the school board to carry out its original decision to desegregate. A nine-day boycott by the parents of white school-aged children ensued.[11]

Fortunately for all families affected, the desegregation of Lexington County District Four did not result in senseless violence as it had in Lamar, South Carolina, where a mob of two hundred whites attacked two buses with bricks, bottles, and ax handles. The passengers escaped before the buses were overturned. Tear gas and patrolmen in riot gear were needed to restore order. The schools were closed for a week. When reopened, 80 percent of white elementary students had left public schools. Of the 120 white students enrolled in the high school, none returned.[12]

White resistors in Swansea employed nonviolent but nonetheless nefarious techniques to express their defiance. According to Robert Maddox, a 1979 graduate of Swansea High School, the eventual successor to Doug Bennett as head football coach (1990-1999) and, a principal at the school, who in 2019 was appointed Superintendent of Schools in Swansea's Lexington County District Four:

"During the boycott, white parents would park across the street from the high school to see which white students were attending school, then call their parents to intimidate them if they refused to join the boycott."

In response to the controversial *Brown* decision, people on both sides of the issue, especially in the South, were moved to action. White parents advocated "Freedom of Choice" desegregation plans, that countered forced compliance with the court's decision, by placing most, if not all, of the burden for dismantling the dual school system on black parents who had to apply individually for their children to be admitted to previously all-white schools. "In practice, freedom of choice maintained the dual race system and gave the school board control over the pace of desegregation."[13]

In May of 1968, the Supreme Court decision in *Green vs New Kent County, VA* stated that freedom of choice plans, which had failed to desegregate schools, would be eliminated. The justices ruled that any plan for integration was insufficient unless it created a system where "...neither black nor white schools existed but rather just schools."[14] Going even further, the Court decided just two weeks later in *Alexander vs Holmes County, MS* that the principle of "all deliberate speed," a resistance tactic adopted in 1955 in the South, was "no longer conditionally permissible."[15] Perhaps unaware of these recent court decisions or in defiance of them, white families in Swansea argued vigorously for freedom of choice, hoping that black parents might not be aware of the resounding defeat of "freedom of choice" and "all deliberate speed," and so choose to maintain the educational status quo.

As a strategy for opposing forced compliance with the *Brown* decision, "all deliberate speed" had initially proven to be successful for its proponents. In 1967, thirteen years after *Brown,* only 7 percent of the black student population in South Carolina had been enrolled by their parents in previously all-white schools. The next year, during which a South Carolina court decision forced the desegregation of the Swansea schools, only 15 percent of black students attended integrated schools in South Carolina. In 1969, the number had risen to 29 percent.

And by 1970, two years after *Green vs New Kent County, VA* and *Alexander vs Holmes County, MS*, the previously "all deliberate speed" had been "accelerated" such that 59 percent of South Carolina's black school-aged children were in desegregated classrooms.

As such decisions had been met in communities throughout the South, white parents in Swansea and surrounding communities, galvanized by their desire to not have "...my kids have to go to school with niggers," soon began to organize and discuss forming a private, segregated academy. They quickly started Sandy Run Academy and later announced their plan to open William Barrett Travis Academy for the following 1969-1970 academic year. Named after a Texan who fought bravely and defiantly at the Alamo, Travis Academy, to a large degree, stood as a symbol of resistance to what many in South Carolina and the Deep South, as well as many throughout the nation, believed to be Big Government's infringement upon American civil liberties.

Some participants in the boycott took a stance of being concerned as parents that the quality of their children's education would be adversely affected by having to go to an integrated school, (the same argument put forward five years earlier by the Charleston Board of Education.) However, it was glaringly obvious that the true motive for many was to protest not the lack of a "freedom of choice," but rather what they perceived to be an encroachment on freedom, primarily the freedom of white people. Other white parents claimed divine inspiration as a reason for removing their children from integrated public schools. When a teacher at Swansea High School resigned to accept a position at the newly formed Travis Academy, she expressed the sentiment of a significant number of white parents when she stated that "I know this school [Travis Academy] will be successful because it is founded on Christian principles."

It is safe to assume that some Christian parents may have taken this position regarding the desegregation of the Swansea schools and the need for a new "Christian" school with some measure of integrity. However, other Christian parents communicated a counter-cultural set of values and set a strikingly different example for their children. Doug Bennett, a Christian parent uncompromisingly committed to his faith and to the education of his children, not only kept his girls in the newly integrated Swansea schools, but also took a stand against the motivation of so many whites who viewed their children as superior to blacks. Of the declaration that William Barrett Travis Academy would become a new bastion of academic integrity and the safe haven for children who should not have to be exposed to inferior children, teacher and coach Doug Bennett asserted that the new private academy had been "founded on bigotry and hate."

Now it is plausible to question whether Coach Bennett's bold stance on the formation of a new school may have been skewed a bit by the fact that the boycott by white families had temporarily reduced the roster of Swansea High's football team. It is equally plausible to consider that Coach Bennett, who had been a stalwart at the high school with coaching experience in every sport, boys *and* girls, may have been approached by some administrators or the fathers of his players who planned enroll at Travis Academy when the school would open in the fall of 1969 and asked to consider becoming the athletic director and/or coach for the Cougars, and to shepherd them into their first season of competitive athletics. He was never approached.

The fall of 1968, the time of the boycott by white parents in Swansea, turned out to be a very significant season regarding the integration of high school and college sports, particularly football in the South. One year earlier, Kentucky had become the first university in the Southeastern Conference (hereafter SEC) to integrate its football team.[16] SEC schools previously had been slow to integrate their teams; most actually refused to participate in competition against teams with black players on the roster.

Both Alabama and Auburn, along with other SEC schools, refused to play opponents with black players on their rosters until 1959, when the legendary Alabama head coach, Paul "Bear" Bryant and university officials agreed to play Pennsylvania State University, whose roster included one black player, in the 1959 Liberty Bowl in Philadelphia. Yet it was not until the end of the sixties, fourteen years after the Supreme Court's 1954 *Brown* decision, that the Auburn and Alabama football coaching staffs began to acknowledge the need to integrate college football in the South.

Post-historical sports mythology provides a story-turned-myth about the integration of the University of Alabama's football program under the leadership of Paul "Bear" Bryant and the implications for high school football in the heart of Dixie. As one would expect, with larger-than-life public figures like "Bear" Bryant, facts or actual events are often "spun" or "massaged" in such a way that it becomes difficult to differentiate fact from fiction.

So the story goes that Coach Bryant was so impressed or distressed by his 1970 team's embarrassing 42-21 loss at home in Tuscaloosa to Southern California, whose roster included twenty or so black players, that he determined that, going forward, he and his coaching staff at Alabama would commit to the recruitment of black high school players so that he could "level the playing field" as expediently as possible. Bryant hoped that, with this decision, he would eventually gain a strategic advantage over any Southern football programs that were stalling with "all deliberate speed" on desegregation. The facts, however, provide a very different picture.

Coach Bryant's staff had begun to identify black high school football prospects in 1968. Perhaps motivated by the successful assimilation of James Owens from predominantly white Fairfield High School into the football program of its archrival Auburn, the University of Alabama signed its first black football prospect, Wilbur Jackson, in 1969, the year after young Mr. Owens's matriculation to Auburn. The next year, Jackson played on the freshman team, thus indicating Coach Bryant's commitment to recruiting black athletes - a full two seasons *before* the infamous defeat at the hands of the USC Trojans.

Also, in 1968, the black and white Alabama high school athletic associations merged, pursuant to a court order, with limited competition between black and white schools starting that fall. That same season, Lexington (SC) District Four desegregated, and Doug Bennett's program experienced upheaval with an influx of black players he did not know and the exit of many white players who had been progressing for years through the Tiger "system." The merger of the two high school associations in Alabama paved the way for white college coaches to recruit minority athletes and provide a way for some economically disadvantaged black youth to earn a college education. In the upheaval of the 1968 season at Swansea High School, Coach Bennett had trouble fielding a competitive starting twenty-two players, let alone identifying any college prospects.

Brown vs the Board of Education was viewed, particularly in the South, as an imposition upon educational freedom in the nation by nine Supreme Court justices (coincidentally, a court composed of nine white males led by Chief Justice Earl Warren); it marked a crossroads after which race relations were further strained. However, in time *Brown* proved to be a landmark decision that provided an impetus for change toward a greater measure of equality. High school and college sports in the South, and especially football, with its larger rosters and its inherent nature as a team game requiring coordination and cooperation between its players to ensure success, provided a mini laboratory for social change."

Coach Bryant, in collaboration with his friend, University of Southern California head coach John McKay, scheduled what he felt would be a competitive game between his all-white Alabama football team and an integrated squad to demonstrate the need to desegregate college football in the South. There is little doubt that the lopsided 42-21 Trojan victory turned out to be more than Coach Bryant bargained for. But the game proved, with time, to be a crossroads for race relations, not only in the heart of Dixie, but throughout the entire country because of the visibility and success of his Crimson Tide program, a watershed game.

For his comprehensive and fascinating examination of this pivotal college football game, Steven Travers interviewed Keith Dunnavant, author of *Coach: The Life of Paul "Bear" Bryant*, who observed:

> I think football is so important, and at Alabama it was the leveler, theopportunity to compete on a level playing field with the rest of the country.
>
> Between those white lines, it doesn't matter who your daddy is; it matters how much do you want to

> win, are you willing to work hard? It is a metaphor for putting forth effort, achieving great things, and taking personal responsibility.[17]

Soon after the integration of college football in the South, there was concern that some university athletic programs, by offering scholarships to blacks, were merely keeping these athletes eligible to play rather than providing them an opportunity to complete legitimate degree programs. Nevertheless, integrated athletic teams, particularly at the high school and college levels of competition, served as symbols of racial progress and provided models for interracial cooperation in the South. Nowhere was this truer than in the tiny rural South Carolina community where Douglas McDowell Bennett had chosen to invest his life.

WE HAVE A DREAM

"THE ONLY THING NECESSARY FOR THE TRIUMPH OF EVIL IS FOR GOOD MEN TO DO NOTHING."
EDMUND BURKE

The postgame environment was hostile and even frightening. The 1975 edition of the football team from Swansea High School (integrated seven years before this night) had traveled twenty-one miles down Highway 6 to face the Wildcats of AAA Lexington High School in the preseason Lexington County Jamboree. After soundly defeating the Wildcats 14-0 in their two-quarter scrimmage segment of the Jamboree, at the end of the countywide event, the Tigers exited the stadium as angry jeers and demeaning insults rained down upon them from Lexington supporters, "Y'all ain't nothin' but a bunch of ignorant rednecks and niggers," being the most memorable.

Prior to the scrimmage, Tiger running back David Streeter informed his teammates that his friends at Lexington High had questioned his decision to transfer to "that redneck, hick town" to play football with so many black players. Streeter warned,

"If we kick their butts," (which he fully expected to happen,) "it could get ugly."

Undaunted, the Tiger football team, now packed tightly together in the yellow Bluebird bus - the oppressive humidity and pungent smell of ammonia comingling in the odorous aftermath of competition - celebrated together, black and white, another decisive victory. Soon a conspiracy was underway as "chant leader" Streeter and team captain Lonnie Simmons composed a hilarious but defiant response to the berating they had just received from a crowd of angry Caucasians.

In a short time, the composers led their teammates in their new ditty: "One, two, three, who are we? / We're the rednecks and niggers from Swansea. / We can't read, we can't write. / All we do is fight, fight, fight!" Their new chant, punctuated with uproarious laughter, filled the bus and spilled out of windows, let down to create some circulation and to provide some relief from the heat all along the return trip to Swansea on Highway 6 East.

Despite the near-flippant response of his team to the ugly scene they had just witnessed, Doug Bennett was concerned about the psyche of his team. After the team had returned to Swansea and emptied the bus, Coach Bennett found his senior team captain Lonnie Simmons and asked him, "What did you think about those people calling us those names? How are you doing, son?" The senior All-Conference middle guard replied, "I'm fine. Coach. Those people don't bother me." And after a brief pause, the young African American added: "Coach, I've been knowin' I was a redneck for a long time!"

* * * * * *

Thus says the Lord God:

> "I searched for someone who might rebuild the wall of righteousness that guards the land. I searched for someone to **stand in the gap** in the wall so that I would not have to destroy the land, but **I found no one.**"
>
> Ezekiel 22:30
>
> (New Living Translation, bold print added).

Prophesying to the nation of Israel in 571 B.C., Ezekiel issues a stern warning to the country's leaders who have compromised and failed in their duty to such an extent that injustice and immorality, oppression of the poor and disenfranchised, even violence and bloodshed plague the land. To fill a grievous void of moral and ethical leadership, Ezekiel declares that God is looking for someone, anyone, to stand up and do something to help restore and revitalize his people, who have forsaken the principles and values their leaders once so diligently taught and modeled for them.

The sad fact is that God found no one: no one to stand up and be counted, no one to recognize injustice and evil and resist those oppressive forces, no one to simply do the right thing.

As in the days of Ezekiel, injustice and oppression, systemic and institutionalized exclusion, pervaded American society in the sixties. At this critical juncture in our nation's history, I believe that God was looking for leaders to "stand in the gap," people who were willing, no matter what the cost, to strive to make a difference for justice and equality. He found more than a few.

As a seventh grader who was serving in the Swansea High football program as a team manager, I had an insider vantage point from which to observe the way Doug Bennett responded to personal and professional challenges during the tumultuous desegregation of Lexington County District Four. During the nine-day boycott by white parents, I went to school. Living with my grandparents following my dad's divorce from his second wife, I was being raised by his parents, Eugene Francis Simmons Sr. and Ruby Burnett Simmons. Owners of the Swansea Variety Store, Gene and Ruby operated their "dime store," one of the few remaining in a nation that was witnessing the emergence of "big box" retailers Kmart and Walmart. Determined not to capitulate to the emerging business "tour de force," my grandparents discovered that they could shop the "blue light specials" at Kmart and buy stock there, often at cheaper prices than those of their wholesale suppliers.

"Mr. and Mrs. Simmons," as they were known in the community, operated their business with policies that took into account that working families, whenever possible, needed a break. Hence, a Christmas season staple was their "layaway" program that allowed folks to secure merchandise, take it off the shelf or sales floor, and "pay it down" with installments until their items were paid in full - just in time to stock Santa's sleigh. Each year I loved my job of assembling bicycles, wagons, tricycles, and other toys; I also loved getting the attention of the older high school girls my grandparents hired as seasonal employees to help out on the sales floor and to wrap gifts. WOW! They sure were pretty!

With words, but more by their example, particularly in how they conducted their business, my grandparents taught me to treat all people with respect. While aware of the differences among their racially diverse patrons, I never really thought about it much. I never saw my grandparents treat any customer with anything but courtesy and respect, regardless of color. In fact, as often as I rode my bike or walked past the local laundromat - just a few doors down on the opposite side of Main Street - it never occurred to me that the hand-painted "White" and "Colored" signage of the plate glass windows was intended to be divisive. It just didn't make sense to me why patrons had to use one side of the painted cinderblock building to wash their whites and the other side to do their colored laundry.

But the impending racial divide and upheaval in our sleepy blue-collar and farming community would soon shatter my childhood illusions. It was after the boycott by white families in 1968 that I would come to understand why our town's two doctors' office buildings were each divided into two separate waiting rooms.

Because of who they were at their very core, at the risk of having their business boycotted, my grandparents stood firm against the pressure within the white community and sent me to school during the boycott. Anything less than that, in their minds, just simply was not right. And because I was going to school, I was able to participate as a team manager while the majority of Coach Bennett's white players were being held out of school by their parents and, according to school policy, could not practice.

As he welcomed a group of players from Monroe Pinkney High into the Tiger football program, Doug Bennett treated each player as a unique, gifted person with some valuable contribution to make to another emerging team. And because he had already demonstrated fairness and equal opportunity with black players Charlie Salley and Willie Wannamaker prior to integration of Swansea High School, members of the black community had already come to regard Coach Bennett as a good coach who treated all players the same and gave each a chance to prove himself.

As it turned out, Bennett's post-integration roster at Swansea High was composed of twenty whites and eleven blacks. Ernest Carter came over from Monroe Pinkney to serve very capably as Bennett's first black assistant coach. Carter had started the football program at Monroe Pinkney just the year before. Much of the equipment for his team had been provided by Bennett, who offered to help in any way he could.

When the players from Monroe Pinkney joined the Tigers, they did not bring a wealth of experience with them. At the beginning of any football season, the Tiger coaching staff welcomed, on average, five to ten new players who were moving up to the varsity from the junior varsity squad. They rarely had any new players they had never coached, much less seen, before. During the nine-day boycott when white parents withdrew their children from the newly integrated schools, rendering them ineligible to participate in school-sponsored activities, Coach Bennett temporarily lost every white player on the roster except for four. With the exception of Charlie Salley and Willie Wannamaker, who had come over from Monroe Pinkney the year before, the rest of the roster was composed of total strangers.

For a couple of weeks, the Tigers had only twelve or thirteen players at practice to prepare for that Friday night's opponent. But Coach Bennett was determined to compete: "As long as we have at least eleven, we're going to honor our contract." The task was daunting, very different than the challenge facing Herman Boone, the new coach at T.C. Williams High in Alexandria, Virginia, three years later in 1971, as depicted in the popular 2006 film, *Remember the Titans.*

In the movie, actor Denzel Washington captures the passion and energy of Coach Herman Boone, the black football coach who is assigned the unenviable task of leading a newly integrated high school, T.C. Williams, through the district's desegregation in 1971. In a story seemingly made for Hollywood, Boone, a successful championship coach from North Carolina, is hired to supplant the highly successful, and hence, popular, incumbent white coach Bill Yoast, who is unquestionably bound for the Virginia High School Coaches' Hall of Fame. After a tense initial encounter and some ensuing struggles, including a breakthrough in preseason camp at Gettysburg College in Pennsylvania, these two strong-willed men set aside their egos and pride to galvanize their racially blended team, and, together, they lead the Titans to the Virginia AAA state championship.

In contrast, the 1968 Swansea prelude to Alexandria's civil upheaval and the ensuing unblemished championship season of the T. C. Williams Titans, did not result in such a warm and fuzzy Hollywood ending for Doug Bennett and the Swansea Tigers who finished the season 1-9 - the worst record of his thirty-nine-year career. And yet Doug Bennett would do nothing during that tumultuous season to shake the confidence of the families of his black players that their sons were playing for a good and fair man.

Although I did not know this during these days that I observed Coach handle this crisis in his school, on his team, and within the community with tremendous poise and dignity, Doug Bennett did not make his decision to stand for what was right in a moral vacuum. Decades before the *Brown* Supreme Court decision in 1954 and the Civil Rights Act of 1964, universities in the northeast had fielded integrated athletic teams.

As early as 1907, the University of Vermont baseball team's roster included two African American students. When the University of Alabama's baseball team, was scheduled for a stop to play the University of Vermont during a road trip through the northeast, Head Coach John H. Pollard demanded that the two black Vermont players be excluded from competition. When Vermont officials refused, Alabama forfeited their two scheduled games and paid a $300 cancellation fee rather than participate in an integrated contest.[1]

Universities with higher athletic profiles such as Syracuse, Penn State, and Michigan State years earlier had taken a stand for equality. Five years after the *Brown* decision and just over fifty years since their refusal to play an integrated team in Vermont, officials at the University of Alabama agreed to play in the 1959 Liberty Bowl in Philadelphia even though Penn State's roster included one black player.

Ironically, it would be the head coach of the Crimson Tide, Paul "Bear" Bryant, who, just over ten years later, would sign Alabama's first African American football player, Wilbur Jackson. A member of the 1970 freshman team during the days when freshmen were ineligible for varsity competition, Jackson watched from the stands as an integrated team from the University of Southern California soundly defeated the still lily-white Crimson Tide, 42-21, with a roster than included over a dozen black players in what has become the most well-known integrated football game played in the heart of Dixie.

In the Deep South, Dean Smith, the head basketball coach at the University of North Carolina, effectively began the de-segregation of Atlantic Coast Conference basketball teams when he signed Charlie Scott, the first African American student to receive a basketball scholarship in that league, in 1966.

Reflecting back on this time of turmoil later in his life, Dean Smith commented: "I must acknowledge that my perspective on integration was significantly shaped by my Christian faith as indeed much of the civil rights activism of the time emanated from the church, with the leadership of Dr. Martin Luther King."[2]

In the fall of 1966, (the semester that Scott was attending his first classes at UNC), Wake Forest fielded an integrated football team that opened its season in the Deep South against Auburn University in Alabama, the state whose governor, George C. Wallace, was a staunch opponent of desegregation. His infamous 1963 declaration "segregation now, segregation tomorrow, segregation forever" and his white supremacy agenda were beginning to crumble. One year later, the University of Kentucky fielded the first integrated varsity football team in the Southeastern Conference (SEC).[3]

The question arises: Is it possible that sports teams, particularly in the South, during this volatile time in America's past, became laboratories, if you will, for social and racial progress? Could it be that integrated athletic teams eventually bonded and provided models for racial cooperation? Equally worthy of consideration is the impact of the young men and women who served as coaches and mentors for these young people, black and white, thrust together by a Supreme Court case from over a decade earlier. Often derided and vilified as "nigger lovers," these coaches, men and women of formidable character, most often did not see themselves as champions for justice and equality, so much as simply coaches who were trying to do the right thing.

To this day, members of the African American community in Swansea remember Doug Bennett as such a man of substantial character who was willing to "to stand in the gap" at a critical time in America's history. In addition to his duties as the head football coach of a recently integrated football team, Bennett was asked, after the 1968 season, to become the interim principal of the junior and senior high schools. With this dual responsibility, he ushered the school and the community through a very tumultuous period, Mr. Bennett, as he was known in his role as an administrator, served as the "interim" principal for five-and-a-half years.

Bennett established credibility and earned trust because of his character and conduct. Yet it was an incident in 1956, when a young Coach Bennett gave a baseball and bat to two black children who were trying to practice baseball with a stick and a crumpled milk carton, that made a positive impression on their families and others in the community who heard about it. Few would have known about this simple act of kindness had it not come up during a black ministers' forum held to look back and reflect upon progress in race relations since the desegregation of Lexington District Four in 1968. When called upon to give his input to the discussion, the retired educator and coach explained what had become a conviction for him. Over the ensuing years, Doug Bennett had become convinced that within the community of those making the transition from Monroe Pinkney High to the previously all-white Swansea High, this incident had resonated and had played a significant role in reassuring parents that their children would receive just and fair treatment in their new school with people like "Mr. Bennett" in charge.

LEE FLAKE
PLAYER 1968-1972

"THE MIND IS NOT A VESSEL TO BE FILLED
BUT A FIRE TO BE KINDLED."
PLUTARCH

Lee Flake's first appearance in a varsity football game for Swansea High School came against Denmark-Olar when Lee was an eighth grader. "Called up" from the "B team" when a boycott by white families during the 1968 desegregation of Lexington County District Four Schools depleted the ranks of Doug Bennett's Tiger football squad, Lee was beyond excited. As a spindly, beanpole of a player at five-foot eight, 105 pounds, Lee was an intelligent and disciplined student but, by his own admission, not the most agile of athletes. He reasoned that starting a varsity game as an eighth grader was intimidating enough, but this Denmark-Olar team was built around the amazing talent of Willie Faust, a five foot nine, 185-pound dynamo who ran a sub-ten-second one-hundred-yard dash.

As a running back, Willie was lightning quick and fast as he shredded and ran away from opposing defenses. But as a defensive end/linebacker who "played bigger" than his size, Willie's lethal combination of speed and strength kept opposing coaching staffs concerned. Of immediate concern to a young Lee Flake, however, was the fact that Willie Faust took immense delight in introducing opposing quarterbacks to the rich green turf of football fields throughout the lower part of the state.

Lee's mom, Lucie, senior postal clerk for the town of Swansea, was beyond nervous at the thought of Lee possibly being broken in two by Willie Faust or some of his teammates. As she and her husband, a retired US Army Reserve Major General "Chippy" Flake walked toward the visitors' sideline before the game, they passed the end zone where Tiger players were going through pregame warm-ups. In this poignant and memorable moment, Lucie overheard senior halfback/linebacker Vernon Lee admonishing his Tiger teammates to protect their rookie quarterback: "Tonight, Lee doesn't get hurt!" As her maternal instincts kicked in, Lucie "…wanted to get him off that field right then and there!"

Proud father Chippy, who served twenty-eight years with the Social Security Administration after he left the active Army, remembers walking through their home turning out lights when he discovered Lee, still up well beyond his normal bedtime on the night before the game, reading a book, *Mr. Quarterback*, as though the fate of the team and his very own welfare depended upon his comprehension and application of the knowledge and wisdom therein.

During the pregame snap-and-step-off drill with the quarterbacks, starting center Donnie Woolsey, who had been called up from the JV team to start his first varsity game, slipped, fell, and severely sprained the thumb on his dominant right hand. After having his thumb pushed back and heavily taped by team physician, Dr. William "Bud" Granger, Donnie improvised and began to snap the ball with both hands since he could not control the football with his right hand. Fortunately, for Lee Flake and the Tiger offense, this improvised snapping technique did not adversely affect the quarterback-center exchange. "I really couldn't notice much difference," recalls Lee.

Preventing an injury to the skinny, speckled eighth grader suddenly thrust into the starting varsity quarterback position would prove to be a formidable challenge. As Lee recalls, "Faust just killed us." But Faust was an even more dominant force on defense: "On offense we were actually calling plays away from him." The Denmark-Olar staff countered by moving Faust from defensive end to linebacker in the middle of the defense to thwart the Tigers' strategy.

One of Lee's most memorable moments in his inaugural varsity contest came on a pass play (which Coach Bennett, in these days viewed as a necessary evil), a play he was forced to call when the Tiger offense fell "behind the chains" and needed more yards than the most productive running plays were likely to yield. As he dropped back to pass, Lee caught a glimpse of a flashing blue jersey just before Faust hit him below the waist. With a move like a wrestling takedown, the linebacker thrust Lee's 105-pound frame onto his broad right shoulder. Flipped upside down by the menacing Faust, Lee was held in the air by his ankles for a couple of seconds that felt like an eternity before being promptly planted in the sparsely grown grass and dirt. From that moment on, knowing exactly where Willie Faust was aligned on defense before every snap became a high priority in Lee's quest for self-preservation.

The Vikings would go on to soundly defeat the Tigers that night. The harrowing experience was a groundbreaking initiation for Lee, and as time would prove, one for the entire Swansea football program. Of Lee's initial performance as a varsity quarterback, Coach Bennett said: "Lee did all right. We played an extremely tough team. Lee got hit a few times on the option, and I told him he should have pitched [the football to the running back] it a few times." Years later, looking back over Lee's career, Coach Bennett noted: "Lee was smart. He was not our best running quarterback, but he was a very good passer. And, of course, he was an excellent leader."

As one might imagine, some of the more memorable moments in a quarterback's career are those where they are leveled by opposing defenders. One such moment for Lee Flake came during his freshman season against Bamberg-Ehrhardt. The Red Raiders had sent forth their Goliath, six foot ten, 260-pound, Wayne Croft, an elite basketball prospect who would later play ACC college basketball for Clemson and who, to the dismay of opposing football coaches, played football in the "off season." But Swansea was led by the freshman signal-caller Flake, who employed a cerebral approach to contests.

Lee's experience with Willie Faust the season before had taught him to be more aware of the alignment of an opponent's best defender prior to each snap. Standing six foot ten, Croft was not hard to find. But locating Croft was only part of the equation. You had to block him as well. And on this night, the Swansea offensive lineman responsible for stopping Croft's pass rush was no match for him.

Since no human has survived being struck by a "Mack truck," we may assume that the impact of Wayne Croft hitting Lee Flake (who now had added muscle and weighed 125 pounds) was slightly less violent. Lee found little distinguishable difference between the two forces. "In all my football career, he hit me harder than I've ever been hit! I had all the symptoms of a concussion: dizziness, nausea, weakness," Lee recalls. Dr. Granger carefully examined Lee, testing and observing his behavior on the sideline before determining that the Tiger quarterback could safely reenter the game. When the Swansea defense forced another B-E punt, Lee put on this helmet, buckled the chin strap, and jogged on to the field.

When two running plays yielded little, Swansea faced another third down passing situation. Once again, the offensive lineman responsible for blocking Croft did not complete his blocking assignment, and the behemoth was barreling into the Tiger backfield with Lee Flake in his crosshairs. Lee proved that his memory had not been impaired when he caught sight of Croft and immediately threw the ball away with little regard for the prospect of gaining a first down.

To this day Lee laughs when he recalls what happened next. When he jogged off the field and took a seat on the sideline bench to watch the Tiger defense try to stop the Red Raiders' offensive march, Bobby Brock, the varsity basketball coach, and perhaps the most physically fit football assistant coach in the Doug Bennett era, sidled up next to Lee and quipped, "You lost a little bit of your courage on that one, huh, Lee?"

Footwork, which served Lee well against opposing defenders like Willie Faust and Wayne Croft, was one of the fundamentals taught by Doug Bennett, the only position coach Lee Flake had during his four years as a starting high school quarterback. Doug Bennett, described by former assistant Coach Steve Carter as "the ultimate coach" had, according to Coach Carter, "...an uncanny ability to identify athletic talent and to put players in the right position where their talent could benefit the team."

But Doug Bennett also demonstrated a knack for knowing when to think outside the box as he did when he met Lee Flake. "Gangly, awkward, and not very athletic," by his own admission, Lee was patiently molded into a championship caliber quarterback by a wise mentor who recognized his obvious intelligence, his love for the game, Lee's discipline, and potential as a leader. Though he might have normally chosen a different athlete for the position of quarterback, Coach Bennett took Lee's abilities and strengthened them while teaching Lee to overcome some of his shortcomings as an athlete with outstanding footwork: "Coach Bennett spent so much time with me on the fundamentals of good quarterback footwork that I literally knew, on every play, exactly where my feet needed to be."

And, as his playing career at Swansea bears out, Lee's feet were in the right position on nearly every single play. Through countless hours of hard work, Lee added the fundamentals of precise ball handling and sought to master the art of throwing the football as he developed into arguably the most fundamentally sound quarterback in Tiger history. But what perhaps gives Lee an edge over other Tiger quarterbacks is his ability to recognize and analyze opposing defenses, a gift that Doug Bennett recognized and nurtured from early in Lee's career: "Coach taught me a lot about what to look for in a defense, the keys that would tip you as to what they were going to do." By early in the season of Lee's freshman year, Coach Bennett had entrusted him with calling his own plays with a "check" at the line of scrimmage - a built-in audible that allowed the Swansea quarterback to make a decision at the line of scrimmage as to which side of the defense to attack. On Swansea's march to the 1970 state championship game in his sophomore season, Lee called nearly every play - except on those occasions when his calls were not going well and Coach Bennett needed to make some of his own calls:

> In games where nothing I was calling would work, Coach would send in a different play, one that frequently did not make sense to me… - but it would work. Or during a timeout he'd give me something else to try. He always calmly got my input and then discussed our options. He was always calm, collected, and focused on the task at hand. By the time I was back in the huddle, I was channeling his calmness and focused on what we had to do to win. Coach epitomized the old saying about keeping your head when everyone around you is losing theirs.

Doug Bennett was a master motivator as he knew exactly which buttons to push with his young quarterback. "Early on, Coach had more confidence in me than I had in myself," Lee recalls: "Coach always talked calmly to me about things. He was always positive and always treated me with respect. He gave me confidence as an athlete that I had never had before." As to the results of this coaching style, Lee adds, "I knew that if I would listen to Coach, I would be able to do what he wanted done on the field."

The confidence Doug Bennett placed in his quarterback and the long hours of working on fundamentals paid their greatest dividends on game nights, when all the preparation counted most. Lee recalls three games that come to mind as the most significant single games of his career.

One memorable contest for the young Swansea quarterback took shape in the 1970 state championship game. Three plays in the Tigers' heartbreaking 16-14 loss to Blackville stand out in his mind. The first was one of two pass plays on which pass interference by Blackville defenders went uncalled:

> "We ran 'Tear Right Pass' - a play-action pass off the action of one of our best running plays. I released the ball when Jimbo [Zeigler] made his break for the post. The Blackville pass defender got off balance as he turned his hips to run with Jimbo and he fell down. [With the Blackville defender now behind Zeigler] he was wide open and my pass was on target. But as he was falling, the Blackville defensive back reached out and grabbed Jimbo by an ankle and tripped him. It was a sure touchdown"

There was a second pass play on which, from the perspective of the Swansea sideline the "refs swallowed their whistles" - another pass interference and no call. The third memorable play for Lee occurred just after Tommy Williams's score set up by Gene Redmond's end around pass to Jimbo Zeigler for fifty-two yards down to the Blue Streaks' two. Down 16-14, the Tigers would attempt a two-point conversion to tie:

> "We were going to run a Wide Quickie left, a down-the-line stretch play. I got up to the line and saw that they were a little weak where we going to run the ball - there was a gap between the tackle and the end - so I did my fake audible to the right side. I started the snap count with "Down,"

> and a linebacker on our left side and one of their linemen jumped off-sides, but they kept coming and grabbed me and picked me off my feet (I think when the refs blew the whistle, our guys stopped). A third guy also jumped off-sides and grabbed me. Then they picked me up and slammed me head first into the ground. The first thing to hit the ground was my shoulder, and I felt like someone had stabbed me with a knife! Donnie Woolsey [Tiger center] and Charles Pound [fullback] thought that I had the breath knocked out of me so they're doing the old thing where they pull me up by my belt to try to get me breathing. But I'm in so much pain that I can't talk to tell them that's not the problem! Finally, one of them helps me up - I don't remember which - and I was taken to the sideline to see Dr. Granger."

Blackville was penalized for roughness and the ball placed on the one-and-a-half -yard line for the conversion attempt. Third-team quarterback "Bobaby" Smith replaced Flake and handed off to running back Tommy Williams, who "apparently pushed over for the score but was thrown back," according to one newspaper account of the game. But the two-point play was ruled unsuccessful, and the Tigers' last possession with forty-eight seconds remaining ended with an interception by Blackville's Michael Lott with nine seconds left.

Lee's collarbone was shattered - and so was Swansea's hope of winning a state title. But the Swansea Tigers playing for a state championship in only the third year after the desegregation of Lexington County District Four transformed a divided community deep in the racially tense South into one where the benefits of integration began to seem at least plausible and the prospect of harmony possible. The juxtaposition of black and white in a state whose political leadership had promised that integration of the schools would never happen was slowly developing into a bond that, over the years, would become one that could not easily be broken.

A second memorable game for Lee occurred during his junior season. With the loss of All-Staters Tommy Williams, Allen Williams, and Jimbo Zeigler from the 1970 State Runner-up squad, the Tigers struggled through the next season. Before 1971, McCormick and Swansea had never met in football. And from the beginning of the game, it appeared that scheduling the Chiefs from the larger Class AAA had been a big mistake.

McCormick jumped out to an early lead when Lee's first quarter screen pass was intercepted by a Chiefs linebacker who dragged Lee the last ten yards before crossing the Swansea goal line for a "pick six." To make matters worse, Lee, who doubled as the Tiger punter, heard the "dreaded double thump" (the name given by coaches for the unforgettable sound of having a punt blocked by your opponent). One of Lee's personal protectors in the backfield of the Tiger punt formation backed up a stride or two too far and, in effect, blocked the punt for McCormick when Lee's extended leg launched the ball into the backside of his teammate. And so, in a game with a disastrous start, the coaching adage about your chances of winning being minimal when you have a punt blocked would prove to be true again.

With the Tiger strategy not working, Doug Bennett abandoned his tried-and-true "run first and play tough, physical defense" game plan and told Lee to "just throw the ball." In today's wide-open "spread offense" oriented game, twenty-five passes are thrown by many teams before halftime. On this night Doug Bennett allowed Lee to call a seventies version of wide-open offensive football. Lee connected on sixteen of his twenty-five passes in an attack that demonstrated a "leap of faith" for Coach Bennett and, more importantly, very clearly demonstrated the confidence he had in his quarterback.

Despite completing 64 percent of his passes, Lee was unable to lead a Tiger comeback from its early deficit as Swansea was soundly defeated by the Chiefs from the larger AAA classification. But there were a few bright spots for the Tigers, some positive moments to build on. Lee had thrown the ball well and, with the exception of his early interception, accurately and on time. From his tight end position, Lee's favorite target, Brette Simmons, caught several of Lee's sixteen completions. A vivid memory from the game for Lee was walking off the field side-by-side with his tight end at game's end, each of them totally exhausted.

As is the case for most young men who play high school football, one's last game is very significant and memorable, if not the most poignant moment of one's football career, even for those players who move on to play in the college ranks. For most, it is their last opportunity to put on the uniform and compete, to experience the gut-wrenching pregame butterflies, to feel the adrenaline rush of running onto the field to the pulsating beat of their school's fight song with friends and family in the stands raising the decibel level with their vocal support.

At home against Elloree, Lee had another highly efficient game connecting on seven of eleven passing attempts for four touchdowns, his single-game best TD production. On the final pass of his career, Lee hit tight end Brette Simmons on a "look-in" from his flex alignment ten yards outside the tackle for his fourth aerial TD of the night. Lee and Brette, who signed with Furman University and was a two-time All-Southern Conference performer at tight end and a team captain for the Paladins, had spent countless hours in the summers working out together, executing route after route, running mile after mile, and sprint after sprint to get better. It was fitting that Lee connected with the junior with whom he had formed a brother-like connection over the years.

Hearing Lee Flake recount with savant-like recall and precision the most minute details from plays forty years prior, one begins to appreciate his brilliance that led many in Swansea to believe he would become a general after having graduated in 1977 from The Citadel as a commissioned officer in the United States Army and winner of the prestigious Granville T. Prior award given each year to the Citadel senior who has the best senior research project in the Department of English, History, and Political Science. Although Lee retired before reaching the rank of general, during his career, which spanned nearly twenty-eight years, the field artillery specialist was entrusted with increasing levels of responsibility.

References to quarterbacks by broadcasters and journalists have produced the "field general" moniker, and Lee Flake certainly lived up to the name during his days under center for the Swansea Tigers. But, more importantly, the leadership lessons Lee absorbed during his time under the tutelage of Doug Bennett enabled him to lead with confidence as a high school football player and served him very well as a soldier. Lee's skills as a leader were challenged right out of the gate as he began his career in Fort Sill, Oklahoma.

Because Coach Bennett had instilled a confidence in him to reinforce the strong love and support he received at home from his parents, "Chippy" and Lucie, Lee was able to lead with confidence while clearly communicating that he cared for his men enough to set high standards and hold them accountable:

> "As a combat arms officer in the Army, leadership was the 'coin of the realm' and necessary for success. So when I found myself as a twenty-three-year-old second lieutenant in a field artillery battery, in charge of nearly forty soldiers and non-commissioned officers, some of whom had been in the Army most of my life, the leadership lessons I had learned from Doug Bennett stood me in good stead."

Lee's first combat deployment came in 1990 when Iraq invaded Kuwait. As a major serving with the 101st Airborne Division, Lee was a part of the first wave of U.S. troops that stood in readiness in the desert in western Saudi Arabia for four weeks until the Gulf War officially began in January of 1991. Throughout his career as a soldier, Lee recalled the leadership principles that Doug Bennett had impressed upon him in his days as a quarterback: "Never blame others when you're in charge and your team fails" and "Never quit, no matter how bad things are and don't let those you're leading ever think you're even considering quitting" are Lee's descriptions of leadership precepts he learned from his high school mentor.

From 1995 through June of 1997, Lee commanded the 1-5 Field Artillery battalion at Fort Riley, Kansas. Lee later served as Brigade Commander of the 41st Field Artillery Brigade stationed in Babenhausen, Germany, charged with maintaining the combat readiness of the brigade from June 2000 through July of 2002. Then for the year immediately preceding the Second Gulf War's inception in March of 2003, Lee served as chief-of-staff of the famous "Old Ironsides" First Armored Division in Weisbaden, Germany. Deployed to Bagdad, Iraq, from May 2003 through June 2004, Lee served as chief-of-staff of the First Armored Division headquartered at what had once been known as Sadaam Hussein Airport.

Soon after the end of the war, Lee went on "terminal leave" before officially retiring from the United States Army on January 1, 2005. A successful ten-year civilian career was launched the next month in February of 2005 when Lee accepted a position with Lockheed Martin in Syracuse, New York. As "director of counter-fire target acquisition radar," he was tasked with a government contract project to design, test, and build a new state-of-the-art defense radar for the Army with solid state components and the capability of searching a 360-degree sector, - one that would replace the outdated "tube" radar from the early 1970s capable of providing target data within only a 90-degree field. On a project that normally takes five to ten years to complete, Lee and his team completed the arduous process of providing a new cutting-edge system - that had never been attempted before in three-and-a-half-years!

On June 10, 2015, after having been under the care of a cardiologist for five years and having passed a stress test in February, Lee suffered a heart attack that got his attention and led to his decision to fully retire in August of 2015. But it was not the long-term pressure of being the leader of troops in combat where the stakes do not get any higher, nor the stresses of civilian corporate work projects that triggered the cardiac event. It was simply genetics. For generations, within Lee's mom's family heart disease had been an ever-present medical issue.

So after nearly twenty-eight years of service to his country and ten years of principled excellence in civilian industry, the history major and Distinguished Army Graduate in Field Artillery from The Citadel retired to the beautiful and historic home of his prestigious alma mater, Charleston, South Carolina. Along with their loveable beagle, Georgi, Lee and his wife Donna enjoy a quiet life of leisure activity including golf, target shooting, camping, and walks on the beach as well as involvement with their local church, First Baptist of Charleston.

A former soldier who became president of the United States, Teddy Roosevelt, once said: "Far and away the best prize that life offers is the chance to work hard at work worth doing." There may not be more appropriate words than President Roosevelt's statement to summarize the life's work of a skinny, gangly quarterback-turned-soldier and the five-foot-nothing giant of a man who would help equip this soldier for a distinguished career of service to his country.

On June 21, 2015, just ten days after his heart attack, Lee returned to the hometown church of his youth, Swansea Baptist Church, for "Lucie and Chippy Flake Day," a special ceremony in which Lee's parents were honored for a lifetime of service to the community and their country. Asked to make a few remarks about his parents, Lee, though struggling through a slow, painstaking physical recovery, spoke about the impact of his mom's love and character on his own identity and choices in life, then he paid tribute to the three most influential men in his life: his father, "Chippy" Flake, Major General, U.S. Army retired, team physician, Dr. William "Bud" Granger, a Citadel graduate who influenced Lee's decision to attend the military college in Charleston and nominated Lee for a prestigious ROTC scholarship, and finally, his high school football coach, Doug Bennett.

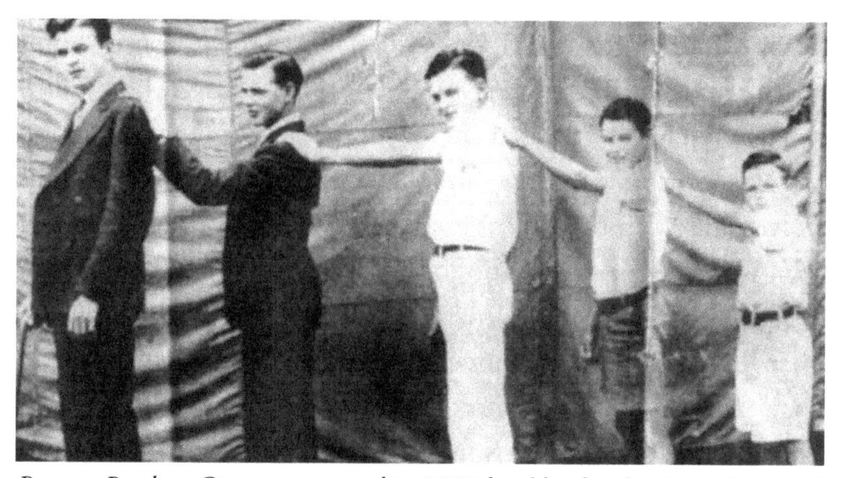

Bennett Brothers Circus was started in 1930 by oldest brother Joe, who served as manager and ringmaster while his younger brothers performed in a variety of acts along with 25 other child performers. Pictured from left to right: Joe, Charles, Bill, Stanley, and Doug.

Big top tent loaned to Bennetts by Barnett Brothers Circus from Canada who made York, South Carolina their winter headquarters. Up to 300 people attended performances for which adults were charged a quarter and children, a dime.

From left to right: Charlie, Stanley, and Joe Bennett

Stanley Bennett, P47 fighter pilot

Doug Bennett, U S Army Air Corps, precursor to the Air Force

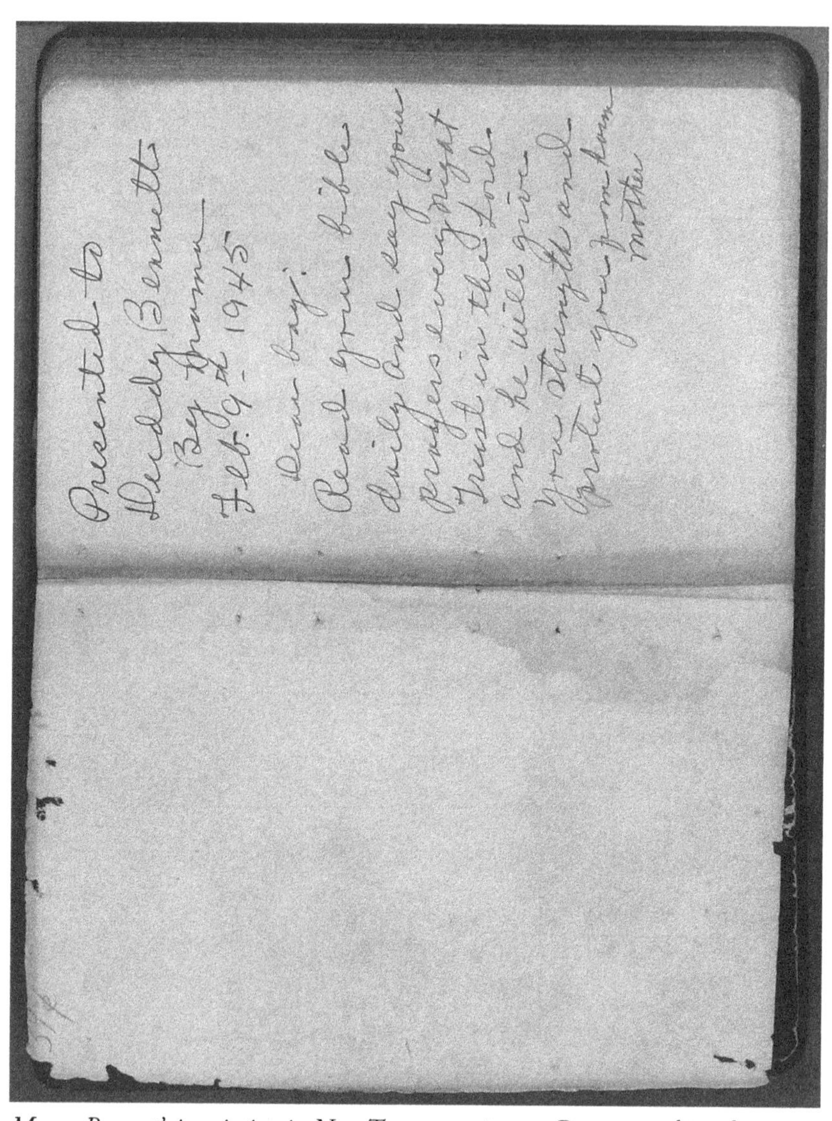

Presented to
Deddy Bennett
By Mama
Feb. 9th - 1945
Dear boy:
Read your bible
daily and say your
prayers every night
Trust in the Lord
and he will give
you strength and
protect you from harm
Mother

Mama Bennett's inscription in New Testament given to Doug upon his enlistment.

Upon arrival at Swansea High School, Doug coached all four sports offered: football, girls' basketball, boys' basketball, and baseball.

One of Coach Bennett's early teams from the fifties

Starting offensive lineup for the undefeated 1956 team

Bennett in his early days at Swansea High

1956 Team – Record 10-0; Coach Bennett's first undefeated team – in his third season

Ready to practice!

Coach Bennett confers with Co-Captains Wannamaker and Lloyd

Doug Bennett diagrams a play for the Tigers

Swansea High's "Block S" Club with Doug Bennett as faculty sponsor

Getting a ground level view

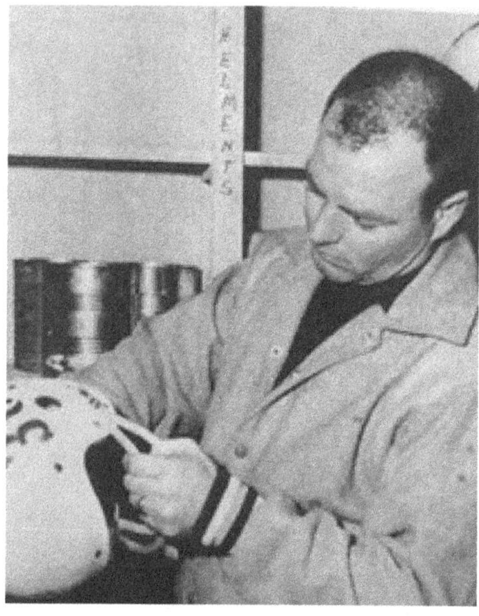

Repairing equipment - one of many jobs of a head coach

Coach Bennett confers with Vernon Lee

1960 Coaching Staff and Captain Johnny King

Starting offense for 1960 Class B State Champions

Tiger players prepare for showdown with Johnston Bears

1960 schedule poster sponsored by Frito Lay

Standout tackle Clark Adkins and Johnny King (South Carolina), another college signee with Adkins (Clemson)

Taking in the action at practice

Coach Bennett moves in closer to emphasize a key point

Doug Bennett keeps an eye on the clock as the game winds down

On the sidelines watching his team execute the game plan

1968 Starting offensive line-up

1968 Team Picture, first season of full integration at Swansea High School. Team posted worst record of Bennett's 39-year career, 1-9. Two seasons later, the Tigers played for the Class A state title.

1968 Team Managers: Brette Simmons, Tracy Woolsey, Tommy Rast

1968 Coaching staff: Top row, L to R: Jimmy Jenkins, Doug Bennett, Bottom row, L to R: Wayne Cole, Ernest Carter.

Coach Bennett exhorts team to play harder and smarter

Tiger players try to stay warm on a cold November night

Charlie Salley, one of two black players, along with Willie Wannamaker, on the Tiger squad the year before full desegregation of District 4, lowers the boom on an opposing quarterback.

Swansea's 1970 All-State Players: L to R: Allen Jeffcoat, Tommy Williams, and John "Jimbo" Zeigler

1970 Class A State Runner-up, with a 9-4 record, just two seasons after going 1-9 in the first year of desegregation.

Players carried Coach Bennett off the field after the Tigers' first-round 22-0 playoff victory over Lockhart.

Game Time! Swansea Tigers' own version of Friday Night Lights!

Bennett addresses his boys

Tiger Staff: Front, L to R: Baxter Gamble, Steve Carter, Back, L to R: Doug Bennett, Allen McNeil, Rudy Cooper

Doug Bennett, a master of half-time game adjustments, outlines the plan for the second half

Tiger Staff: Front, L to R: Joel Thompson, Doug Bennett, Bob Novinger; Back, L to R: Tommy Williams, Fred Orr, John Petrey

1974 Class A State Champions, #2 in Conference 5-A, #1 in the state!

1975 Class A State Champions, Undefeated, 14-0 Record, 19-game winning streak

Workhorse running back, Aaron Pinckney

Diminutive dynamo, Rickey Sturkie, gave the '74 Tigers a powerful one-two punch at running back with Pinckney

'74 Defensive tackle, Stevie Raulerson, the oldest of five brothers to play for Coach Bennett

Tiger Homecoming, 1984

Standout linebacker, Barnell Mack, has an extraordinary blocked punt against Bamberg-Erhardt, takes the ball off the punter's foot and scores a touchdown, one of the single greatest plays in the history of Swansea Football

Tough, physical, swarming defense: a Tiger trademark

Another one bites the dust!

Four Championship Caliber Quarterbacks

Called by Doug Bennett, the best option quarterback he ever coached, Bobby Frederick led the Tigers to the 1974 Class A title. Said Coach Bennett, "Bobby never missed a pitch."

Lee Flake surveys the defense vs Blackville in the 1970 State Championship game. His outstanding regular season performance against undefeated Chapin, generated momentum that propelled the Tigers toward the state finals.

Kit Jackson, a great all-round athlete who changed schools but kept the same mascot when he signed with Clemson after the 1963 season. He was a three-year starter at defensive back for Clemson and a high jumper for the track team with a career best leap of 6'8".

Perry Adkins quarterbacked an undefeated squad to the 1960 Class B title, before signing a scholarship with the University of South Carolina, the arch-rival of the Clemson Tigers, who signed his brothers W.B. and Clark Adkins.

Tiger fans start early in Swansea and the surrounding communities

Swansea's cheerleading squads, throughout the years, helped to generate momentum on the field with their enthusiasm and energy

Doug Bennett was blessed with competent and loyal support from: L to R, Dr. Bill Wilkes and Harold Witt, film and videography. Raymond Johnson did an excellent job keeping accurate statistics for all Tiger games.

Dr. William H. "Bud" Granger and the mascot always had the cure for whatever was ailing the Tigers. Dr. Granger began working with the team in 1962 and faithfully served the Swansea program for 31 years.

Swansea High administrative assistant, Jewell Riley presents documents for Principal Doug Bennett's signature. Bennett served as the school's "interim" principal from 1969 to 1974.

Principal Douglas McDowell Bennett: Class Act!

After 5 ½ years as "Interim" Principal, Mr. Bennett stepped down at the end of the 1973-74 academic year. The school's yearbook, The Swansean, was dedicated to his honor that spring.

Jane and Doug Bennett

Bennett Family on the field as Coach is recognized for his 200th win at Swansea: Coach, Beverly, Susan, Jane Ann, and Jane.

Doug Bennett: Fierce Competitor, Humble Gentleman

Coach Bennett's induction into another Hall of Fame

Coach and His Girls: L to R, Beverly, Susan, Coach, Jane, and Jane Ann

Coach Bennett and nine of his ten grandchildren

South Carolina's fifth-winningest coach in 1989

Coach, with press box for Doug Bennett Stadium as a backdrop

Coach Bennett the holds the banner provided to his parents, C.P. and Olive Bennett, with each of six stars representing a Bennett son serving in World War II. In a war in which 416,800 American GIs lost their lives, all six Bennett brothers returned home.

EYE OF THE TIGER

"IF YOU CAN MEET WITH TRIUMPH AND DISASTER
AND TREAT THOSE TWIN IMPOSTERS JUST THE SAME,
YOU WILL HAVE CLASS."
RUDYARD KIPLING

Doug Bennett was something of a coaching paradox. Many of his opponents described him as a fierce competitor; but, foremost, as a Christian gentleman. He loved to win, but he would not compromise by striving to win at any cost. His assistant coaches embraced his refusal to take ethical shortcuts to winning such as bending the rules or recruiting players from other communities.

On the high school level, Doug Bennett was a consummate "coach whisperer." Assistant Steve Carter points out that Coach Bennett had principles that were far higher than what most coaches choose as standards of excellence:

> "He did not count wins and losses as a measure of one's success. He evaluated his successes purely on the merits of whether he helped someone mature, grow, and become a better individual. He always

> stressed God and family. Academics came before athletics. He knew that the best way to help young people learn was by his setting a good example."

Doug Bennett stood for more than just winning. He wanted to win the right way - with dignity and class. He was gracious in victory and humble in defeat. His Swansea teams, over the years, developed heated rivalries with some of South Carolina's most successful high school football programs including Batesburg-Leesville, Blackville, Bamburg-Earhardt, Olympia, and Chapin.

Two of these programs had sustained success over many years as they enjoyed the benefits of head coaches with long tenures: Bamburg-Earhardt under Leon Maxwell and Chapin under Cecil Woolbright and his successor, Eddie Muldrow.

CECIL WOOLBRIGHT HEAD FOOTBALL COACH, CHAPIN HIGH SCHOOL

The rivalry between Swansea and Chapin has been one of the best in the history of South Carolina high school football. Chapin's legendary head coach, Cecil Woolbright, (1968-1980) was well known among his coaching peers for his ability to instill physical and mental toughness in his players. His teams were predictably strong and machinelike in their efficiency, a product, strangely enough, of Coach Woolbright's counterintuitive approach to preparing a team. His out-of-the-box methods worked quite well as the Eagles posted a 111-30 record during his thirteen-year tenure.

Many of the head-to-head battles between Coach Woolbright and Coach Bennett were the stuff of high school legend. From 1968 through the 1980 season, the series was deadlocked five to five, with a four-year hiatus, 1972-1975, when the two teams were reclassified into different conferences. According to *schighschoolfootballhistory.com*, the two schools played twenty-seven times from 1959 through 1989,

Doug Bennett's last season as Swansea's head coach. Bennett's career record against the Eagles was 23-13. In 2015, Coach Woolbright was posthumously inducted into the 2015 South Carolina Coaches Hall of Fame, in the same class with his competitor and friend, Doug Bennett.

Prior to coming to Chapin, Cecil Woolbright had squared off against Doug Bennett's Swansea teams when he was the head coach at Cardinal Newman, a parochial school in Columbia that competed in a public-school conference. He won only twice in six meetings. But his first two years at Chapin, the Eagles won convincingly with his oldest son, Marty, a six-foot five quarterback, leading the Eagles to 33-0 and 28-6 victories. Marty went on to star at the University of South Carolina, where he was converted to a tight end and drafted as a senior by the NFL's New York Giants.

When his playing days were over, Marty followed his dad into the coaching profession as the head coach at Lower Richland, Gilbert, and Clover in South Carolina before accepting a job at Audrey Kell in Charlotte. Like his dad, he faced Doug Bennett-led Swansea teams - but only twice while at Gilbert High School - defeating the Tigers in Coach Bennett's last two seasons, 1988 and 1989.

From his first day as head coach of the Eagles, Cecil Woolbright was a nonconformist and a bit unorthodox in his coaching philosophy. He was unconcerned about appearances and cared nothing about having (or, for that matter, his assistant coaches having) the latest in coaches' apparel. His short-sleeved, white button-down Oxford cloth shirt with a pack of cigarettes in the front pocket and khaki pants was his uniform of choice for practices and games alike. He shunned the standard issue coach's whistle, much preferring to stop action at practice with a deep-throated "Whoa! ...Whoa!" Chapin practices were not today's highly organized and regimented sessions with twenty-four (or more) five-minute periods, each transitioned to the next by a blast from an air horn.

Of the many hard-fought games in the Swansea-Chapin rivalry, it is the 1970 meeting at Chapin that is the most memorable for Swansea fans - for reasons beyond the game's final score. Coming into the contest, Chapin was 6-0 and riding the crest of a 27-game regular season winning streak. In his first two seasons at Chapin, Coach Woolbright posted a 20-1 record. The Eagles, who had soundly beaten the Tigers in the previous two meetings, were not particularly hospitable hosts for visiting teams having won twenty-seven straight games, half of them at home'

After having started six games as a freshman, Swansea quarterback Lee Flake views this rivalry showdown as the "biggest game" of his young career. Lee was extremely nervous and was putting intense pressure upon himself to perform well against the Eagles. The breakthrough play for Swansea came late in the first quarter. Operating out of the Tigers' "pro" set, Lee sprinted to his right and hit former quarterback-turned-running back Tommy Williams in stride as he ran a crossing route against the flow of the play and sprinted thirty-three yards to paydirt. Williams's touchdown culminated a seventeen-play Tiger drive that, to the frustration of Chapin's Woolbright, ate up nine minutes of the clock.

To the shock of fans on both sides of the field, Swansea led 20-0 at halftime. The Tiger offense struggled in the second half until they went to the well a second time on a successful play from the first half: "I knew Coach Bennett had confidence in me when we came back and ran the same play (that Tommy had caught for a TD in the first half) from the 'con set,'" Lee recalls. This time Lee found the dynamic Stanley "Bobaby" Smith, again running across the grain, for a fifty-nine-yard score with one minute and ten seconds remaining in the third quarter for a comfortable 26-6 lead. Smith, a diminutive, lightning-quick back, who was difficult for opponents to tackle, went untouched on his jaunt to the endzone.

Chapin responded with two second half touchdowns and a two-point conversion, but it proved too little too late. In the most pressure-filled game of his young career, Lee Flake connected on five of seven passes for 157 yards and three touchdowns. This stunning 26-14 victory over the previously undefeated Eagles would prove to be the impetus that propelled the Tigers, now 5-2 into the 1970 state championship game in Orangeburg. It was the only game that Chapin lost that season.

Not used to seeing their team lose much and certainly not at home in recent seasons, a few distraught Chapin fans were at a loss for how to respond. After the teams were off the field at game's end, a fight broke out between Chapin and Swansea fans - not the players! And while there are few reliable accounts of exactly what set off the scuffle between a few fans, it was remembered for many years by fans from both communities.

EDDIE MULDROW
CHAPIN HEAD COACH
1981-2005

Eddie Muldrow, who played collegiately as a wide receiver at the University of South Carolina, joined Coach Woolbright's staff in 1976. Muldrow was hired to serve first as the head coach for the Eagle junior varsity program as well as an assistant for the varsity coaching staff.

When he became the head coach for the varsity team in 1981, Coach Muldrow instantly began to develop a special bond with Doug Bennett as the highly competitive rivalry between Chapin and Swansea opened a new chapter. That fall, Eddie Muldrow's debut as the Eagles' head coach was the season opener against Chapin's long-time nemesis, the Swansea Tigers. Despite being reclassified into different conferences, Chapin and Swansea continued their series for many years. This night Swansea triumphed 27-17.

Coach Muldrow recalls meeting Doug Bennett - whom he had come to admire during his years as a Chapin assistant as a "first-class gentleman" - at midfield for the traditional post-game head coaches' handshake: "Your team fought hard and made very few mistakes. You're doing things the right way...Y'all are gonna be okay" he remembers the veteran Swansea coach reassuring him. Muldrow quips today, "As it turned out, this was one of the few times when Coach Bennett was wrong. We went 2-8 that year. Folks here weren't quite ready for that."

Over the nine years that his teams faced Doug Bennett's Swansea teams, Muldrow knew his Eagles would face Tiger teams whose players were "well-prepared, tough competitors who would play whistle-to-whistle, but without cheap shots. Coach Bennett sought to control games with the running game and tough defense. As a young coach, I wanted my teams to learn to play like that."

Coach Muldrow's record against Coach Bennett was 5-4. And despite Bennett's competitive intensity in this rivalry, it was the quiet force of the Swansea veteran's character that impacted the Eagle's young head coach. Muldrow recalls three specific encounters with Doug Bennett that made a lasting impression.

"First of all, when we traveled to Swansea, rather than sending one of his assistants, Coach Bennett always met our bus and greeted the coaches before directing us to the facility where our team was to get suited up for the game." Coach Muldrow recalls one visit to Swansea during which he enjoyed a conversation with Coach Bennett shortly after the Chapin bus had arrived. After exchanging some of the normal pleasantries, he and Coach Bennett discussed how on every high school football team there are some players who seem to be more motivated by some of the perks of being a member of the team rather than by a love for the game.

Besides enjoying a certain level of status among their peers, high school football players enjoy the common practice of team members being issued their game jerseys on Thursdays after practice so that they can wear them to school the next day - game day. Lamenting the fact that this benefit and little else seemed to motivate a few of his Chapin players, Coach Muldrow revealed to Coach Bennett that the Eagle staff privately referred to these payers as "jersey boys."

In similar fashion, it seems that certain Tiger players were also motivated by another school tradition at which the Swansea booster club provided a meal after Thursday's practice consisting of grilled hamburgers and all the accompanying trimmings. In discreet conversations among the Swansea coaches, a few players in the Tiger program were known as "burger boys."

In recalling another of his "meet the bus" conversations with Doug Bennett, Coach Muldrow remembers thinking that Coach Bennett's practice of greeting the visiting team's bus may have been part of a greater strategy for success on game nights when Coach Bennett commented, "You've got a pretty big squad there, coach." Bennett's observation, in turn, led Coach Muldrow to counter that in preparing to play the Tigers that week the Chapin staff had noticed "two of the biggest players we'd seen all year [Barrett Black and Doug Robbins]. They would put those two big boys in there side-by-side in the middle of that defense to stop the running game."

Not to be outdone in this tongue-in-cheek verbal sparring, Coach Bennett reassured the Chapin head coach that "those two boys will not be in there at the same time tonight because when they are in there, they sweat too much!" When he pressed Coach Bennett for an explanation, the Swansea mentor quipped, "Yeah, we can't play those two together in our 6-2 defense because they sweat too much and their perspiration is killing my grass!" Legendary for his meticulous care for the grass on his game field, it seems that Coach Bennett was willing to sacrifice a possible competitive advantage to make sure that the Tigers' playing surface endured the wear-and-tear of the season without losing a large section of turf permanently.

Finally, Coach Muldrow recalls an incident a few years later - after Swansea and Chapin were placed in different conferences - where his superintendent came to him with a request to change what had become a traditional opening nonconference game between the two schools. The newly opened Dutch Fork High School would be competing without a senior class, and the Chapin administrator saw an opportunity to gain a notable victory over a much larger school with a predictably weaker squad. Coach Muldrow was reluctant to call, but nevertheless picked up the phone and dialed the Swansea athletic department number. Essentially, he asked Doug Bennett to drop a game that had already been set by contract: "Coach Bennett was gracious and let us out of the contract." But as Dutch Fork High School grew and stronger classes of seniors emerged, Chapin dropped the game and reestablished their opener against Swansea.

In recalling his days as an assistant on Cecil Woolbright's staff, Muldrow says he was grateful for the opportunity to become a part of the legendary coach's staff, despite a rather inauspicious beginning to his long career at Chapin. In the one staff meeting held just a few days before the opening of the preseason in August, Muldrow, who just the year before has served as a graduate assistant coach on Jim Carlen's staff at South Carolina, raised a question near the end of the meeting as to what coaches should wear to the Eagle's first practice since they had not been issued any coaching practice apparel.

Coach Woolbright, dressed in his standard short-sleeved white Oxford cloth buttoned-down shirt and khaki pants said,

"I'll probably wear this." Long-time Chapin Defensive coordinator, W.F. Sullivan, dressed in his standard coaching outfit - a pair of cutoff jean shorts and a white V-neck T-shirt - added, "This is what I'm wearing." Muldrow was soon to learn that coaching apparel and even equipment such as whistles for his coaches were not high on Coach Woolbright's priority list.

Later in his career, after succeeding Cecil Woolbright as the Chapin coach, Muldrow had an opportunity to re-hire his former mentor to serve as an assistant on his staff. In a very awkward moment for Coach Muldrow, he interviewed the cagy veteran coach. Known for his rugged toughness, this man of few words was not one to elaborate on his many qualifications for the job. He said simply, "Look, I'm not much on making up practice schedules or breakin' down game tape - you know my assistants always did that. But I can water and cut the grass and line the field for games, I can drive the bus and I can do laundry."

And so, Coach Muldrow had his man.

LEON MAXWELL
1952-1991

Doug Bennett's his first contest with a Leon Maxwell-coached squad was in 1976, a season in which the formidable Raiders went 9-3 after going 13-1 the two previous years. It was Swansea's first season in Class AA after winning back-to-back Class A state titles.

After arriving in Bamberg in 1970, Leon Maxwell had quickly established the Raiders as one of the top AA programs. From 1973 through that 1976 season, Coach Maxwell's teams went 45-7. In 1973, 1974, and 1975, Bamberg-Erhardt also played in three consecutive state finals, losing to AA powers Chapin twice and Woodruff once.

In this inaugural meeting, Swansea prevailed 20-10 in the type of hard-fought battle that would come to characterize these matchups. But this first encounter between these coaches began not only a series of competitive games, but a friendship built on mutual respect. As Randy Maxwell, son of the late Coach Maxwell points out: "They were fierce competitors; but they were friends."

Although Bennett's teams would go on to establish an 11-3 edge in the series, seven games would be decided by a touchdown or less, with four decided by only one point. Randy relates that once Doug Bennett told him, "There's nothing that I like better than beating your daddy's football teams." Not to be outdone Maxwell replied, "And there's nothing he likes better than beating yours."

From 1952 to 1991, Leon Maxwell established himself as one of the most successful and respected coaches in South Carolina. He began his career at Latta and spent eight highly successful years there. In 1960 he became the head coach at St. Stephen, where he posted a 62-30-1 mark in ten seasons including an undefeated state championship team in 1962.

In 1970, Maxwell inherited a Bamberg program that had won only fourteen of forty-seven games in the previous five years. In Coach Maxwell's third season, he won six games, and in his fourth season, 1973, his team posted a 10-3 mark and played for a state championship. After finishing 13-1 each of the next two seasons with the only loss occurring the in the state finals, he would go on to play for two more state championships, winning a title in 1990, a season after reaching the state finals again and a year before he retired. From 1989 until his retirement after the 1991 season, Maxwell's teams went 34-8 and played for the state title twice. He finished his career with 297 wins.

This first meeting between Maxwell and Bennett was the first game the two schools had played since 1969 and "the fight," as it is known in each of these small towns to this day. Swansea was trailing 8-6 late in the fourth quarter when Vernon Lee broke a long run and tightrope-walked the last five yards for an apparent touchdown. However, one of the referees raced in from midfield and ruled that Lee had stepped out of bounds at the five-yard line. Despite the protests from the Swansea sideline, a first-and-goal series began from five yards out.

After three unsuccessful attempts to score, Vernon Lee crossed the goal line, and a fight broke out - first among the players and soon after between the fans. Wayne Croft, a six foot- ten defensive end with a cast on his wrist and hand came off the Bamberg-Ehrhardt sideline and was hitting some of the Swansea players with his casted hand. To stop him, Swansea tackle Robert Jumper performed a perfect form tackle on Croft, driving him to the ground. As Jumper, at 260 pounds, sat on Croft, teammate Gene Rowell, a fullback, punched Croft until the fighting stopped.

To bring order and peace to the chaos, Bamberg-Erhardt officials temporarily turned off the stadium lights. Then the B-E band director led his charges in the playing of the national anthem. By that time most of the fighting had ceased. Doug Bennett remembers that he and his coaches had gotten their players off the field and that they were standing at attention for the playing of the anthem. Since play was interrupted before the conversion, both teams had to return to the field. Swansea was successful on a two-point run by Stanley "Bobaby" Smith for the game's 14-8 final score.

Jumper and Rowell were two of three Tiger players - along with Bruce Rucker - involved in the melee who, ironically, would go on to become ministers. Croft signed a basketball scholarship with Clemson.

Coach Bennett's contention was that when one of the referees called Vernon Lee out of bounds from nearly fifty yards away, his decision set up a new series of downs during which drama and tension rose and erupted when Swansea scored on fourth and goal. Giving credit to both teams, Bennett felt "the fight" would never have happened had the official gotten the call correct.

Although Leon Maxwell did not arrive in Bamberg until the next season, 1970, he soon heard about the incident from the 14-8 loss to Swansea the previous season. It would be seven seasons before the two teams would play again. But the people of both towns talk about "the fight" to this day, fifty years later.

From 1976 to 1982, Randy Maxwell served as an assistant at Edisto High School and faced the usually unpleasant task of competing against his dad's teams. "I think we won once," Randy recalls. "Coaching with him was a far better experience than coaching against him." But it was uncomfortable for Randy on a personal level as well as professional: "It's not like I wasn't invited for Christmas dinner," he recalls with a laugh, "We just didn't talk about it."

Near the end of his dad's career, while he served as an administrator Randy would scout Bamberg's upcoming opponent on Friday night. He also coached the junior varsity. When Leon Maxell began to talk about retirement, Randy told him that he might want to reconsider since a group of talented players on the junior varsity that he had been coaching was about to move up. Leon Maxwell decided to postpone retirement for a little longer. That group of JVs comprised the nucleus of what would become the 1990 state champions.

It was during his time earlier as an assistant coach at Edisto that Randy Maxwell came to know Doug Bennett. From getting to know him over time, Randy Maxwell says of Bennett: "He was a gentleman first, a competitor, smart. His teams were well-prepared, disciplined. If you made mistakes against them, it cost you. Coach Bennett was one of the people who did it right. He was everything you wanted in a small-town coach."

Doug Bennett respected his worthy opponent, Leon Maxwell: "First of all, Leon was a good man. He obviously was a good coach; his record clearly demonstrates that." Bennett may not have always known what to expect from Bamberg strategically, but "I knew they would be coached well."

The approach to coaching the game of football for these two competitors was similar. Both Bennett and Maxwell believed that a winning program was built upon a tough, fundamentally sound defense. Randy explains, "Daddy was primarily a defensive coach. Over his career, he taught and employed most of the basic defenses, except for the six-man fronts. He would study film of an opposing offense and move his defense around to stop it."

Offensively, Coach Maxwell started his career running the single wing, which was in vogue in the fifties. Next came the straight T, the wing T, the split back veer, even the wishbone. Over the years Maxwell developed an arsenal, and he taught his teams to employ certain offensive formations in specific situations to try to create a mismatch or numbers advantage. He maintained a flexibility to adapt an offensive system or formations to the players he had any given year.

Another similarity between these two fierce competitors was an emphasis on positive coaching. Randy Maxwell observes: "Daddy was a very positive coach. After studying film and practicing a couple of times, by the middle of the week he thought we could beat anybody." He was right more times than not.

Other than the close margin of victories in this series, another trend emerged. Some years, the team who lost the regular season match up would win the rematch in the playoffs. Although Swansea won the initial contest between these two coaches, Bamberg-Ehrhardt won the rematch in the second round of the 1976 state playoffs. In 1990, Bamberg-Erhardt won the annual meeting on the fourth Friday in September, 20-13. However, in the state playoffs in November, Swansea defeated the Raiders in the first year after Bennett's retirement.

The two coaches also had a similar philosophy about how to conduct a business meeting for the coaches in the conference. If you wanted to continue to enjoy the convenience of hosting these meetings instead of having to travel to another school, you'd better make sure that good food was served! The success of these meetings was judged, in large part, by the quality of the meal.

Leon Maxwell retired with a career record of 297 wins, 121 losses, and 4 ties, which ranked third all-time in South Carolina football history at the time of his retirement. Coach Maxwell and Doug Bennett were both inducted into 2015 class of the South Carolina High School Football Coaches Hall- of -Fame. Chapin's Cecil Woolbright was inducted posthumously with these two friends. Maxwell and Bennett had previously been selected to the South Carolina Athletic Coaches Association Hall-of-Fame in the same 1995 class.

1960 STATE CHAMPIONS

"IF ONE ADVANCES CONFIDENTLY IN THE DIRECTION OF HIS DREAMS, AND HE ENDEAVORS TO LIVE THE LIFE WHICH HE HAS IMAGINED, HE WILL MEET WITH A SUCCESS UNEXPECTED IN COMMON HOURS."
HENRY DAVID THOREAU

Bennie Shivers was exhausted. The junior halfback had just run for five touchdowns and passed for a sixth to lead his undefeated Swansea Tigers to their seventh straight victory, a 48-0 rout of Wagener. But the exhilaration of victory mitigated his fatigue. To that point, the Tigers owned a perfect 7-0 record. The stout Swansea defense had yielded a mere twenty-five points in those seven games; (they would give up only twelve in the remaining six games.) For Shivers and his teammates, a state title was a realistic goal. A 40-6 crushing of winless Whitmire that would follow in the next game featured the Swansea defense holding Whitmire scoreless until Robert Jones ran for a two-yard touchdown with four minutes remaining in the contest. Expectations were rising.

"This is certainly one of the best teams I've ever had," said Doug Bennett, in his seventh year at Swansea. "The boys are intelligent, experienced, eager, and hardworking. You can't beat that. The teamwork is excellent. The club seems to be able to take advantage of the other team's mistakes and also make its own breaks."

Batesburg-Leesville

The closest game up until now had been the Batesburg-Leesville game, a 19-6 win in the season opener. After a 6-6 tie at half-time, Swansea was able to take advantage of two Batesburg-Leesville errors. The first was a fumble that Swansea recovered at the B-L thirty-one. Shivers capped the short drive to paydirt with an eleven-yard run, putting the Tigers ahead 12-6.

The second Panther miscue came in the fourth period when Rollin Saylor blocked a B-L punt and Alvin Chavis recovered it at the two. Perry Atkins scored on his second attempt and Bennie Williams ran for the extra point and the final 19-6 margin. It was only the first game. But the Tigers had beaten a perennially tough opponent. Convincing wins followed Swansea's opening contest: a 40-7 rout of Barnwell, a 33-6 defeat of Andrews, and a 41-0 blanking of rival North.

Lower Richland

In their fifth win of the season, the Tigers overpowered Lower Richland 37-6. Halfback Larry Sturkie got Swansea jumpstarted with a fifty-two-yard touchdown run on the second play of the game. One series later, Bennie Shivers galloped fifty yards for another Tiger score. Johnny King kicked the extra point to make the score 13-0 at the end of the quarter.

Midway through the second period, King raced twenty-three yards up the middle for a touchdown. Swansea closed out the scoring in the first half when Perry Adkins sneaked over from the two for a 25-0 Tiger advantage.

Swansea scored again early in the third period when Adkins sneaked over from three yards out. Lower Richland got its only score in the game when Alvin Phelps ran seventy-three yards with an option pitch. The attempt for the extra point failed, bringing the score to 31-6. In the fourth quarter, the Tigers added their final touchdown on an eighteen-yard yard run by Shivers.

Irmo

Swansea picked up its sixth win of the season with a 29-0 shut-out of Irmo in a Conference 4-B contest. For the second consecutive game, Larry Sturkie scored on the second play of the game when he raced eighty-six yards for a touchdown. Johnny King kicked the first of his three extra points for a 7-0 lead. Later in the quarter, it was King's turn as he ran fifty-three yards for the second Tiger touchdown. In the second quarter, Bennie Shivers slashed fourteen yards for a score, and the two teams broke for halftime with Swansea owning a 21-0 advantage.

The second half was played in a downpour, but the deluge did not deter the Tigers. In the third period, end Arthur Chavis recovered a fumble at the Irmo twenty-one to set up Perry Adkins's sixteen-yard yard pass to Shivers for a touchdown. In the final period, Swansea's defense had Lower Richland backed up and punting from its own end zone. Irmo punter Richard Johns mishandled the snap, and the ball rolled out of the end zone, resulting in a safety and the final 29-0 score.

Johnston

As one sportswriter phrased it, Swansea's unbeaten Tigers "bruised" Johnson 36-0 for their ninth victory. The lopsided win gave Tiger fans plenty to cheer about and sparked optimism, as Johnson was the defending state champion.

Again, the Tigers got off to a fast start, racing to a 20-0 halftime advantage. Short runs by halfbacks Bennie Shivers and Larry Sturkie and another by fullback Johnny King gave Swansea an insurmountable lead. In the second half, end Arthur Chavis scored when he scooped a Bear fumble and raced thirty-three yards. Quarterback Perry Adkins added a one-yard plunge for Swansea's fifth touchdown. King, who kicked three of five extra points, added an eighteen-yard field goal in the second half.

With the regular season winding down, end Davie Craft revealed what may have been one secret to the Tigers' success: "...a gold-colored pair of custom-made underwear that my mother would sew the game scores on. It was a good motivator in the locker room before each game."

Chapin

The Tigers extended their winning streak to ten with a 32-0 win over rival Chapin. In this one, Swansea scored quickly, tallying three touchdowns in the first quarter. Larry Stuckey sprinted eighty yards, Bennie Williams ran five yards, and Bennie Shivers passed twenty-three yards to Arthur Chavis to give the Tigers an 18-0 advantage after one period. Near the end of the quarter, Johnny King intercepted a pass at midfield and returned it to the Chapin ten. Two plays later, he slammed over for the score. King kicked both second half extra points for the Tigers. With the win, the Tigers were conference champions and headed to face Buford in the quarterfinals of the state playoffs.

After ten games, the Tigers were averaging 301 yards of total offense and yielding a mere 77.8 yards to their opponents. More importantly, Swansea was scoring 35.5 points per contest while giving up just 3.1 points per game. Despite their dominance, the Tigers would not have an easy path to a championship.

Buford

In the Tigers' quarterfinal matchup with Buford in Lancaster, quarterback Perry Adkins climaxed a forty-yard drive in the opening period when he scored from the one. Johnny King's kick for the extra point was good for a 7-0 Tiger lead. From the outset, the Tiger defense served notice that yards and points would be hard to come by for the Indians. A scoreless second quarter followed.

In the third quarter, the Swansea offense marched seventy-five yards with Perry again scoring from one yard out. The Tigers wrapped up their scoring - and the game - when King passed thirty yards to Davey Craft, who scampered the remaining ten yards for a touchdown.

The Tiger defense again turned in a stellar performance as they recorded their fifth shutout of the season. The win propelled Swansea to a semifinal game against Johnson, a rematch of their regular season contest, which the Tigers won 36-0.

Johnston

In their semifinal match with Johnson, Swansea faced the daunting task of playing a team they had already beaten handily. Although the Bears had fallen to the Tigers 36-0 just three weeks prior, they were the defending state champions. To be sure, their pride would be a factor in this rematch. Bennett was concerned about how the large margin of victory in the first meeting might affect his team: "This may be a psychological hindrance against us."

Lest they be beguiled by overconfidence, the Tigers faced the sobering reality that they would enter this game without the services of their top two running backs, Bennie Williams and Bennie Shivers. Williams had suffered a broken collarbone at practice earlier in the week. Shivers had injured his knee and took part in only one play. Fullback Johnny King would step up to carry much of the load in the running game with these two outstanding backs unable to play.

As might be expected, both teams struggled to generate any offensive threat in the first quarter. Early in the second period, Swansea drove to the Bears' four but lost possession on a fumble that was recovered at the two. When Johnston was forced to punt, Monroe Swearingen got off a poor kick and Swansea got the ball at the Johnston thirty. From there, Perry Adkins completed the short drive when he sneaked over from the two. Johnny King kicked what would prove to be the all-important extra point.

Johnston got their lone score of the game when they drove eighty yards with halfback Billy Miller slashing in from four yards out. Miller's attempt to run wide for the extra point was stopped by Adkins and King. But Johnson was not finished. In the fourth period they drove to the Tigers' twenty-one trailing only by a point. But Perry Adkins's interception of a Bear pass ended the threat.

In this defensive struggle, Swansea prevailed 7-6 and earned the right to do something unprecedented in the history of the school - to play for a state championship in football.

St. Matthews

As his team prepared to face St. Matthews in the state finals, Doug Bennett was asked what he thought were the keys to the Tigers' undefeated season this far:

> "We've got good material. In fact, we've got three college prospects on the team, and if the rest of them were big enough or seniors, they could play college ball too. Secondly, we've had a lot of spirit all year. When you're winning I guess it's easier to keep the boys happy. Third, I have to say our overall balance is just about all you could ask for. We've been getting excellent defensive, play, and our passing and running have been above average.
>
> St. Matthews entered the championship game coming off a 14-0 upset of powerful Lamar. "And they'll be tough tomorrow night," Bennett declared. "But we're so close to that title that I don't think the boys will let them take it away from us."

Swansea's inaugural appearance in the state final could not have been much closer to a home game than in Orangeburg, thirty miles away. St. Matthews, playing in their third straight championship game, was even closer. Nearly four thousand fans - more than the combined populations of both towns - turned out and watched Swansea complete a perfect 13-0 season with a hard-fought 7-0 victory over the Yellow Jackets.

Swansea drove forty-four yards for a first quarter touchdown and then relied upon their stingy defense the rest of the way. In the lone scoring drive of the game, Johnny King had a fourteen-yard carry before he plunged in from the one. His kick for the extra point was good, as he accounted for all the Tigers' scoring.

For the remainder of the game, fans witnessed a defensive slugfest. Each team was fighting for first downs (Swansea had nine for the game and St. Matthews five). However, in the third period, Swansea drove all the way to the St. Matthews half-yard line. There the Yellow Jacket defense stiffened and got the ball back on downs.

With two and a half minutes left in the game, St. Matthews had one last attempt to even the score. But an incomplete pass was followed by a completed jump pass that was jarred loose and recovered by the Swansea defense. It was their second recovered fumble to go along with two interceptions for a total of four defensive take-aways. The Swansea offense, which committed no turnovers in the game, ran out the clock.

After the final whistle, it seemed most of the town of Swansea rushed the field as a - triumphant celebration ensued. In a surge of euphoria, students, families, and fans embraced their Friday night heroes. Players and coaches hugged one another, elated that their hard work together had paid off.

End Davie Craft explained what had been a driving force for him and his teammates over the course of their championship season: "Us senior boys figured that 1960 was our last chance to win for Doug Bennett and for Swansea High School."

In his typical understated manner, Doug Bennett told reporters, "We're mighty happy we won."

DAVIE "LEWIE" CRAFT PLAYER 1957-1960

"HARD WORK BEATS TALENT WHEN TALENT DOESN'T WORK HARD."
UNKNOWN

On August 18, 1957, there was a horrible car accident involving six Swansea football players just three days before the start of the season. Herbert Stabler, the Tigers' center, had his back fractured in fourteen places. Davie Craft said, "Coach Bennett told us what happened and that we were still going to play. Then he added, "Davie, you will play center."

Davie was shaken by his lack of experience since he had not played much as an eighth grader: "I spent that whole season learning how to put my uniform on and how to travel away from Swansea in a bus." But even more challenging was the fact that he had never snapped a football. Davie began his crash course that afternoon by practicing snapping the football to Tiger quarterback Billy "Bones" Mack. "We worked on it in the next morning's practice and in a scrimmage against Olympia that afternoon."

Davie's self-described "baptism by fire" came the next night as Swansea traveled to Ninety-Six to play on a field that was saturated with three days of rain. Davie described the challenges he faced in his first-ever varsity game:

"One, I did not know how to snap a wet and muddy football. Two, I did not know even one blocking assignment. Three, I had just turned fourteen and weighed 142 pounds soaking wet. Four, my opponent weighed 240 pounds. Five, their line averaged 235 pounds. Six, them boys were young men; in those days you could play until you were twenty (years old.)."

Davie said that these older players at Ninety-Six taught him a few physics lessons:

"The first lesson was how a small human body could be knocked backwards in midair for about five yards with your helmet and shoulder pads - first hitting the wet, muddy grass first - with your cleats still high in mid-air."

Davie alternated at center with Arthur Chavis in the first half. At halftime, a solution presented itself. Roy Jeffcoat, Davie's cousin who had played football at Swansea, asked Coach Bennett, "Coach, let me show Davie how to crab block." And since Coach Bennett had plenty of other concerns, he said, "Take him." So Roy took Davie behind the bleachers and taught him how to crab block so that Davie could stay low and "get in their way a little bit." Davie survived the game, which he described as a "physical beating," but he had a new skill in his toolbox - crab blocking - which eventually helped him against larger opponents.

The next week against Great Falls, Davie's opponent was a six foot one 215-pound middle guard who was reported to be the best in the state and was being heavily recruited by Clemson. "I got one block on him all night," an exasperated Davie said.

Just before that one block, halfback Donnie Kirkland had told Davie, If you don't block, I'm gonna run up your back." And he did: "I had cleat marks under my shoulder pads. Donnie got our only touchdown on that play."

Davie and his Swansea teammates ended the regular season and would face, to Davie's dismay, Ninety-Six for a second time. "About all that had changed from the first game was that them boys had gotten themselves into better physical condition," Davie observed. Determined not to be denied in their quest for a state championship, Ninety-Six was aggressive and physically punishing. Ninety-Six won this matchup and would go on to win the state championship. But Davie learned a lesson after this second physical test in which he was undersized and overmatched. He learned to fight back (legally) with his blocking and to no longer be afraid: "I took an aggressor frame of mind. If they are going to hit me that hard, why don't I take it to them as hard as I can."

Davie kept working. He continued to try to master the techniques of the crab block since he was small in stature and that technique gave him a measure of equilibrium with his larger opponents. "I either moved out on all fours and made contact very low, or I stepped out - a bit higher and dropped low into a crab block. Option three was if my man stood straight up and took a step to the rear, I could move up on him to "pop" him in the ribcage. That gave me just enough variety to keep my man guessing."

As much as he respected the physical conditioning of his opponents and sought to improve his own to keep pace, Davie was given a great example from one of his older teammates. C.L. Wise, a guard from the undefeated 1956 team, set a standard. C.L.'s family lived about two and a half miles outside of

Swansea. He drove a school bus like many of his fellow students. When Davie's dad offered to give C.L. a ride home after practice, C.L. said, "I don't need a ride because I run to and from practice." Somewhat skeptical, Davie, an eighth grader, decided to follow C.L. home after practice. He discovered that C.L. ran two and a half miles home. "I was amazed! I took notice of how C.L. rather briskly ran the four laps before practice. I gave it a try and found that I could make the four laps faster than most players. Once I knew I could do this (consistently), I started pushing the other players to kick on around on their four laps. So C.L. Wise set a high standard for me, and I passed it on to my teammates thus raising the conditioning level of Swansea Football for my four years."

Through hard work and dedication, Davie kept improving. By his junior season he discovered a secret to success: "I tried to play my best on a consistent basis, but I think that my positive attitude and performance at the practices had as much to do as my game play…for me receiving the most valuable offensive lineman award as a junior." Davie also possessed a quality not found in many athletes – he enjoyed practice! "I must have been the only nut to have enjoyed practice as much as I did."

Doug Bennett fostered an environment at practices that did in fact make them possible to enjoy. He was not a yeller and a screamer. Player mistakes did not result in a volcanic eruption. Coach Bennett's philosophy was "if you are going to make mistakes, make them now (in practice) before the game." In one effective coaching approach to a player not doing something correctly, Coach Bennett would say to a nearby player, "Give me your helmet." He would then put the helmet on and demonstrate the correct technique with the entire team looking on. His standard statement was, "Now that's how I want it done."

Bennett had a cerebral approach to analyzing football that involved, of all things, grass! He chewed, one blade at a time, as he crouched and watched the action on the field. Davie spoke for his teammates in expressing their confidence that Doug Bennett could analyze and make the adjustments needed by his team: "He had a certain way of moving his head back and forth from side to side as he was diagnosing a play on the field. It worked for him because he usually saw enough from the sideline to give us players a solution to our problems on the field."

In Craft's view, another motivating factor for Bennett's early squads was that because the overall numbers of football players were lower than in his later years, Bennett was able to dress players in grades eight through twelve. And even though everyone was not playing, they were able to observe, and absorb the atmosphere and learn from the experience:

> "Everybody traveled to games. Everybody got a full dose of winning Swansea football. Practice, games, players' attitudes, AND the attitude of the people in Swansea and the area was about winning. You did not waste a minute thinking about losing. You ate, slept, and lived to win for Swansea High!"

Bennett saw his role as more than just training football players; he was molding the character of young men. With this approach, Bennett knew that his own character and conduct had to be exemplary to have the effect he desired in the lives of these young men. Davie Craft observed, "We were blessed to have a man such as Doug Bennett to lead us into the young man's game of football battles. He molded us boys into young men both physically and mentally."

Since the action in a football game begins with the snap of the ball, as the Swansea center, Davie Craft felt in the middle of all the action:

> "Once the center position grows on you, then you come to like the idea that whatever is happening, you are in the middle of it. You never have a left-out or excluded feeling. Sure, you're at the bottom of the pile, and it seems like them lazy jokers will never get off of you. In most of the games we had, I tried to hit at least one opponent. Then I would get up after hitting one opponent and hit another. I once blocked five opponents on one play. I loved to knock one down, get up, and knock another one down."
>
> Davie continued, "A good center knows how important his job is. It's a lot of hard work and physical abuse; but you have to grin and bear it and say to yourself, Nobody else wants to hear about it. Such is the life of a center. I loved it!"

In his senior season, Davie was moved from center - where he had started for three straight years - to end. Wayne Jumper was an adequate center, and the team needed an end more, so Davie was asked to move there. The Tigers would go on a magical run to an undefeated season and the Class B State Championship.

Including that storybook season, Davie had several fond memories of his days playing football at Swansea High:

> "I still have a gold - colored pair of custom-made underwear that my mother would sew the game

> scores onto. It was a good motivator in the locker room before each game"

"To this day I see a number and visualize the face of my Swansea football teammate."

Senior classmates recognized him a football player with the most team spirit after Swansea won the 1960 Class B state championship. Five members of Swansea's 1960 squad earned scholarships to play college football: Clark Adkins, Perry Adkins, Benny Shivers, Benny Williams, and Johnny King. But Davie never saw football in his future after high school. That fact was never clearer to him than on the morning after the championship game:

> "I woke up that morning knowing that six years (grades eight through twelve) of struggle and enjoyment were suddenly over. Period. No more playing Tiger football! And just when I was getting the hang of this thing called football, and I was almost big enough to play too. Whatever I had done for Tiger football was in the books. From now on the Tiger games are played in your memory, and with the latest Tiger team on their field of dreams! Once a Tiger, always a Tiger!"

Craft, recognized by his teammates as their most spirited player, added, "I never thought that football was going to take me to college. I tried to savor each-and-every moment of the high school games and even the practices. I doubt that anyone enjoyed high school football more than I did."

1974 STATE CHAMPIONSHIP

"ONE WHO GAINS STRENGTH BY OVERCOMING OBSTACLES POSSESSES THE ONLY STRENGTH WHICH CAN OVERCOME ADVERSITY."
DR. ALBERT SCHWEITZER

During the 1970 season, when Swansea lost 16-14 to Blackville in the Class A state championship game, Bobby Frederick quarterbacked the Tiger junior varsity team to an undefeated record - as an eighth grader. During all the excitement of that magical season in which the Tigers captured the conference title, in large part propelled by a decisive 26-14 victory over previously undefeated Class A power Chapin on the road, the undefeated season of the junior varsity team was somewhat overshadowed. With back-to-back playoff victories over Lockhart and Buford by the varsity, most of what the Tiger JVs had accomplished faded into the background, obscured by the varsity's heartbreaking loss in the title game.

However, just how much that early success could mean for the future of the Swansea football program was not ignored by the

Tiger coaching staff, and Bobby Frederick would go on to play an instrumental role in that future. But before he found himself in the position of starting quarterback in one of the state's most successful high school football programs, Bobby Frederick had to overcome numerous setbacks, bide his time, and wait for his turn.

It has become cliché now that the best job in the National Football League is that of the backup quarterback. After all, he is paid quite handsomely to "hold a clipboard" and, more times than not, is a fan favorite (until he sees action and demonstrates *why* he's the backup.) Those who find themselves in the position of the backup have certain advantages, other than a greatly reduced risk of injury. For those who seize the opportunity to learn as an understudy - with far less pressure - and for those who carefully observe, from a unique vantage point, both the strengths and weaknesses, the successes and failures of the starter, there is much to be gained.

Bobby Frederick seized just such an opportunity. After leading the Tiger JV team as a "Tenderfoot," (Boy Scouts' rank for a beginner Scout) to that perfect season record, Bobby steadily progressed through the Tiger football program, though not without setbacks. He missed the entire 1971 season and in fact the entire sporting year, as a ninth grader with a severely separated right shoulder.

As a sophomore, in his return to action for the 1972 season, Bobby led the Tiger JVs under Head JV Coach Steve Carter in his second season on the Swansea staff. Carter instilled in these young players a championship mentality and recognized something in Bobby Frederick that would pay dividends in the near future: "Bobby was a good athlete. You can do a lot with a good athlete at quarterback."

In a manner similar to the way he progressed through the series of merit badge challenges and advanced through the Boy

Scout ranks to reach the pinnacle as an Eagle Scout, Bobby Frederick applied himself and learned and grew into a championship-caliber quarterback. Though he insists that "I was not a very good quarterback," pointing out that he "...threw a football like a baseball," Bobby persisted and persevered and learned from the example of older players - Lee Flake, in particular: "During one game, Lee broke the thumb on his throwing (right) hand when it hit the helmet of a rushing defensive lineman as he attempted to throw a pass. He was in severe pain, but I just remember Lee begging not to be taken out of the game." That brief but poignant snapshot of Lee Flake's courage and determination impresses Bobby to this day.

Despite Lee's insistence that he could get the job done, Coach Bennett, always concerned about the safety of his players, took Lee out of the game, replacing him with his first backup, junior Billy Mills. Billy struggled to generate any type of momentum for the Tiger offense, and Bobby was called on for his first action in a varsity game. Team physician Dr. Bud Granger had re-set Lee's dislocated thumb and taped it heavily, but the Tigers' senior quarterback was unable to reenter the game. And so Bobby finished the offensive snaps for the Tigers that night. Bobby Frederick had gotten his first taste of competition at the varsity level. And he liked it.

Bobby began his junior season, - again a backup quarterback - to senior Billy Mills. According to Billy:

> "We won our first game over Wagener-Sally 16-0 - no big deal. But the next week Blackville-Hilda smoked us! I didn't get the job done at quarterback. And about the only real excitement I felt in that came was when I was playing safety and Blackville

> threw a pass on an early down. I read the quarterback's eyes and was anticipating a swing pass when he threw the ball to their running back Ronnie Razor, a Georgia signee, as he ran an arc route out of the backfield. So when I broke on the ball, I was thinking to myself 'I'm gonna light this joker up!' But before I could get there, Brette Simmons (playing linebacker on the same side of the defense where the pass was thrown) beat me there and hit that back so hard that his helmet went flying and he went down like a sack o' taters."
>
> Mills, beloved by his teammates and the Swansea High student body for his zany antics and quirky sense of humor, handled losing his starting position with class and focused his energies on helping the team as a safety on defense. As Billy admits to this day, "Coach decided to make a change. And truthfully, I was glad. I didn't like the pressure." But the defensive back techniques that he had learned from Tiger assistants Wayne Cole and Steve Carter over his career as a two-way player had prepared him for this move to focus on defensive play and staying prepared as a backup quarterback. That season, Billy led the state of South Carolina (all classifications) with seven interceptions and was recognized by coaches and the media as an All-State performer.

The 1973 team, as seniors from that squad contend to this day, "set the table" for what would transpire during Doug Bennett's second state championship season. After a 32-15 defeat in game two at the hands of nonconference opponent Blackville - their nemesis from the 1970 State Title contest - the Tigers would go on to win seven of their next eight contests to finish the season 8-2. However, the 1973 fall season was the last in South Carolina in which only conference champions made the postseason playoffs, (the 13-6 loss to St. Angela in game five cost Swansea the conference title). The Tigers, despite winning their last five games and fielding what many observers felt was a team good enough by season's end to contend for the state championship, remained at home. As the starting quarterback, after replacing Billy Mills for the third game of the season - a 24-0 shutout victory over Strom Thurmond High School - Bobby led the Tigers to within a touchdown and two-point conversion of making the state playoffs again.

What came next for Bobby and the Tiger program is viewed by many as the most awkward and yet revealing transition in Doug Bennett's 36-year tenure at Swansea. Allen McNeil, who had played for South Carolina high school coaching legend "Mooney" Player at Lower Richland High School and who went on to star as a quarterback at Presbyterian College, was hired as the coach who would coordinate the Tiger offense. As is common practice for offensive coordinators at the college level - but not as common in high school football programs - McNeil was allowed to install the offensive system with which he was most comfortable, one that he felt he could best teach to high school players.

As a feisty 150-pound quarterback who set a school single-season passing yardage record as a junior at Presbyterian and was named to the Little All-American team as a senior co-captain, McNeil possessed the knowledge of the quarterback position and the leadership experience essential to gaining credibility. However, the same confidence and self-assurance that had served him well was as a record-setting college quarterback may have become something of a hindrance to him developing another quality demonstrated by highly effective teachers of young people - humility. Viewed by many as cocky - and lacking the proper level of respect for the veteran coach who had given him a great opportunity as a young assistant - McNeil was nonetheless a bright, capable tactician with a clear vision of what he wanted to accomplish with the Tiger offense.

As a quarterback in the Swansea program, Bobby Frederick had grown accustomed to being prepared by Coach Bennett to be aware of how the Tiger offense could exploit opposing defenses. The senior had "paid his dues" in the Tiger program and had been trusted by his mentor in the previous season to call the majority of plays in a game. But Bobby never called a play during his senior season. He felt, in some ways, like he had as a "Tenderfoot" in the Boy Scouts.

Recognizing that new and different concepts being added to Bennett's offensive system could create an extremely steep learning curve for the Tiger players, the coaching staff decided to make a change in the normal preseason routine at Swansea. While it had become common practice for high school teams to travel away from the comforts of home to train in a different location for a week during the preseason, this expensive privilege had never been considered as an option at Swansea since so many of Coach Bennett's players worked on family farms or needed summer jobs to pay for necessities. Not only did the 1974 Tiger squad go away for preseason camp – the Tigers moved into the barracks at the Marine air station base, the companion training facility to Marine Corps basic training grounds on Paris Island near Beaufort.

For a week, in addition to learning a new offensive system, they lived and trained and ate and slept (as little) as Marines! And in deference to the discipline and sharp appearance of a Marine, any Swansea player who had showed up for camp with his hair too long was promptly coiffed, Marine style, to maintain the Tiger's new "esprit de corps." The Tigers got a taste of what the brave men and women who have made it through the hell of marine basic training have experienced - well, except for those "Hollywood Marines," who train in San Diego. And they were better for it.

One might argue that such measures were too extreme and even, at best, unnecessary. Perhaps the Tiger coaching staff realized that unless something very different were done to capture the attention of their players, such a major transition might be too much for them to handle. Assistant Coach Steve Carter admits that initially he was not a proponent for going to camp. "But after we went through it, I thought it was good. It unified us as a team, brought us closer."

And so, in the fall before he graduated from Swansea High School, Bobby led the players from that undefeated JV team on a somewhat improbable - and even more thrilling - journey to the 1974 state title. The only way the 1974 could have started worse was if the Tigers had suffered all of their three losses of that season in the first three weeks. Instead, the opening 20-18 loss to Wagener-Salley was followed by dropping their second game to perennial Class A power Blackville. After two losses there is little doubt that some - including more than a few Tiger players - may have been second-guessing the new offense schemes and wondering why the hell they had spent that grueling week on Paris Island. For this?

And then it happened. It is now cliché among coaches that the most improvement in a football team occurs between the first and second games of the season. Well, in the case of the 1974 edition of the Swansea Tigers, that improvement came a week later: an 8-0 victory over Batesburg-Leesville, a AAA power expected to contend for a state title. Ray Whitaker, a starter at fullback and "monster back" on defense, remembers that the coaching staff, after the two frustrating losses to open the season, took time to evaluate and make some strategic changes: "A lot of us were playing both ways and getting worn out, so the coaches cut back on that, and we started a two-platoon system with only a few of us playing on both sides of the ball. The Batesburg-Leesville game was a slugfest. But because very few of us were playing both ways, we had more energy in the fourth quarter and that made a huge difference."

"At the time, very few of the larger 3-A and 4-A schools were able to play two-platoon football. And yet Swansea, one of the smallest Class A high schools in South Carolina, fielded a football team with enough athletes to employ this system. Doug Bennett, through the years, had built and established a community-supported program where boys played football early and grew up wanting to become a Swansea Tiger. When the district desegregated in 1968, Monroe Pinkney High had only fielded a football team for one season. Thus, there was not a sudden infusion of experienced football talent with the merger. But desegregation added players to the program, and eventually this increased the competition within the team for playing time. After going 1-9 in 1968, two seasons after integration the Tigers played for a state championship.

Top assistant Steve Carter had coached Bobby Frederick and the 1972 JV squad to an undefeated season. That undefeated JV team formed the nucleus of the 1974 varsity squad. The addition of three full-time assistants in McNeil, Rudy

Cooper, and Ed Pauling, all knowledgeable and capable coaches, allowed for more individual instruction of players. But the three new assistants, having played for the highly successful Mooney Player at Lower Richland High School, had been well coached themselves, and they brought some fresh ideas and experience that enhanced the Swansea staff. The coalescence of all these factors led to what may now be seen as a "perfect storm." The hard-fought victory over Batesburg-Leesville in a test of grit and determination was, as Whitaker saw it, "the turning point." The next four Tiger opponents - Holly Hill, Gilbert, Buford, and St. Angela - were left in the wake of this storm of rising momentum.

Next came conference opponent Cardinal Newman, undefeated and ranked third in the state in Class A. But the Tigers were playing at home. And few teams in South Carolina, in any classification, enjoyed a greater home-field advantage than Swansea. Ray Whitaker grew up in a home where the stadium lights illuminated parts of his backyard. "Our fan support was phenomenal. It was 'Friday Night Lights.' I grew up just wanting to play in front of them…it just gave me goose bumps!"

Swansea assistant Phil Williams, who coached on the last Swansea staff to play for a state championship under Doug Bennett in 1980, recalls his first encounter with a rabid Swansea fan who issued him a tongue-in-cheek warning: "You better hope your house don't catch on fire on Friday night…cause that thing's gonna burn to the ground. Ain't nobody gonna leave a Swansea game to go put out no fire."

Well, truth is that someone's home actually did catch on fire on the night of a Swansea home game. Doug Bennett, who himself served as a member of the Swansea Volunteer Fire Department, recalls that "Harold Witt (town mayor and member of the volunteer squad) who filmed the first half of all of our games, and some others had to leave the game around halftime." Then, with a laugh, he added, "But as I recall we were pretty far ahead." Coach Bennett stayed.

Billed as the Columbia area's "Game of the Week," Cardinal Newman arrived in Swansea sporting a 7-0 record. Off to their best start and with a shot at the conference championship for the first time in several seasons, the Cardinals, led by first-year head coach Al Checca, were confident and prepared to go toe-to-toe with the Tigers: "This will be our biggest test of the year. They have the biggest team in the conference and are very physical." Checca, who had watched the Swansea program for years, added, "This is just like every Swansea team I've ever seen. They always seem to get better as the year goes on. Those two games they lost were the first two of the year. In both cases they just ran out of time."

"We don't have anything sewed up this year despite our present record," Checca continued. "We still have three games left, and there are several teams which have good conference records at this point. Right now we're sky high. We haven't had a chance to win a conference title in some time. I just hope we can keep it going for a while longer."

The Cardinals' unbeaten streak of seven straight wins came to an abrupt halt as Swansea struck for two quick first quarter touchdowns before Cardinal Newman could run a play from scrimmage en route to a 14-0 victory that was more convincing that the score would indicate.

The Tigers took the opening kickoff and quickly marched to the Cardinal three behind the one-two punch of Aaron Pinckney and Ricky Sturkie. Quarterback Bobby Frederick slashed in from there and then passed to Sturkie for the conversion. The Tigers then recovered their onside kick at the Cardinal Newman forty-eight. In three plays, Pinckney put the Tigers up 14-0 on a twenty-eight-yard draw play. The conversion failed.

A couple of Swansea fumbles prevented possible additional scores in the first half, in which the Cardinal Newman offense had only one first down - the result of a penalty on the Tiger defense. This dominant win for Swansea came despite several missing players. "Two of our best backs, Hozell Mills and Bernard Fields were injured going into the game, "observed Bennett. Aaron Pinckney suffered a hairline fracture of a bone in his leg. Said Bennett, "We hope Pinckney won't be out too long." Also absent from the Tiger roster were defensive tackle Steve Raulerson with a broken arm and offensive tackle Buddy Harley with the flu.

The swarming Tiger defense stifled the Cardinals allowing a mere thirteen yards of total offense. "Our defense played a super game, and we are extremely pleased with them. To win a big game like this with some people sick and injured is really great," said Bennett. And, as happened on so many of those Friday nights in Swansea, another opponent went down in defeat in front of nearly every able-bodied person in the town and the surrounding area.

Jackson

Injuries are a part of sports at all levels, and for their most critical game of the regular season against Jackson, the Tigers were hit especially hard. Their four top running backs - Aaron Pinckney, Bernard Fields, Hozell Mills, and Ray Whitaker - missed the game with injuries, a debilitating loss for the Swansea offense.

The winner of this showdown would represent Conference 2-A as champions. The loser would go to the playoffs as the second or third team. With their win over previously unbeaten Cardinal Newman, the Tigers had positioned themselves to represent the conference as champions with a win over Jackson.

But as the Tigers appeared sluggish and out of sync, Jackson was dominant in the first half, twice driving inside the Swansea ten before failing to score. However, they mounted a seventy-four-yard drive with Willie Bates scoring from the one. A fifteen-yard facemask penalty against the Tiger defense was a key play in the drive.

After two scoreless quarters, Jackson drove sixty-one yards after Alonza Pressley recovered a Swansea fumble at the Jackson thirty-nine. Bates scored on a fifty-two-yard run, but a clipping penalty nullified that run and the ball was placed at the Swansea thirty-nine. Bates scored five plays later on a twenty-yard jaunt. The two-point conversion pass from Ryan Timmerman to Don Boyd was complete.

The loss dashed Swansea's hope of winning the Conference 5-A championship outright. It was particularly frustrating to the players and coaches, knowing that they played without several key players who likely would have made substantial contributions. Losing took a lot out of Bennett's squad:

> "After a football game you're exhausted - you're exhausted even when you win. When you add losing to the equation, then all the pain is multiplied by two or three. When you think about what it feels like to lose a football game, Lombardi's quote doesn't sound too over the top anymore: 'Winning isn't everything. It's the only thing.'"[1]

After a 28-6 victory over Elloree in the final regular season game, the Tigers finished with a 7-3 record and second place in the conference. A year earlier, their season would have ended. Fortunately for the Tigers, the South Carolina High School Coaches Association had voted, prior to the 1974-1975 academic year, to expand the football playoff format to include more than just the champion from each conference. And the Tigers, many of whom were on the '73 team that had finished with an 8-2 record but were not eligible for the playoffs as a conference runner-up, resolved to seize this opportunity, this second chance, and make the most of it.

And seize it they did.

H.E. McCracken

Despite finishing as the conference runner-up, Swansea opened the playoffs with a home game. Their scheduled opponent, Blackville, was ousted from the playoffs because of an unsportsmanlike incident in their previous week's game. The Tigers' new opponent was H.E. McCracken, coached by former Swansea assistant Mickey Gardner. Suddenly placed in the unenviable position of coaching against a veteran head coach and a mentor, Gardner explained, "I just hadn't planned on playing Doug this soon."

It didn't take long to understand why Coach Gardner would have preferred to face the Tigers later. After the Tigers' unfruitful first possession, Ray Whitaker scored on a short touchdown to get things going. Bobby Frederick added the two-point conversion. Ten seconds later, Otis Lykes picked up a fumble and returned it thirty-seven yards for a touchdown. Aaron Pinckney, back after missing two weeks with an injury, added the two-point conversion.

After McCracken scored on a fifty-yard pass and a two-point conversion, a Ray Whitaker interception set up the Tigers for a short touchdown run by Pinckney. Ricky Sturkie ran twenty-two yards and Pinckney added the two points to close out the Tigers' scoring in the first half and give them a 30-8 lead with thirty-two seconds on the clock.

The third quarter featured more of the same Tiger dominance when Otis Lykes scored his second defensive touchdown on a ninety-one-yard interception return. Bernard Fields added the two-point conversion. Aaron Pinckney ran twenty-five yards late in the third quarter for another Swansea score. Buddy Harley added the two points. The Tiger lead after three quarters was 46-8.

In the fourth quarter, McCracken mustered a short-lived rally, scoring two touchdowns on Tiger reserves. The 46-22 victory propelled Swansea into a second-round matchup with Holly Hill, whom they had defeated 48-24 in the regular season.

Holly Hill

Swansea wasted no time in getting the upper hand with two early touchdowns in the opening period of this quarter-finals matchup. The Tigers took their opening possession eighty yards behind the running of Aaron Pinckney and the passing combination of Bobby Frederick and end Otis Lykes. Ricky Sturkie blasted off tackle for twenty-two yards to cap the drive with the Tigers' first score. Frederick passed to Lykes again for the conversion.

Swansea then successfully executed an on-sides kick. Five plays later, Frederick hit David Wayne Pinckney for a thirty-one-yard touchdown and a 14-0 lead with 4:16 remaining in the first period. The conversion run failed. Late in the second quarter, the Tigers mounted a ninety-eight-yard march that culminated with Ricky Sturkie's eleven-yard burst just before the half ended. Aaron Pinckney's successful run for the two points gave the Tigers a 22-0 halftime advantage.

Despite being down by three touchdowns, Holly Hill attempted a second half comeback with a fifty-yard drive at the beginning of the third quarter. Jerome Benjamin scored on a twenty-five-yard run for the Bantams with 9:50 remaining in the period. Neither team scored again until the Swansea defense recovered a Holly Hill fumble, setting up Frederick's run for the remaining five yards of a short Tiger drive. The run for the two-point conversion was unsuccessful. Down 28-6, Holly Hill scored a final touchdown with Benjamin pushing over from one yard out near the end of the game.

McColl

Swansea's reward for defeating Holly Hill for the second time in the 1974 season was a semifinal showdown with the top-ranked team in Class A, the McColl Red Devils. The previous year's state champion, McColl had run off twenty-five consecutive victories coming into the contest with the Tigers.

Swansea used a powerful running game to slowly bury McColl 34-14. Ricky Sturkie scored the Tigers' first touchdown on a twenty-yard scamper that closed an eighty-yard drive. Bobby Frederick ran for the conversion and an 8-0 lead. After each team had fruitless possessions, the Tigers went into a hurry up mode to move sixty-two yards and scored again when Frederick found David Wayne Pinckney on a twenty-three-yard pass on the final play of the half.

In the third quarter, the Tigers went up 20-0 when Bernard Fields raced twenty-six yards on a reverse to cap a sixty-nine-yard drive. The Red Devils got on the scoreboard for the first time when Jerry Coles ran ten yards later in the third period. The McColl drive was kept alive by a successful fake punt. Ricky Sturkie notched his second touchdown of the game when he slashed eight yards to push the Tiger lead to 26-8. Larry Patterson added a five-yard score for the Red Devils' final score. Swansea ended its scoring when Aaron Pinckney plunged one yard to culminate a fifty-six-yard march.

In this game, the previously dominant team was dominated. Swansea piled up 392 rushing yards to 112 by McColl. The Tigers rolled to twenty-two first downs compared to eight for the Red Devils. Once again, the Swansea defense showed its mettle by holding McColl scoreless for most of three quarters while their teammates on offense built a 20-0 cushion.

This convincing win propelled the Tigers into the state championship game to face a familiar opponent, the Jackson Indians, who had handed them a bitter defeat and claimed the Conference 5-A championship - on the Tigers' home field.

Jackson

Wayne Merchant and his Jackson Indians no doubt came to regret the decision by the SC High School Coaches Association to include conference runners-up in the state playoff field. Faced with the unenviable task of preparing to play an opponent for the second time in the same season - and one you had defeated during regular season - what Merchant and his team were not aware of was the number of key Tiger players who had missed the previous matchup.

Coach Merchant dismissed any notion that his squad was overconfident going into the title game: "We took them seriously. I think we were ready to play." The three Tiger players who scored touchdowns for Swansea on its way to a 20-0 blanking of Jackson in the state championship game had all missed the conference showdown with injuries; this time, they were ready to play.

After neither team scored for most of the first half, Swansea struck quickly to close out the half. Ray Whitaker scoped up a Willie Bates fumble at the Jackson twenty-three and sprinted untouched to the end zone. Bobby Frederick's pass to David Wayne Pinckney fell incomplete. After the ensuing kickoff, Jackson fumbled again at its own eighteen and Alton Harley recovered for the Tigers with only eighteen seconds before halftime. Aaron Pinckney then banged his way through the Indian defense for a thirteen-yard touchdown with five seconds remaining in the half.

After a scoreless third quarter, the Tiger runners started to dominate play, and the Indians could do little to stop them. On the second play of the fourth quarter, Pinckney hit Bernard Fields on an eight-yard halfback pass. Frederick ran for the two-point conversion, boosting the Tiger advantage to 20-0 with 11:13 left in the game. Jackson did muster a threat in the fourth quarter when Indian quarterback Marty Harper completed two straight first down passes. But an ineligible receiver penalty nullified Jackson's best scoring opportunity when a pass to Raymond Timmerman had the Indians inside the Tigers' ten-yard line.

Despite losing six fumbles - either forced by a hard-hitting Swansea defense or else committed by the poor concentration of unforced errors on the part of the Indians - Jackson players and even, it seems, Coach Merchant himself, were reluctant to give Swansea credit for the shutout: "Other teams hit us harder than they did. We just couldn't hang on to the football." Jackson quarterback Marty Harper insisted, "We knew what they were going to run and they knew what we were going to run. It was just the fumbles that beat us."

Of his team's failure to protect the football Coach Merchant said, "They (Swansea) were going for the ball, but we just weren't holding on to the football." He added, "Sometimes mistakes can come from trying too hard."

Despite the 0-2 start to the 1974 season, the Tigers had rallied to win ten of their last eleven games, including the one that counted the most. As the Chinese calendar announced, 1974 was the "Year of the Tiger." And as the T-shirts they wore under their pads during the game declared during their public unveiling after the game, Swansea was:

#2 in Conference 5-A

#1 in the State

There were ten Tiger seniors on the '74 squad. Most had played on an undefeated JV squad. Since that undefeated season as an eighth grader, Bobby Frederick had encountered obstacles and setbacks, but he did not allow this adversity to deter him in his efforts to become a quarterback capable of leading his teammates to a state championship.

By now, the desegregation of Swansea schools in the fall of 1968 had been generally accepted in the community and the diversity welcomed, if not quite yet embraced. The 1968 season's 1-9 record - something of a disaster by Swansea football standards - seemed like a distant memory. With one exception, since integration, Bennett's teams posted progressively better records culminated by the 1974 state title.

In view of the impact of high school football in the Swansea community, as in countless other small towns throughout the South, some questions arise. Did acceptance of the 1968 integration by the community and a spirit of cooperation make possible a unity among the players that strengthened their resolve and led to success on the field? After all, other than the nine-day boycott by white parents who removed their children from classes temporarily, desegregation of the Swansea schools had been a transition without the intense opposition and even violence that occurred in far too many instances in the South.

Or, is it possible that the success of the Tiger football team and the overall improvement of athletics at Swansea High School somehow produced common ground upon which two races of mankind could stand with community pride and learn to trust the other just a little bit more? Sociologists believe that in many instances, particularly in the South, football teams, which by the very nature of the sport engender a spirit of cooperation, served as laboratories for acceptance and change. The outcome of the 1975 season at Swansea High would further validate that line of thinking.

1975 STATE CHAMPIONS

"FRIENDSHIPS BORN ON THE FIELD OF ATHLETIC STRIFE ARE THE REAL GOLD OF COMPETITION. AWARDS BECOME CORRODED, FRIENDS GATHER NO DUST."
JESSE OWENS, GOLD MEDAL WINNER, 1936 OLYMPICS

The Swansea Tigers led 6-0 at the half, but had you been in the locker room at the intermission, you might have thought they trailed 36-0. Doug Bennett was steamed:

"Dadgummit, boys, the defense is giving it 100 percent, and y'all are just sleepwalkin'! If y'all want to win, y'all are gonna' have to play harder!"

Undefeated, and ranked number one in the state, Swansea had scored early in the first quarter on Bernard Fields's sixty-three-yard jaunt. But the Tiger offense had done little since. As the only Class A program in South Carolina that was playing two-platoon football, the Tigers' halftime routine was to meet in separate areas of the locker room for the coaches to review the first half's action and to make any needed adjustments and to then communicate the second half strategy to their players.

As the head coach who had chosen to work exclusively with the defensive unit, Doug Bennett did not usually speak to the offense until the two units came back together, when he would address the whole team just before they went back out to play the second half. But this night was different. All-Conference 5-A and All-State center Andy Williams, who had plans to enroll at Clemson University to study industrial engineering the next fall, recalls of Coach Bennett on this night: "You could tell he was mad if he took off his hat or if he said 'Dadgummit.' That night he did both!"

Before leaving to meet with the defense, Coach Bennett turned to offensive coordinator Allen McNeil and said, "Okay, tell 'em what we're going to do." And he left. Coach McNeil then said to the offensive unit, "We want to see if you guys want to win. We are not going to call anymore plays tonight. You can run one play the rest of the game: 44 c and g. You can run it right or left, but that's all." Then he walked away too.

Andy continued. "We went back out for the second half with our one play and scored twenty-one points in the third quarter. Our quarterback, Johnny Huggins, each time in the huddle would ask, "Who wants to run it this time? Bernard? David? Hozell? Okay, which side to you want to run to, right or left?" During the Tigers' third-quarter offensive explosion, the other Tiger back who had been asked the same questions in the huddle, David Streeter, scored on runs of four and forty-five yards before Ray Whitaker, the Tiger fullback whose main role during the season had been primarily to block for a bevy of other backs, hit pay dirt on a nine-yard burst to cap a sixty-yard drive.

The Jackson players were more than caught off-guard by the different team that came out of the Swansea locker room for the second half. Andy relayed that "...midway through the third quarter one of the Jackson linebackers asked me, 'Are y'all just runnin' the same play every time?" Now one might expect a cocky, taunting response from a player whose team had found its rhythm and was clearly dominating their opponent. But, instead the Swansea senior, (now working in research and development as a compliance engineer with Tetronic Industries in Anderson, South Carolina) - offered a calm, cerebral - one might even call it compassionate - response to his opponent: "I told him, 'yes, we are, and if he wanted me to, I would tell him which side we were going to run to each time. He just shook his head and said, 'Man, y'all are good.'"

As it happened time and time again over his career, Doug Bennett had accurately assessed his team's first half performance, and he had responded in the way that seemed most appropriate under the circumstances. This night he was angry about the lack of concentration and effort by his offensive players. He did not hide his displeasure. After the offense responded to his challenge to "play harder," the defense continued its excellent first half play and held Jackson to a mere yards ten rushing for the night. And, as if to add insult to injury, the defense capped the scoring for the Tigers with a safety as Swansea dominated Jackson, their conference rival and their opponent in the 1974 state championship game, 29-0. Over the past two meetings with their conference opponent, the Tigers had scored forty-nine points while holding the Indians scoreless (for eight quarters.)

As it had in the previous preseason when the Tigers went away to camp in early August and trained at the marine basic training site on Paris Island, a week of practices at Camp Blue Star near Hendersonville, North Carolina, brought the 1975 team closer together. In addition to the bonding that occurs on a football team when the players strive together to push through and finish practices when they are tired, sore, hot, and sweaty, the Tigers found a way to create some levity and have fun together.

Running back David Streeter, who had transferred to Swansea from much larger Lexington High School just before the Tigers' run to a state championship the season before, had emerged as the team's "chant leader." And when the team traveled en masse to and from the dining hall that served meals of mostly kosher food, Streeter led the team in a song/chant that would become a favorite for the Jewish children from the northeast who were attending the traditional family camp at Blue Star:

> "We are the Tigers (We are the Tigers)
> The mighty, mighty Tigers (The mighty, mighty Tigers)
> Everywhere we go (Everywhere we go)
> The people want to know (The people want to know)
> Who we are (Who we are)
> So we tell them (So we tell them)
> We are the Tigers…"

In fact, to show their amusement with and appreciation for this group of guys practicing a game that most of them did not understand, the campers put on a skit at the end of the week that included their own rendition of the Tigers' team chant.

As a break from their two-a-day practices and the additional midday meeting to watch film, the Tiger staff arranged for a team swim at the camp's swimming area. For safety purposes, the Swansea players were lined up to be cleared by the lifeguards as capable swimmers who could tread water before being permitted to enjoy the water. When his teammates realized that Joe Nathan Davis had disappeared, they were concerned. Tiger assistant Steve Carter, a certified lifeguard, dove in after Joe Nathan and found him sitting on the bottom, paralyzed in fear, with his legs crossed underneath his torso. Joe Nathan emerged from the water gasping for air, and one of the camp's lifeguards immediately asked him, "Why didn't you tell us you couldn't swim!" Joe paused for a moment and then casually replied, "Well, you didn't ask me."

The 1975 edition of Swansea football broke camp after an exhausting but very productive week, full of optimism and the quiet confidence that winning engenders. As the season approached, expectations were running high. After winning their last five games the season before - including a shutout of Jackson, who had beaten them during the regular season to win the conference championship - the Tigers welcomed the start of a new season.

Like Bennett's 1961 squad, Swansea was declared the media favorite to repeat as state champions. But the 1961 team had failed to repeat, losing to East Clarendon 13-7 in the state final. How would this team respond to the challenges and pressure as the reigning champion? Upon their return to Swansea and the start of a routine of practices after the school day, Coach Bennett and his staff were determined not to allow a repeat of the 1961 shortfall.

Professional and workmanlike in his teaching style, offensive line coach Rudy Cooper challenged his players to improve with each practice as they approached season's opening game. Like the other Swansea coaches, Cooper pushed his players and would not allow even the slightest hint of complacency. Departed from last year's championship line were starters L.H. Peele, Marty Wise, and Class A Lineman of the Year Buddy

Harley. With Andy Williams at center and Joe Nathan Davis and Robin Rucker at guard, Cooper knew he had a reliable pair of bookend tackles, massive senior Gregory "Coo Coo" Williams, and junior All-State candidate Marshall Riley, in only his second year of high school football. Cooper realized he had a very capable unit, and he planned to utilize Riley as a pulling lineman and on devastating double-teams.

Doug Bennett's time-tested coaching philosophy had been to win with sound, punishing defense and a physical running game with enough play-action passing and misdirection plays to keep the opposing defense off balance. The Tiger offense, with Allen McNeil in his second season as the coordinator, returned experienced running backs David Streeter, Hozell Mills, Ray Whitaker, and another All-State candidate, Bernard Fields. Departed All-State quarterback Bobby Frederick, who Coach Bennett regarded as the best he had coached at executing option plays because "he never missed a pitch," had been replaced by Johnny Huggins, a sophomore. And ends Jimmy Smith and Elvin Jeffcoat were good blockers and capable receivers for the play-action passing game.

At six-foot-four and 230 pounds, Marshall Riley was one of the most gifted athletes to ever put on a Swansea uniform. And he played in the offensive line. He was, many say, the most dominating and devastating blocker in the history of the program. But his path to becoming the Class A Lineman of the Year during Swansea's magical journey to their second consecutive state title in 1975 had a somewhat tentative beginning.

Marshall Riley did not play football until his sophomore year. He had sustained a serious eye injury when he was cutting sheetrock in a summer job. The injury prevented him from participation in athletics as a freshman. After his eye injury healed, his mother was still not particularly keen on the idea of her "baby" risking injury in a very physical sport. His dad said he needed Marshall to work. But the Swansea coaching staff was able to convince Mr. Riley of the benefits, both present and future, of Marshall playing football.

Before the 1974 season, Marshall, a sophomore offensive lineman, had never started a game in any sport at any level. He had never experienced "the butterflies," the nervousness and accompanying churning stomach that routinely strikes many athletes just before competition. It took him the first two or three games of the 1974 season to learn how to cope with the nerves - (the Tigers, incidentally, lost the first two games of the 1974 season – perhaps, in part because the young man who later that season would develop into a dominating blocker - was too nervous to be effective). But once he became more comfortable and confident, opponents took the brunt of his "country strong" blocking ability.

Starting center Andy Williams, recalls an incident from Marshall's junior year, the 1975 season, with him now playing with a whole season under his belt: "One game, Marshall Riley was pulling as our lead blocker and just leveled their defensive end to that side and broke some of his ribs." Andy remembers that the player had to be carted from the field by paramedics and was rushed to the hospital.

But the outcome of that devastating hit and injury to an opponent created an opportunity for both Marshall and Andy to discover something about their head coach that made them respect him even more than they already did. The next week at practice, Andy recalls, "Coach had us sign a get-well card for that player, and he took it and paid that kid a personal visit in the hospital. That made an impression on me - how he always cared for others." It was a love and respect for their head coach and his coaching staff that drove Marshall, Andy, and the rest of the 1975 Tiger team to play their hearts out on an undefeated run to their second straight state championship.

H.E. McCracken

After an undefeated run through ten regular season games, Swansea faced H. E. McCracken in the opening round of the 1975 playoffs. The Tigers got off to a fast start with Bernard Fields scoring two touchdowns and two conversions in the first quarter. Fields scored on a sixty-yard run to open the scoring. David Streeter completed a halfback option pass to Fields for the conversion.

Less than two minutes later, Ronald Jeffcoat recovered a McCracken fumble at the fifty and returned it twenty yards to set up the Tigers' second touchdown. Behind the capable running of Streeter and Hozell Mills, the Tigers drove to the eight, where Fields ran for the second Swansea touchdown. He added the conversion for a 16-0 lead.

Calvin Mack recovered another McCracken fumble at the five-yard line and ran it in for a touchdown. Mills was successful on the conversion run to boost their lead to Ray Whitaker closed out the Tiger scoring with a five-yard run in the third quarter. Once again, Mills added the conversion. The final score was 32-0.

The Swansea defense was dominant, holding McCracken to seven first downs and a paltry thirteen yards rushing. Tiger defender Calvin Mack proudly observed, "Our defense did a tremendous job." Running back Bernard Fields expressed his appreciation for the defensive effort, "If we hold everybody like we did tonight, we can't be stopped," declared an effusive Fields.

Holly Hill

After a scoreless first half, the quarterfinal matchup between top-ranked Swansea and second-ranked Holly Hill was shaping into the hard-fought battle that was expected. The Tigers had defeated Holly Hill 48-24 in the regular season and now faced the challenged of playing a formidable opponent for the second time,

Starting center Andy Williams was injured on the third play of the game when massive Holly Hill defensive tackle John Robinson landed on his right (snapping) hand. Andy's hand swelled to nearly three times its normal size, so he could no longer grip the ball to snap it. Robin Rucker replaced Andy at center for the remainder of the game. Neither team was able to generate much offensive momentum the rest of the first half.

With their first possession of the third quarter, the Tigers drove seventy yards. Hozell Mills scored from the one to cap the drive and then added the conversion for an 8-0 Swansea lead. The opportunistic Swansea defense once again set up the offense with a fumble recovery at the Holly Hill twenty-four. On a fourth-down play, Johnny Huggins passed to Ray Whitaker for a score. Holly Hill thwarted the two-point conversion attempt. The Tigers held a 14-0 advantage. Holly Hill drove fifty-five yards in the fourth quarter and scored their lone touchdown on an eleven-yard pass. They kicked the extra to make the score 14-7 with 5:12 remaining. The loss was the second in twelve games for Holly Hill - both to Swansea.

After the game, offensive line coach Rudy Cooper told Andy, "You're going to have to learn to snap with your left hand, Andy. We need you." "I was in a lot of pain on our bus trip home," said Andy. "When we stopped at a Burger King to get something to eat, after I got my food, Coach Bennett came over and helped me unwrap my burger since I was one-handed."

Well, the truth was that Andy was not the only center on the Swansea roster. But he was a senior, and the "captain" of the offensive line, and he was a player of such caliber that he would be named All-State at the end of the season. He learned to snap with his left hand during the next week, but he found that he was not moving off the line and out of the way when guard Joe Nathan Davis was pulling. So Andy adapted and learned to snap with both hands in time for the semifinal playoff matchup against Blackville.

Blackville

The Swansea Tigers, with the state's longest active winning streak seventeen games, and Class A's number one ranking, entered their semi-final showdown with the Blackville Hawks, another long-time bitter rival. Swansea had defeated the Hawks during the regular season. Just one season after their 1974 state championship, the Tigers now faced the same challenges that their conference foe Jackson had faced in that championship matchup: playing a conference opponent you had already beaten in the regular season but a team that had improved and had momentum in the playoffs.

Blackville Head Coach Ken Singleton assessed the rematch: "We feel like it will be a defensive struggle. Our offense has scored some points, but we haven't played a team like Swansea much." Doug Bennett agreed that defense would play a critical role in the outcome: "We teach a swarming, gang-tackling defense. We stress that especially against good backs like Blackville has." Then Bennett related a recent conversation with a former Tiger defensive player that demonstrates the teaching effectiveness of the Swansea defensive coaches through the years: "A former player of mine came down from Cleveland a couple of weeks ago. He told me he saw two of my players loafing on a play. I asked him how they were loafing, and he said they weren't on the pile. (Nine other Swansea defenders had been in on the tackle.) That's what we want."

Singleton expressed further concern about the Hawks' upcoming opponent: "Their offense could be the real key. They'll probably try to run right at us and we'll have to stop that run if we plan on staying in the game...We'd like to think our kids would play harder since that first loss to Swansea. I think they want to show everyone that they've improved."

The Blackville head coach's comments leading up to the contest proved prophetic. However, the defensive struggle that he and his staff had envisioned - and were hoping would ensue - never really happened. In fact, the only defense that struggled was his own as the Swansea offense, with machinelike efficiency, blew open a close game - a 22-14 halftime lead for the Tigers - by scoring nineteen points in the second half as their cohorts on defense held Blackville scoreless, and Swansea overwhelmed the Hawks 41-14.

Blackville effectively dashed any hope of a close game by fumbling on the opening play of the second half at their own twenty-nine-yard line. Swansea marched the remaining yards in six plays with Hozell Mills scoring on a two-yard run. The Tigers' try failed, and they led 28-14. The Swansea defense then forced a twenty-one -yard Blackville punt that set up a Swansea touchdown only forty-seven seconds later. Fullback Ray Whitaker rambled into Blackville territory on the Tigers' first play of the ensuing possession and then, on the next play, sprinted the remaining thirty-seven yards for a touchdown, putting the Tigers up 34-14 with five minutes remaining in the third quarter.

To Blackville's credit, the Hawks had come back in the first half after falling behind 16-0 in the first quarter on two-yard scoring runs, first by Bernard Fields and then by Hozell Mills. Quarterback Johnny Huggins passed for both two-point conversions to ends Jimmy Smith and Elvin Jeffcoat. The Hawks cut the lead to 16-6 on a fifty-three-yard bomb from Ronnie Martin to Willie Lee Thomas. But the Tiger defensive staff made an adjustment after the deep scoring pass by Blackville: Swansea's All-State safety Horace Bookman, was instructed by the defensive coaches to align a few yards deeper after Blackville's deep scoring pass: "Our coaches told me to play back a little deeper since our line was handling the run so well. We just didn't want to give up the big play." The change in strategy soon paid dividends when Bookman returned an interception twenty-six yards for a score and a 22-6 Tiger lead. The Hawks countered with Floyd Calhoun's three-yard scoring run and his pass to Jerry Washington for the two-point conversion to pull within eight. The score was 22-14 at the half.

On their nineteen-point blitzkrieg in the second half, the Swansea offensive line continued to pave the way for the Tigers' deep backfield. Hozell Mills started the second half scoring. With time running out in the game, Horace Bookman grabbed his third interception of the night and his second touchdown interception for a touchdown. Team captain Lonnie Simmons added the two-point conversion.

As it turned out, the most prophetic statement made by Blackville Coach Ken Singleton in his remarks leading up to the game was his observation about the Tigers' two-platoon system. Indeed, perception became reality on this night as the Swansea offense amassed 353 yards rushing and 104 yards passing while the Tiger defense gave up only seven first downs and held the Hawks' vaunted backfield to only forty-seven rushing yards.

Swansea had punched its ticket for a second consecutive trip to the State Class A Championship game.

Calhoun Falls

During the week leading up to the championship game, Calhoun Falls coach Joe Rossera made some observations about Swansea's two-platoon system and the advantage that created for the Tigers: "They run two teams while we play fourteen (players.) As far as manpower is concerned, they seem to have an edge. They do so many things on offense and do them all well. They have four good backs and real good tackles and they have confidence in what they're doing."

Swansea entered the 1975 state championship game with an eighteen-game winning streak. But a virus was running through the squad the week leading up to the game. Quarterback Johnny Huggins was one of the Tigers players most affected, as was the Tigers' Doug Bennett. More than with the illness that had taken away much of the volume of his voice, the veteran coach was concerned about their opponent, Calhoun Falls, who entered the matchup 10-3. Of the Blue Flashes' old-fashioned single wing offense Bennett observed: "We haven't seen the single wing in years. It will present some problems for us. It's entirely new to our players."

Bennett's concerns seemed unwarranted when running back David Streeter scored from one yard out early in the second quarter. The ailing quarterback Johnny Huggins ran left for the two-point conversion and a 22-0 Swansea lead. All-State running back Bernard Fields had run fifty-five yards for a score on the Tigers' first possession. Hozell Mills added the two-point conversion to put the Tigers up 8-0. Then on their second possession, Johnny Huggins threw a thirty-three-yard scoring pass to end Jimmy Smith. The conversion failed, and Swansea held a 14-0 lead. Calhoun Falls did get points before the half - when Swansea, backed up near their own goal line, took an intentional safety. The score at halftime was 22-2.

The performance of the Swansea offense in the third quarter was what the coaches may have feared and even warned about during the intermission. The Tigers, demonstrating lapses in concentration, incurred far too many penalties. Neither team scored in the third period. Then Calhoun Falls, their seniors watching time wind down on their final game of football – ever - made a run at the undefeated Tigers. Ricky Boggs hauled in a fifty-four-yard scoring pass from Clarence McIntyre, who later in the final stanza scored on a three-yard plunge to close the gap to 22-14.

The Swansea defense, with their offensive teammates struggling to establish any momentum at all in the second half, rose to the occasion and thwarted the Calhoun Falls rally. Doug Bennett told reporters afterward: "I thought our defense did a good job holding them off there at the end. Our offense was having trouble with penalties and our defense had to do the job. I knew we had a strong offense, and I thought we could score on anybody. The only thing I was concerned about was the defense."

When the clock hit all zeroes, the jubilant Tigers stripped off their shoulder pads to reveal the motivational T-shirts supplied by the coaching staff with the declaration that all involved with Swansea football were hoping to experience: "It Is Nice To Win It Twice."

The momentum of the 1974 state championship team had carried over into the 1975 season as the Tigers replaced four offensive line starters and their starting quarterback on offense and two ends and a linebacker on defense, but they had younger players step up to fill the voids. The season began with a five-game winning streak from the previous season. Each week the 1975 Tigers added another win all the way to an undefeated 14-0 season mark and a nineteen-game program winning streak.

Winning begets winning. The next seven Tiger teams all made it to the playoffs while posting a 67-18 composite record. During the decade of 1973 to 1982, Swansea posted a 100-24 record, a dominance similar to Bennett's teams in the fifties and sixties.

COMMUNITY SPIRIT

"LEADERSHIP IS THE POWER TO EVOKE THE RIGHT RESPONSE IN OTHER PEOPLE."
HUMPHRY MINORS

Doug Bennett held so fast to his principle that "you're no better than your help," that through the years he surrounded himself with competent people who made valuable contributions to his football program.

Dr. William H. "Bud" Granger moved to Swansea in 1962. One evening, he was performing preseason physicals for the Swansea football team when he asked Coach Bennett if he needed a team doctor to be on the sideline for games in case players had injuries that needed a doctor's immediate care. For his first eight seasons at Swansea, before Dr. Granger volunteered his services, Coach Bennett had no such arrangement. He gladly accepted the young doctor's offer. With this agreement, "Bud" Granger went on to serve twenty-seven seasons during Bennett's tenure and for four years afterward. He performed preseason physicals for the team during the entire time at no charge. Before games, Coach Bennett taped the ankles of players who needed taping. Dr. Granger did any type of specialized taping that was needed.

When asked about the most serious injury that Dr. Granger treated during a game, Coach Bennett was unsure of the most serious. But he did recall perhaps one of the most hilarious injury incidents. In 1967, in a game against rival St. Matthews, center/linebacker Robbie Lee Stabler came to the sideline as his pinkie finger had been dislocated and was grotesquely twisted on his right hand. Dr. Granger calmed Robbie down and grabbed his hand and reset the dislocated pinkie despite Robbie's screams of pain and protest: "All I could see was stars!" He then taped the pinkie finger to the ring finger to stabilize it. When he finished, Dr. Granger told Robbie Lee, "Son, you're cured. Now get your ass back out there and play some ball."

But Dr. Granger's commitment to football in Swansea extended beyond the players and coaches. "He would do anything for the team and the people that supported them," said former mayor Harold Witt. "He wasn't about to let a player or a supporter miss a game with an illness if he could help them." His service to the Tiger football program continued through the 1993 undefeated state championship season. He died in the spring of 1994.

"Dr. Granger meant so much to our program" said Coach Bennett. "It was a relief to have someone on our sideline who could treat our players immediately if they were injured. We didn't have anyone at Fort Mill (where Bennett was an assistant for two years) or at Sharon (when he was a first-year head coach in 1953.) And we did not have that at Swansea (for eight years) until Dr. Granger moved here in 1962."

One of the most basic means for evaluating an athletic team's performance as well as the performance of individuals is film or video. Early in his career, Doug Bennett had the services of skilled cameramen. Landis Sharpe, who ran a TV repair business, owned an 8mm camera that he offered to make available to the young coach. In 1958, Sharpe began filming Swansea games from a six-foot platform. Bennett was one of the first coaches in South Carolina to film his team's games. When his team marched to the state championship in 1960, he was able to exchange films with only a couple of opponents as this practice, which later became a requirement by the rules, was not commonplace at that time.

Later, to elevate the vantage point for filming, Jack Rucker built a press box using four telephone poles. Harold Witt, who owned a local hardware store and also served as the town's mayor, teamed with Dr. Bill Wilkes, the town's pharmacist, to film games, each filming one half of the game. After the games, the two took the film to Southeastern Films in Columbia to have it developed. At times, they were so excited to see the results that they waited for the film to be developed and then watched the game as the film processing was being completed.

Al White served as game announcer for all Swansea home games until he moved to Florida in the early sixties. He was succeeded by Charles Goodwin, who continued as the game announcer until the school system desegregated in 1968 and he quit. One of Coach Bennett's former players, Charles Rucker, became the Tigers' announcer, a role he continued in even after Doug Bennett retired after the 1989 season. Raymond Johnson served as the team statistician from 1968 through the tenure of Doug Bennett. Former player, Bruce Rucker took over keeping team statistics during games in 1990 when Bennett continued his involvement with the Tiger program under Robert Maddox.

Ann Witt, Harold's wife, ran the concession stand for Tiger home games for fourteen years. "I can remember cooking four hundred to five hundred corn dogs prior to games and taking them to the stand. We're a family during football season, and those kids playing are like our own. The town comes to life every fall when the season begins."

Sherrie Manual, representing the hundreds of young women who have served as cheerleaders for the program, said in 1994, "Football is just about everything here at Swansea. We just praise the Lord that the new coaches are Swansea boys and have followed in Coach Doug Bennett's path. It all started with him and his love for the kids."

Although there may be many who would view themselves at Swansea's most loyal fan, few have demonstrated the dedication of former player Tommy Manuel. Having lost both legs to illness, Manuel has been a regular at Swansea games, home and away. "Just being there is a tradition for my entire family. I guess it goes back to being a country boy and having a plow-mule mentality, but football is a true display of what a young man is capable of achieving in his life."

JIMBO RAULERSON
PLAYER, 1976-1979

"POWER IS OF TWO KINDS. ONE IS OBTAINED BY THE FEAR OF PUNISHMENT AND THE OTHER BY THE POWER OF LOVE. POWER BASED ON LOVE IS A THOUSAND TIMES MORE EFFECTIVE AND PERMANENT THAN THE ONE DERIVED BY THE FEAR OF PUNISHMENT."
MAHATMA GANDHI

When Steve and Ruby Raulerson moved their family of seven from Perry, Florida, to Swansea in 1968, their third son, Jimbo, had to repeat the second grade. In the destructive wake of Hurricane Alma in 1966, Perry schools were forced to cancel classes and close for reconstruction. The next year as a second grader, Jimbo missed too many school days with a severe case of pneumonia and was not able to attend the required 180 days. When he was enrolled for second grade classes in Swansea, Jimbo was nearly two years older than his classmates. These unfortunate circumstances and setbacks at an early age would, with time, provide Jimbo with certain unanticipated advantages in the football-crazed small town that became his new home.

It took little time, with five boys ages four through eleven, for the Raulersons to get caught up in the small-town infatuation with and excitement for Swansea Tiger football. Jimbo recalls standing-room-only crowds that forced fans to arrive very early to get good bleacher seats high enough to see over the small throng of ex-jocks and wannabes who roamed up and down the sidelines following the team's every move from field level. While Steve, Sr. took the boys inside the fence and paid for their admission, Ruby Raulerson, in poor health and fighting a severe case of rheumatoid arthritis, remained outside the fence in the family vehicle parked strategically with a clear line of sight to the field from behind the south end zone.

When some of the women of the community learned that Ruby was in that 1974 Ford pickup truck, they brought their lawn chairs and positioned them close by outside the south fence to sit with Ruby so that she would not have to watch the game alone. It was here, on the white-striped field of green that the two oldest of the five Raulerson boys, Stevie and Stanley, would compete for Doug Bennett's Tiger teams before the three youngest, Jimbo, Johnny, and Paul completed their playing days at the newly constructed Doug Bennett Field completed and dedicated in 1978.

Stevie, the oldest, and the second son, Stanley, were key contributors to Bennett's back-to-back state championship teams in 1974 and 1975, the school's second and third appearance in the state finals by the midpoint of the decade. Both defensive tackles, Stevie was a mainstay and an emotional, team-oriented leader while Stanley was recognized by opposing coaches as an All-Conference performer. While his two older brothers experienced the rare thrill of back-to-back state championships, Jimbo, a ninth grader, played JV football and competed against the varsity in practices during each game week, biding his time until he might get his opportunity to move up to the "Big Team," as Swansea players referred to the varsity.

That opportunity to move up to the "Big Team" came in 1976 when Coach Bennett told Jimbo that he needed him on the varsity because "I can't have a team without a Raulerson on it." With duties divided between the members of his coaching staff, Coach Bennett had responsibility that season for the offensive line. Jimbo desperately wanted to play on offense, to have Coach Bennett working directly with him. But Doug Bennett explained that this particular year he would need Jimbo to follow in the footsteps of his older brothers as a defensive tackle and, despite being on the opposite side of the ball, he would, as Coach Bennett reassured him, "...be playing just as much for me" as a defensive player as he would have been as an offensive lineman.

While Jimbo and younger brother Johnny did not experience the same level of success with the Tigers enjoyed by Stevie and Stanley, they were important contributors to Bennett teams that compiled a 25-11 record from the 1976 through 1978 seasons, winning three consecutive conference championships, including the "extra special" title Jimbo's and Johnny's senior year. Included in Jimbo's senior football player class was Robert Maddox, who would, in the 1990 season, become the successor to Coach Bennett as the head coach, and would lead the Tigers to three consecutive state championships during the '91, '92, and '93 seasons.

Nicknamed "Ram" by his teammates, Robert Maddox, an undersized offensive guard, was, according to the third Raulerson defensive tackle, "the hardest hitting little fella I ever seen." With a determination and intensity that far surpassed his smallish frame, Maddox, according to Jimbo, would get "very upset when he messed up." And if "Ram" was frustrated with his performance, he ramped up his effort and his hits on defensive players got even more violent. Raulerson recalls once respectfully requesting that Tiger Assistant Coach Phil Williams back off a bit on his spirited corrections of "Ram's" mistakes in one memorable practice period because of the potential repercussions for him and his other defensive line teammates. Jimbo recalls, a little over a decade later, watching with delight as his former teammate, now "Coach Ram," led the Tigers to three consecutive state titles with Jimbo's nephew on the team.

Tragically, four members of Jimbo's class, Bill Adkins, Lee Etheridge, Mark English, and Rhett Flake, all left this world, from a human perspective, far too soon - the youngest at thirty-eight years of age and the oldest fifty-two. In the 1978 team picture, Etheridge and Adkins were beside one another on the back row, and Jimbo was next to English. While Jimbo describes all of his teammates as "family," he felt a special bond with Bill Adkins, whom he met while attending Faith Baptist Church together on Sundays and with whom he became fast friends in his class at Swansea Elementary. Learning of Bill's early death from a skin melanoma on his fair-skinned arm that metastasized "...tore me up," laments Jimbo.

Years after his playing days at Swansea High, Jimbo reflected on his experiences under the leadership of the Doug Bennett and came to appreciate his coach's brilliance and skill as a motivator: "Coach Bennett treated each one of us like a family member." Through personal attention and "father-son talks," as Jimbo describes them, the Swansea head coach communicated his strong, positive affirmation while clearly delineating the high expectations he had for each of his "sons" in matters of personal character, conduct, and academic performance, ahead of their play in practices and games. His "four priorities": God, family, schoolwork, and football - in that order - were the foundation from which any rules or principles of discipline were derived. Each of Doug Bennett's players knew clearly where he stood and what he expected, as well as the consequences of unwise choices or an unfortunate "rearranging" of priorities.

Perhaps because of the disruptive beginnings of his early education, Jimbo occasionally struggled in his "schoolwork," often frustrated by his difficulty with time management, trying to balance the demands of homework and studying for tests with rigorous physical, mental, and emotional demands of high school football practices. "Make sure you do as much homework as you can during your study hall" was Coach Bennett's advice to his players, understanding the challenges that studying at night after exhausting practices would present.

Yet as committed to football as Doug Bennett was, he refused to let any player, regardless of his ability, just get by with sloppy academic work. "If you didn't perform up to speed in the classroom, his wild card was "you can't play football," Jimbo recalls. Though he never proselytized nor tried to force his faith on any player, if circumstances were tough in a young man's life, either on the field or off, Coach Bennett would, Jimbo remembers, "…pray with you if you needed it."

Because Doug Bennett was so consistent in his coaching methods and in his character, Swansea players always knew what to expect from him. Jimbo recalls, "If you looked from the field over to the sideline and Coach Bennett was taking those short, quick steps as he paced back and forth, you knew it was not going to be good!" Jimbo remembers with a laugh one game at Bamberg-Ehrhart when a much smaller offensive lineman was getting underneath his pads when they engaged at the line of scrimmage. Being in the lower position of this initial deadlock, his smaller opponent was able to gain leverage on Jimbo and control him, moving him out of the path of the ball carrier or chopping his legs out from underneath him if he was unable to move Jimbo.

As he jogged off the field after another frustrating series of plays, Jimbo saw the "short, quick steps" as Coach Bennett approached him. On occasion, Coach Bennett would reach up and place his hand on a player's face mask - not the out-of-control grabbing of a face mask that was so in vogue during this era - in order to be able to look his player in the eye. This was one of those moments. What ensued was one of Coach Bennett's "energy talks" as Jimbo calls them: "He's whippin' you. He's getting' his pads under yours and just whippin' you! Golly buck, Jimbo!" Coach Bennett continued: "But I believe in you. You're better than that. Now go out there and show him you're from Swansea!"

Properly admonished by his "daddy-figure" coach, Jimbo, from that moment on, totally dominated his smaller, pesky opponent, and by game's end, heard the "I knew you could do it" exclamation from his coach after a decisive victory. One of the key plays occurred when Jimbo drove his smallish pest deep into the backfield and into a collision with the quarterback, who fumbled. Tiger safety Mark English, son of former Lexington District Four Superintendent Robert English, deftly performed the "scoop and score" drill practiced so regularly at Swansea by returning the muffed football for a key touchdown.

Another of Coach Bennett's highly effective motivational techniques was the standard awarding of helmet decals for big plays, but with an interesting twist. To the delight of Jimbo (who might have also been nicknamed "Jumbo") and other

Tiger linemen with large appetites, Coach Bennett provided discounted meal tickets from the extremely popular Shoney's Big Boy restaurants in nearby Columbia. Ever the gregarious teammate, Jimbo liked to accumulate his tickets and then take other players out for dinner (or, more accurately, "supper," as it is known in the South.)

Around 1976 or 1977 (Jimbo can't quite recall), Coach Bennett implemented his ingenious post-practice ice cream motivational program. During the hot months of August and September, when a Swansea player had a particularly good practice, he was awarded his choice of an ice cream sandwich or a "Nutty Buddy," a waffle cone filled with vanilla ice cream and topped with nuts and a milk chocolate coating. At certain poignant moments in a drill or scrimmage after an outstanding play, Coach Bennett was known to call out a player's name and declare, "That's a Nutty Buddy!"

Players who did not enjoy a particularly good practice, however, still did not go without some type of cool refreshment. Those whose practice was acceptable but not exceptional, received a flavored two-stick double popsicle. But anyone whose performance in practice was substandard, perhaps because he had arrived preoccupied with a girlfriend or even more serious problems at home, had to suffer the ultimate indignity of having a two-stick popsicle broken in half to be shared with another slacker.

Coach Bennett's most powerful and motivating quality, however, may have been his calm demeanor in the face of adversity. Jimbo recalls:

> "More times than I can count, we would come in at halftime, and,we, as players, we were done. We felt we were hopelessly behind and saw little hope

> of victory. Coach would listen carefully to the observations of his assistant coaches, and then he would bring us together and explain very logically what the problems were and how we could fix them. Then he would give us an "energy talk," telling us that he had watched us practice all week and that the coaches had not kept us out on the practice field for nothin'. We were better than we were playin'. Then Coach would say something like, "We know who we are but we haven't shown them yet. Let's show them what it means to be a Swansea Tiger!'"

Ready to "eat nails" and "run through brick walls" for the man they so loved and admired, more times than not, Swansea overcame halftime deficits and went on to win in convincing fashion.

When the Tiger football team began playing its home games in the newly dedicated Doug Bennett Stadium in 1978, Jimbo's senior year, his mother's declining health prevented her from attending the games. Jimbo recalls a family dilemma: "My daddy kept going to the games, but my mother was really bad off by this time and had to have round-the-clock care. My daddy felt so bad about leaving her at home, but she told him to go to the games." But an area radio station had begun airing Tiger football games, and Ruby Raulerson, her body racked with pain, was able to follow the fortunes of her sons' team.

In 1983, the year that Paul, the youngest Raulerson brother, finished playing football and graduated, Ruby Raulerson, having developed a severe fibrosis in her lungs, moved quietly into eternity. As though she had been waiting until her last son finished playing for Doug Bennett and graduated, Ruby's death came on August 13, just a week before the start of the first season in ten years without one of her boys on the Swansea roster.

Perhaps no moment better illustrates the powerful influence of a humble high school football coach who taught his players by word and deed to serve others and do the right thing than the day Jimbo Raulerson, a thirty-six-year-old resident of Swansea and member of the town's volunteer fire department was alerted and called out during a Sunday morning worship service at Swansea Baptist Church. On this otherwise quiet and peaceful morning, a large, raging woods fire was being fanned by 50 mph winds and threatening several nearby homes in a neighborhood just off Highway 6. As he performed his duty manning one of the water lines, Jimbo and several other of the volunteer firemen were still dressed in their "Sunday best" attire under their standard issue protective fire gear.

After a long battle on a main hose, Jimbo was relieved of his duty on the front line of the efforts to control the blaze. As he was walking toward one of several firetrucks that had been summoned from throughout Lexington County and even from other surrounding counties, he heard a familiar voice, one that called to mind a flood of memories. There, dressed in his "Sunday best," offering Jimbo some water before he himself would don his fire gear and take his place in the battle with the blaze, stood volunteer fireman Doug Bennett.

IN HIS OWN WORDS

"BE SOMEBODY WHO MAKES EVERYBODY FEEL LIKE SOMEBODY."
GREG VISHNEPELSKI

When coaches are asked to communicate their coaching philosophy, many describe at great length and in great detail the principles and strategies upon which they have built their programs. Doug Bennett's coaching philosophy, by comparison, was simple. His was a straightforward approach to teaching the fundamentals of the game of football while seeking to have a positive influence upon the lives of his players. What follows are the key elements of Bennett's plan for making a difference.

"God, /Family, /Academics, / Football"

What became known as "The Four Priorities" were the foundation stones for Bennett's program. From the outset of his coaching career, Bennett was firm in his convictions about keeping first things first in these four areas, listed in descending order of importance. He wanted his players to maintain balance and perspective on what was most important in their lives.

Bennett taught these principles, first by example in his own life. He emphasized avoiding the impulse to place too much importance on football because of the instant gratification or recognition one might receive from participating. He wanted them to place a priority on their relationship with God and upon relationships in their family. Academic effort and success were valued over football to such degree that if a player was not performing up to standards in the classroom, he was not allowed to practice and play. He had to spend time on studying and improving his grades.

This balanced approach enabled Coach Bennett to keep things in perspective in his own life. In coaching and in life, this is extremely difficult to do. But Bennett did this better than most. Early in his career when "If they play it, you coach it" was his motto as he coached every sport offered by Swansea High School, Bennett taught himself how to relax by pursuing other interests such as hunting. This ability to decompress enabled him to stay in a business where stress and burnout overwhelm many.

"If you don't have 'em, you can't help 'em."

Doug Bennett's approach to teaching the game of football and to building a team was more inclusive than that of many of his contemporaries. He believed that the benefits of playing high school football should be enjoyed by the many and not just the few. Thus, unlike some other coaches, he never "cut" players from the team's roster, regardless of their lack of proficiency in the skills needed to play well. Bennett, instead, wanted to keep young men involved in his program for how they might benefit, not just for how they might help enhance his record as a coach.

Bennett knew that a freshman could become a much more skilled player as he matured physically and emotionally. He needed time to develop. Nor was Coach Bennett anxious to get rid of players who were trying the game for the first time. Even seniors who had never played football were permitted to become a member of the team.

Bennett's was no "My way or the highway" or "This ain't no democracy" authoritative coaching style: "I think football is the most democratic sport out there. You can take a kid from the poorest and the richest neighborhoods in the town, and as soon as they become teammates, they become family. One's contribution determines the other's success. They work together, play together, pray together, and stay together. When it's all over, it's not a team anymore, it's a close-knit family."

Coach Bennett also demonstrated a respect and appreciation for boys who were not particularly athletic, but who were, at least, trying. Some of these young players went on to enhance the team's on-the-field success. Others played little, but they had a head coach and a staff who made them feel like somebody with a valuable contribution to make to the team in whatever role they found themselves.

In Swansea, football provided a guardrail for some young men who needed discipline and guidance regardless of their athletic ability. Bennett had a strong conviction that he and his staff, even the game of football itself, could make a difference in the lives of the young men under his charge. Those who stuck around were better for it.

"You're no better than your help."

Doug Bennett understood delegation better than many corporate CEOs. He trusted his assistant coaches to carry out their assigned duties and offered them guidance and assistance where needed. Bennett understood well the value of having capable assistants and demonstrated the wisdom to develop them without micromanaging them. Steve Carter, a member of Bennett's staff from 1971 to 1979, describes his mentor's leadership approach:

> 'He gives you ideas, works with you and allows you to develop your own potential. Every assistant coach he has ever had, he allowed them to have an area of responsibility. He'd treat you as if you were the head coach in that area. It would be yours to run, but we always looked to him for guidance."

"If you want to win, you've got to have good material."

On the evening of his retirement ceremony on June 2, 1990, Doug Bennett offered a few reasons for his longevity and success at Swansea: "If you want to win, you've got to have good material. We've been very blessed to have had a lot of good athletes."

On no Doug Bennett team was this truer than on his 1960 Class B state championship team, which had five players who earned major college scholarships. Even much larger schools in the state were not blessed with this much talent. Through the years, Swansea and the surrounding area have produced an unusually high number of talented athletes, especially considering that Swansea High School has competed in the lower classifications.

As far as talent on an individual basis, it is difficult to single-out Bennett's most athletically gifted player. The veteran coach says that he's had so many good players that it's difficult to pick one. However, in the opinion of many, that distinction goes to Ryan Tillman "Kit" Jackson, III, the quarterback and safety on Swansea's 1962 and 1963 teams. An all-around athlete who once scored forty points in a basketball game against Olympia, "Kit" stood out in football and track.

According to Coach Bennett, Kit "was good at everything" as a quarterback: "We ran a lot of run/pass option plays because he read defenses so well." During Kit's tenure, "he was our best running back as a quarterback," says Bennett.

In one of "Kit's" more amazing feats, he flew into Columbia from his senior class trip in New York City on a Saturday morning to compete in the state track meet. With no practice during the entire week before, Jackson won the state title in the high jump and placed second in both the high hurdles and low hurdles events.

His knack for creating big plays as a quarterback, his ball-hawking ability as a safety, and his electrifying skills as a punt returner drew the attention of several college recruiters. "Kit" signed a football scholarship with Clemson where he became a 6-2 180-pound starting safety during 1965-1967 ACC Championship seasons. As a sophomore, he was the first Clemson player to intercept three passes in a single game - against Wake Forest - a record that has since been tied four times, but not surpassed. Jackson also competed on the track team as a jumper: high jump, triple jump, and broad jump.

While at Clemson, "Kit" jumped 6'8" before the Fosberry flop revolutionized the high jump. He used the "western roll" technique, in which the jumper approaches the bar from the left side and jumps off the left foot. He then thrusts his right leg vertically and performs a half-body roll and kicks with the right leg to help propel his body over the bar. The western roll is considered a much more difficult high jump technique since speed and momentum do not factor in as much as they do with the Fosberry flop.

"Kit's" sons, Michael and Ryan, each played a couple of seasons for Doug Bennett. "Kit" eventually moved to Rocky Mount, North Carolina, where he enjoyed golf and turkey hunting in retirement while volunteering with Meals on Wheels as well as with United Community Ministries until his death in May of 2018.

"The steam that toots the whistle don't turn the wheel."
Doug Bennett had a healthy disdain for braggart players or coaches who talked a good game, even if, in fact, they possessed one. Despite his coaching success, Coach Bennett demonstrated a gracious, humble attitude toward competitors, in victory or defeat.

One Bennett assistant, Tommy Williams, relates a story of the impact that Doug Bennett's humility and self-control had upon others:

> "My most memorable event about Coach was not on any athletic field, but in a crowded gym during a pep rally. The students were really wound up and loud, but when Coach Bennett walked to the microphone, it immediately got quiet. He didn't have to yell or scream or threaten these students. All he did was walk to the microphone to speak. These were all types of students, some who played for him, but others who just knew him as 'the coach.' I had never witnessed, nor since have witnessed, such a display of respect for someone. The respect was not out of fear, but more out of love for a man that has given his life to a school as well as a community."

"Lead by example."
As he did in every aspect of his demeanor and behavior as a coach, Doug Bennett exhibited unusual patience in dealing with player mistakes. As though practices were a sort of laboratory in which failure was a necessary means to success, Bennett never belittled or cajoled. Instead, he demonstrated the techniques he wanted implemented and, when he felt it necessary, he went a step further.

One day, a player was repeatedly making a mistake when Bennett took matters into his own hands. He said to a nearby player, "Gimme your helmet." He put the helmet on, demonstrated the technique, took the helmet off, and said, "Now that's how I want it done." Parents of Doug Bennett's players could not have asked for a better leader by example in matters of character and good conduct. He was fair and just in his dealings with players and a role model of moral and ethical excellence.

"If you don't have a sense of humor, you don't have any business being in coaching."
A quiet man of few words, Doug Bennett is, ironically, a gifted storyteller with an impeccable memory. He takes immense delight in telling a humorous story, punctuating the ending with a hearty laugh. Here are just *a few* of Bennett's favorites:

One Skilled Bus Driver
It seems that after the 1976 regular season ended with another playoff berth, Swansea High administrators had difficulty securing an adequate bus for transporting the team to their first-round contest at Loris. On the day of the game, a rickety, poorly maintained Greyhound bus showed up. But as disconcerting

as the appearance of the bus was, when the driver got off to introduce himself, he offered his left hand for a handshake greeting - the only hand he had! The driver's right arm had been partially amputated at the elbow, leaving only a nub, which his new passengers would soon discover was highly functional.

A short distance into the trip, Doug Bennett got the attention of Coach Orr, who was sitting next to him. "Look at that," he said as the driver, a self-made master of compensation and adaptability, reached across his body to change gears with his left hand and arm, while steering with his nub. However, the most unsettling development with this bus operator's adapted driving method would occur when the driver later reached into a small cooler and pulled out a bologna sandwich, which he held in his left hand as he steered with his nub. Equally impressive and nerve-wracking was the driver's coordination as he casually took a bite of the sandwich, set it down in his lap to change gears, and picked it back up to take another bite, all the while using an amputated arm to guide the bus.

Fred, a man of faith who would later serve as a Baptist minister after his coaching career, recalls that it was after watching this man's highly skilled sandwich consumption that Coach Bennett turned to Fred and quipped, "I'm just praying that we make it!"

The Thirteenth Man

In a game with rival Olympia High, the Tiger running game was in high gear, and the Red Devils were unable to slow it down, much less stop it. Olympia Head Coach Bobby Giles, was extremely frustrated with the officiating crew as well as his defense's ineffectiveness. After exhausting every conventional counter move at his disposal, Coach Giles decided to test the referees by sending in a twelfth defender in hopes of stopping the Tiger offense. Even against twelve Olympia defenders, Swansea kept methodically racking up yardage and first downs.

When the officiating crew did not recognize that there were twelve Red Devils on the field, Coach Giles was even more incensed with their incompetence, and he sent in a thirteenth player. Even with a two-man advantage, Olympia could not stop Swansea. Finally, Coach Giles took off his hat, threw it to the ground, and removed his two extra players. Some suggest that even a fourteenth player would not have stopped the Tigers on this night.

Sack 'o Taters

In the fourth game of the 1968 season, Swansea traveled with fourteen players to Jackson High and played in a torrential downpour. First-year Swansea running back Sammy Colter was hit hard and injured and had to be removed from the game. After he was brought to the sideline, one of his teammates, Curlee Brooks, was concerned that Sammy was going to get soaked - like everyone else present - and needed to get out of the rain. Unaware of Coach Bennett's sideline protocol, Curlee hoisted Sammy and threw him across his shoulder like a large sack of potatoes and started off to the locker-room.

With Sammy and Curlee now away from the sideline, there was only one remaining Swansea player not in the game. As Curlee was carrying Sammy, an ambulance was closely following the pair with the driver blowing the horn and trying to get Curlee to let them carry Sammy in the vehicle. Curlee was undeterred. After successfully completing his mission, Curlee returned to the Tigers' sideline.

Bleacher Coach

During one season after he had retired from thirty-nine years of coaching, Doug Bennett attended a Swansea High game and occupied an unusual vantage point for him: a seat in the home side stands in the stadium named in his honor. It seems that throughout the course of the game, one particularly vocal Swansea fan was expressing his displeasure with the coaching strategies and results. After listening to this man's long litany of complaints, Fred Orr turned to his mentor and asked, "Coach, who is that guy? And with the wry, tongue-in-cheek delivery that is his trademark, Doug Bennett quipped, "I don't know, Fred, but he's been coaching Swansea since long before I did."

BARNELL MACK
PLAYER, 1977-1980

"IF YOU WANT TO LIFT YOURSELF UP, LIFT UP SOMEONE ELSE."
BOOKER T. WASHINGTON

Unlike his participation in the sport of football, Barnell Mack began wrestling at Swansea High in the ninth grade with no prior experience. He had older friends who wrestled, but he had never learned from them any wrestling moves or techniques. In addition to his inexperience in the sport, another challenge Barnell took on with determination was getting into shape to wrestle, a very different type of conditioning than is required for football.

Typically, when football players transition to participation in wrestling, they have to lose weight to qualify for lower weight classifications. But for Barnell, "there wasn't any weight to lose," he declares with a laugh. Wrestling requires a different type of physical conditioning than football, in which plays involve short, explosive bursts for four or five seconds with longer rests after each play. Much more endurance is required in wrestling, which is structured with three intense periods each lasting two minutes with only a brief break in the action for the referee to flip a coin to determine the starting positions of the two contestants before each period. Wrestling puts "more demands on your wind," Barnell explains. In those two-minute periods, "you're thinking more, and your body is moving a lot."

Barnell proved to be a quick learner and a superbly conditioned athlete. During his wrestling career, he won four state championships, each in a different weight class: 135, 145, 155, and 165 pounds. This feat has since been duplicated, but Barnell still holds the state record for the most wins in back-to-back seasons.

His enviable success as a wrestler notwithstanding, football was Barnell's first love. He began playing the game at "ten or eleven" on the "midget" team in the Lexington County league. Barnell started out at multiple positions: running back, linebacker, and defensive back and enjoyed certain aspects of each position. Coincidentally, these were the positions he would play years later on the junior varsity and varsity teams at Swansea High School.

Practices and a few games were held at "the county field just above Coach Bennett's house." Parents served as coaches. Most of the league games were played in Lexington, the county seat, and in other small communities such as Pelion and Gilbert. With most of their games being played away from Swansea, the parents organized transportation to the other game sites. Barnell recalls with a laugh how he and his teammates loaded up pickup trucks to the point that "the bumpers were nearly draggin' the highway." A local grocer, Charles Goodwin, loaned parents a utility van in which the merchant hauled food as another vehicle in the caravan. "Our parents really kicked in and stepped up to help us in our journey."

When Barnell became a parent and his son reached the age for eligibility to play in the county league, "there was no little league football going on." At the county field in Swansea, the goalposts had been removed, and what once had been a football field was being converted to a soccer field. Barnell wanted his son to play football, so he appealed to the county recreational administrators to re-establish a football team. "They told me that if we could get enough players, we could have the football field back."

Barnell was able to generate enough community interest to get players registered for two teams of the youngest players, "termites" and "mites." The goalposts were re-installed, and youth football games were again played in Swansea. Barnell's son, Brandon, was too old, by two months for county league football, and he ended up playing eighth grade football with Sand Hill, which was coached by the junior varsity coaches at Swansea High.

Barnell served as the lead organizer the first two seasons of the newly established county league teams in Swansea. He took responsibility for helping secure sponsorship for the teams to provide uniforms, and he communicated with county recreation officials. From among the parents, he recruited coaches, including Zach Smith, "who has been coaching ever since."

When Barnell started playing football at Swansea High as a freshman on the junior varsity team, many of the opposing teams were comprised of players he had played against in the county's youth football league. After games, the players would talk to one another and reminisce about their community teams competing against one another. Barnell adds, "We would keep up with the stats of players from county ball all the way through our senior year."

Like Swansea, these teams represented one-school communities. Players competed against one another year after year. This familiarity, instead of breeding contempt, more often generated respect for one's opponent. Though the competition was fierce, most often friendships endured regardless of the outcome - even in rivalry games.

Barnell recalls Coach Bennett speaking to the Tiger JV team when they had gotten off to a quick start and were winning every game. Bennett spoke to the team about continuing to work hard to finish the season strong. He pointed out that when they moved up to the varsity team, they would be playing with the same teammates from the JV squad and that if they continued with a good work ethic, they could enjoy a similar type of success at the next level in the Swansea program. Coach Bennett also pointed out that, as members of the varsity team, they would continue to compete against these familiar opponents they had faced in youth football.

Barnell was moved up to the varsity team as a sophomore, but this transition was anything but smooth. As a backup defensive back, Barnell was frustrated that he was not playing in games right away as he had as a member of the JV team, where he had played on offense, defense, and special teams: "I just wanted the action." Especially tough on Barnell was hearing his former teammates on the JV team at school on Friday, game day for the varsity, describing their exploits after the season's first two Thursday night games. Barnell was going through something he had never experienced before - sitting on the sidelines and watching the action. This was very different from his days during the back-to-back state championship years in '74and '75 when he had followed the action from behind the steel cable that ran the length of the field and served to separate fans from the bench area. He was no longer a kid enthusiastically following the exploits of his heroes. He was supposed to be playing.

After not playing in the first two games, Barnell took advantage of an unexpected opportunity. Linebacker coach Phil Williams needed another player: "I'll take anybody who wants to play this position," he declared. Though smaller than the typical high school linebacker, Barnell moved over from defensive back. He made an impact right away. In his first action as a linebacker, Barnell recorded two sacks and four solo tackles against rival North High in the Tigers' third game. With this performance, he became the starting linebacker, a position he held for the remainder of his career at Swansea.

Perhaps because he had played the position in the county youth league, Barnell wanted to play running back in addition to being a linebacker. As a junior, he went to running backs coach Bob Novinger and asked to be given an opportunity: "I'm what you need. Give me one game, and I won't harass you anymore," he insisted. Barnell reasoned that his experience as a defensive player responsible for tackling runners gave him an advantage: "I know how to shuck and jive a defensive player. (As a defender) "...you don't look at a runner's eyes; you look at his waist. Ninety percent of defensive players look at his eyes." If allowed to play running back, Barnell had a plan to elude defenders: "I'm gonna get their eye contact and let hips and legs do the rest. I also had a technique where I could spin around and keep my balance."

Even though the Tigers had good depth at the running back position, Barnell was given an opportunity to play in certain situations. At times when the Swansea offense needed a first down, "...the coaches would let me go in to run the ball."

Most often, Barnell was called on to block for David Smith when the Tiger offense got inside their opponent's thirty-five-yard line. What Barnell lacked in size as a lead blocker he made up for with sheer athletic ability: "I would jump vertical and sideways to shield defensive players from David so that he could get through." Barnell added, "I knew I had a racehorse coming behind me, so I just opened things up for him."

Barnell Mack's incredible athletic ability had always created opportunities for him. He was a pole vaulter and a high jumper all four years for the Tiger track team. As a junior and senior, he won the lower state titles in each event. He also ran the high and intermediate hurdles even though he "didn't have speed. I just had instincts." But perhaps the singular moment that best exemplifies Barnell's career as an athlete came in the 1980 season, against rival Bamberg-Ehrhardt, when he executed one of the most memorable plays in the history of Swansea football.

Trailing by a touchdown, the Raiders' drive stalled on their side of the fifty-yard-line, and they elected to punt to try to pin Swansea deep in their own territory. As a linebacker lined up close to the long snapper when opponents punted, Barnell had been watching the snapper closely and had picked up on a habit that tipped when he was going to snap the ball: "I watched the movement of his hand. When he put pressure on the ball, his hand turned totally red." Barnell was so confident he was going to block the punt that he told the referee and his teammates what he was going to do. "I am going to touch the (punted) ball, so look for the ball."

"When he started to move the ball, I was standing up, and I jumped over the snapper flat-footed, (with no running start)" Barnell rushed toward the punter, and just as the punter's foot made contact with the football, "...my hand caught it and

I brought it down to my stomach. He fell down, and I just kept running (twenty-eight yards for a touchdown.) I knew I was going to touch it, but I had no clue I was going to get that much of it," Barnell said afterward. Coach Bennett told Barnell, "You timed that just perfectly." Barnell explained, "It was there all night. I just took advantage of it."

More than the individual plays or exciting moments, Barnell remembers and treasures his relationships with teammates. With many of Swansea's players having been on teams together from an early age, a comradery developed and grew as the years went by. "The main thing I enjoyed about playing for Swansea was the guys I was playing with. It was like a brotherhood." As a part of a long-time successful program under Doug Bennett, Barnell and his teammates "had the respect of the student body." Having that respect, Barnell insists, carried a certain responsibility: "Since they look up to you, we couldn't let no one bully other students. We tried to stop things before teachers would need to know anything about it."

One of the things Barnell learned from Coach Bennett's example affected his own decision-making and conduct: "What you do has an impact on other people's lives because you don't know who's watching. Respect is one of the biggest things he taught us. In anything you do, have respect for yourself and others will respect you." Being treated with respect by an adult mentor and learning to respect oneself enabled Barnell and others to make good decisions at an age when peer pressure overwhelms many.

The disappointing loss in the 1980 state championship game against Woodruff served as a reminder of another principle that the Swansea coaches had instilled in their players. "Coach Bennett and his coaches taught us that when times get bad, you don't give up. Even if you don't win, if you give 100 percent, you don't feel as bad. You still have a strong mentality that you can accomplish certain things. Mainly you have to suck it up and take the bad with the good." In 1980, there was more good than bad for the Tigers as they finished with an 11-2 record. During Barnell's varsity career, Swansea had season marks of 8-3,8-5, 11-2, a combined 27-10 record and a lower state championship.

Barnell Mack was recognized by teammates and other students as a leader who cared about people. As such, peers often sought him out for advice. On many occasions his recommendation was that his friend discuss a problem in his family or some other personal issue with the man Barnell had come to trust. Barnell's advice: "Talk to Coach Bennett, and he'll tell you which way to go."

Trust must be earned. Throughout his career, Doug Bennett earned the trust of students and peers because of his character and his consistency. Barnell explains, "Coach Bennett was a person you could go to like a father. He didn't speak over your head with great big words." Because Doug Bennett was caring and approachable, Barnell often accompanied friends when they wanted to discuss a problem. "I'd go with them and get the conversation going and then leave when I knew the conversation was about to get more personal."

Over the years, Bennett mastered the art of establishing rapport with others. He often accomplished this by telling a joke or a funny story to get the other person laughing, putting them at ease. He was a good listener who patiently sought to understand the nature and scope of the issue before speaking to it. When he spoke, he did so in a non-judgmental manner without compromising on what was true and virtuous. His advice was sound, the right thing to do. And the listener knew it.

Claudette Lucas, a student at Swansea High remembers:

> He cared about his students. I got called to his office (when Bennett was still serving as "interim" principal) when word got to him that I was dropping out to get married. I never forgot that he cared so much and tried his best to get me to stay in school. He knew how important it was. I didn't stay, but did return a few years later in adult education and graduated - Class of 1974 became Class of 1977, ...something I'll never forget."

Bennett's wise counsel was most often received because people knew, without question, that he cared about them. He was interested and present in the moment. He made people feel special. Barnell describes the impact Doug Bennett had on himself and on other people this way: "Whether you played for him or not, he always had a good word to say to you. He made you feel like you were somebody."

ROBERT MADDOX PLAYER, 1976-1978 AND HEAD COACH, 1990-1999

"A DISCIPLE IS NOT ABOVE HIS TEACHER, BUT EVERYONE WHO IS FULLY TRAINED WILL BE LIKE HIS TEACHER."
JESUS CHRIST (LUKE 6:40)

One of Robert Maddox's first decisions as a new head coach was to invite his former head coach, Doug Bennett, to be involved in the Swansea program to any extent that he wished even though he had retired. Maddox today counts it a privilege and a blessing that Bennett agreed to serve the program for Maddox's entire tenure from 1990 to 1999. "There wasn't any aspect of our program in which we didn't want his involvement, as long as he was willing to be a part of it. "declared Maddox*

But before Coach Maddox accepted the offer to succeed his mentor as the leader of the Tiger program, he lobbied for his best friend and coaching compadre, John Petrey, to be hired as the athletic director. Maddox was able to convince school officials that Petrey, a former player and assistant coach for Bennett, would indeed be a capable athletic administrator and defensive coordinator. Said Maddox at the time, "I would not have come to Swansea without John." He added, "Not only did I think he belonged here at Swansea, but he's a great defensive football coach and I wanted him with me. He's as much a head coach in our program as I am."

With Coach Petrey in place and with Doug Bennett agreeing to serve in an advisory capacity without coaching a position, Maddox assembled a staff which included Bob Novinger, who had served under Coach Bennett, David Heilesen, Lee Sawyer, and Ben Killian. In putting together his first staff, as well as throughout his entire tenure as head coach, Maddox was blessed to serve under an administration who worked with him to hire excellent teachers for open positions who could also be excellent football coaches.

With Maddox's new staff providing skillful coaching and leadership in the technical and motivational aspects of teaching football, the new Swansea head coach called on his mentor at the beginning of each season to provide a history of the program and to share life lessons from the game that would have meaning for high school students. As the season progressed, Coach Bennett attended practice every day and offered input on what he observed. Maddox and defensive coordinator John Petrey relished the insights from Bennett whether the advice might be on the technical aspects of a drill or wisdom on how to handle a player issue. On Saturdays after Friday night games, Bennett joined the staff to offer input on the previous night's game regarding things the Tigers did well and how they might improve. Bennett also served, along with Ben Killian, as a coach for the "B Team" (about fifty middle schoolers).

In his first year at Swansea, Robert Maddox taught biology and chemistry with one open planning period, which he used for lesson planning. Thus, he was unable to use an open period on Fridays of a home game to line off the football field. For his first home game, Coach Maddox had to request a sick day to have time to fulfill the obligation of field preparation. However, after Doug Bennett saw the results of the first-year head coach's effort, he volunteered to handle that duty going forward. With thirty-six years of experience few, if any, coaches could do a better job of lining a football field with precision than Doug Bennett. And, as one of the premier "grass men" as a football coach in the state of South Carolina, Coach Bennett passed on what he knew to the new Tiger head coach to help ensure that Swansea's teams had the finest playing surface possible.

Sports journalist David Shelton says that to hear Robert Maddox outline his coaching philosophy is like listening to thirty-six- year veteran and Hall-of-Famer Doug Bennett:

> " I don't believe in winning at any price. To me, the effort to win is more important. We judge success by how close we come to fulfilling our potential. We set realistic goals, things that we can work on every day. We set a goal to do the things that are going to get us in position to have a chance. There's no reason we can't be the hardest-working team in the state. There's no reason why we can't have as much character or class as anybody else. Those are things we can control."
>
> Maddox adds: "I hate losing, but I'm not going to work any harder after a loss than I do after a win.

> I'd say the effort to be the best is more important than winning. We try to emphasize having fun and to enjoy the game. In order to have fun, it takes a lot of hard work. It isn't fun if you can't compete. Winning is the result of doing a lot of things right."

One of the lasting lessons Coach Maddox learned while playing for Bennett was more of a relational nature than of the technical aspects of coaching: "He cared about all players, and he tried to be fair. He also wanted to be a good example in the way he lived his life."

Like his mentor, Maddox enjoyed the benefits of having a program that was situated in a small town and drew students from the surrounding area. "The thing I like about (the) AA (classification) is that a lot of the schools are named after the town they're in. There's a community with its own identity that also has its own team. There's one school and one team to rally around, and when all of the energy and support is focused on one thing, it makes for a really special situation." Tiger defensive coordinator and athletic director John Petrey described this support in terms of an advantage: "The biggest thing I can remember as a player was all the fan support. We knew they would be there for us. We tell the kids they are very lucky to have the support we have here. It's something special. The coaches know it, and the players do as well."

That throng of Tiger supporters enjoyed an unprecedented run in the first five years of Maddox's tenure. In his first season at the helm, Swansea qualified for the playoffs and advanced to the third round, finishing with an 8-5 record. The next year, the Tigers appeared in the program's seventh state final, where they lost to Abbeville and finished 12-3. What happened next had never happened before in the history of Swansea football.

The Tigers duplicated the efforts of the teams from 1960 and 1961 who appeared in back-to-back state finals. But in 1992, the Tigers defeated Batesburg-Leesville for the AA state championship after losing three of the first four games, igniting a streak that would end with three consecutive state championships. The 1993 season was perfect, 15-0, with Swansea winning its first five games by a combined score of 160-0. Maddox explained how this was a special team and season:

> The first thing that stands out about the 1993 team was their ability and talent, and, second, their ability to stay focused on working hard each week to get better. They had a lot of high expectations and a lot of people talking about how good they were, but they never let it go to their head. Those kids loved to play the game. I won't ever coach a team that loves to play as much as they did. They loved to compete with each other, and that competition within the team helped them improve a lot. We had some real solid leadership on that team.

In 1994 the Tigers achieved a "three-peat" with a 27-0 win over Pageland Central in the state final after losing eleven starters from the year before.

Maddox, with his teams having run off a 60-13 record and four state championship appearances in his first five years as a head coach, said that the longer he stayed in coaching, the better chance he had of experiencing the other side of the spectrum - losing. Maddox's words proved prophetic as the Tigers went 4-7 the year after their three-peat of state championships. Following a 26-12 run during the '96, '97, and '98 seasons, Maddox's team posted a 2-8 mark in his final season as the Tiger head coach. "We were not as talented, and we had some injury problems. And it was my first season as a head coach without John Petrey, our excellent defensive coordinator, who had decided to go into school administration. I hated it for our seniors."

Robert Maddox's worse loss, however, was not experienced on the field of play. After each had left coaching to become school administrators, John Petrey, with whom Maddox had coached his entire career in high school and who had become his closest friend, was diagnosed in June of 2009 with glioblastoma, a cancer of the brain with a 100 percent mortality rate. During his treatment, John received compassionate and skillful care at Duke University Hospital, where Senator Edward Kennedy had been treated for the same disease.

Maddox recalls taking a walk with John during which his dear friend spoke of the pain of his imminent death and having to leave his family: his wife, Gay, and his sons, Tanner and Grant. On another occasion, John called Robert to ask if they could have lunch together. After spending two hours together, Robert had just returned to his office when Gay called to tell him that John had just had a seizure. On Sunday June 13, 2010, John died. Robert is immensely grateful that in John's final days, he was able to have that precious time over lunch with his long-time friend before he left this life.

Robert and his family faced another formidable opponent after he had left coaching. Robert's son Jess was diagnosed with Wilms tumor a week before turning three years old. Jess's radiation and chemotherapy treatments went on for over a year, with Jess's weight dropping seventeen pounds at age four before he entered periodic monitoring for recurrence. A year later, he began the "late effects" protocol to monitor the effects of treatment. Jess is fully recovered now and twenty-two-year-old senior mechanical engineering student at the University of South Carolina.

When his family reached the other side of this battle, Robert was able to focus more on his new career as a school administrator. In his role as the superintendent of Lexington County District Four schools, Maddox has applied many of the principles and lessons from his days as a football player and coach. "It's important to set priorities, to have a good work ethic, and to plan well. But, just as in football, execution is the key." Maddox adds, "Leadership is developing people to leverage resources in a team effort. To me, it's just common sense. You want everybody in the organization doing well."

As a player, Maddox was fortunate to have observed leadership principles modeled by his mentor Doug Bennett. And by soliciting the assistance of Doug Bennett in a collaborative role after his retirement, Maddox provided a platform for his own players to benefit from the wisdom and experience of the "Head Coach Emeritus." Through his continued involvement in football at Swansea High School during the tenure of his protege, Doug Bennett had a significant role in a total of ten state championship appearances with the Tigers capturing six titles. While Coach Bennett would modestly minimize the importance of his role, especially after his retirement, Maddox has a different view: "There's no way to quantify the contribution that Coach Bennett made to our program. Our players were able to come as close as possible to the experience of having Doug Bennett as a head coach without him actually in that role."

BEYOND THE GOALPOSTS

"PREACH THE GOSPEL AT ALL TIMES AND, IF NECESSARY, USE WORDS."
ST. FRANCIS OF ASSISI

The Boy Scout law has twelve tenets: "A Scout is trustworthy, loyal, helpful, friendly, courteous, kind, obedient, cheerful, thrifty, brave, clean, and reverent." For decades, Boy Scouts in America and around the world were encouraged to strive for excellence in each of these qualities. Perhaps the most difficult of these principles for an adolescent boy to understand, though, is the idea that a Boy Scout is to be reverent. But in Swansea, many a young man, including myself, learned what it is to be reverent, not in a church building, but in a football locker room.

In our present day, concerns about the "separation of church and state" are, it seems, exaggerated far beyond the original intent of the founding fathers in such a way that any expression of faith is considered a "threat" or potentially offensive to some. Doug Bennett, a humble man with strong convictions about a faith-based life, if he were still coaching today, might be unfairly labeled as "extreme." But during his coaching career, his reverent and genuine prayers in the locker room with his players were welcomed and appreciated. After leading a sincere prayer for the safety of the young men on both teams, Doug Bennett led his team in The Lord's Prayer, with his team joining in unison, just before the team left the locker room for the field.

We will leave it to the theologians to debate whether God is even remotely concerned about the outcome of any athletic contest. I suspect that He has far greater concerns about the universe. But what Doug Bennett was communicating to his team was his belief in a personal God who was concerned about all the details of each human being's life and that even the smallest details, like the number of hairs on our head, as Jesus said in Matthew 10:30, were not overlooked.

This awareness of a God who cares about human beings and who is for their good began at a tender age for Doug in the Bennett household. His mother had a deep spirituality and spent much time in prayer for her children. The family attended the Associated Reformed Presbyterian Church in York, where the children were involved in Sunday school classes. After receiving a New Testament with the psalms from his mother upon his enlistment in the Army Air Corps, Doug began to read the Bible regularly. Its tenets impacted his view of the world and shaped his moral compass.

Since his arrival in Swansea, Doug Bennett had been involved in Good Shepherd Lutheran Church, which was next door to the home in which he lived as a boarder. Doug held a variety of leadership positions over the years, including serving as superintendent of the Sunday school, and as president of the Lutheran men. He also served two four-year terms on the church council. For several years he taught an adult Sunday school class while also participating as a member of the choir, which he does to this day.

But Doug Bennett's faith was not confined to sacred acts of devotion in a church building. Coach Bennett was a member of the community of Swansea serving on the town's volunteer fire department. He was a member of the American Legion Post 156 and the Lion's Club. As an educator and a coach, he was in the public eye and subject to scrutiny on many levels. Yet his reputation in the community is that of a man of integrity.

In a letter supporting Coach Bennett's nomination for the South Carolina High School Athletic Coaches Hall of Fame, Jim Moore, owner of Todd & Moore, a sporting goods store in Columbia, did not cite Bennett's outstanding coaching credentials but rather his character:

> "He is a fine Christian gentleman who walks his talk. Doug's character traits of truth, integrity, sound judgment, fairness, diligence, combined with unselfishness and his ability to work in harmony with others makes him an excellent nominee."

When one considers that our society envisions an energetic, dynamic speaker as the ideal personality most capable of influencing others, one question arises: What explains the far-reaching and powerful impact of the life of a humble, unassuming, mostly quiet gentleman? Two word-pictures from the Bible offer insight into this question. The first analogy portrays God as a potter and the believer as clay to be molded and shaped into an object with beauty and function. Isaiah 64:8 reads, "Yet Lord, You are our Father; we are the clay and You are the potter; we all are the work of Your hands" (Holman

Christian Standard Bible). Moreover, there is a relationship between the potter and what he has made: "You have turned things around as if the potter were the same as the clay. How can what is made say about its maker, 'He didn't make me'? How can what is formed say about the one who formed it, 'He doesn't understand what he's doing'?" (Isaiah 29:16, HCSB).

Eileen Weissner, an artist living in Lake Royale, North Carolina, whose mediums include writing, painting, and pottery, describes pottery making as a two-step creative process: preparation and shaping. During preparation, the potter selects the clay based upon the type of object she wants to create and upon its designed purpose. If the end-product is to be an object of beauty, she chooses porcelain clay. If a more functional dinner plate is the goal, then stoneware clay is selected.

The "wedging" phase of preparation resembles the kneading of dough in breadmaking, but it is more difficult and lengthy. It is essential that the clay selected be wedged until consistency is achieved, resulting in a fully pliable and moldable raw art form. Says Weissner, "If not done properly and thoroughly, the results will be disastrous."

The shaping phase is done on the potter's wheel. During this stage, the potter focuses on nurturing the clay - painstakingly shaping and manipulating the clay to enable it to become the vessel it is destined to be. To this end, the potter applies appropriate pressure to the clay at the proper time necessary for shaping it to the original design. Throughout the entire shaping phase, the object's ultimate purpose is foremost in the potter's mind. For the clay to become what it is destined to be, an intuitive feel for how to work with the clay is required. If the design is for a bowl, then it must not be too small; if a mug is the goal, then it must not be too big. From time to time, the potter has to reshape the clay or make corrections. However, if the clay is "uncooperative" or nonresponsive, the potter then is forced to change the original design.

The second illustration focuses on the design and purpose for the potter's creation. Notice that the clay vessel cannot create itself; it must be shaped by the potter. Further, this process takes time - it cannot be rushed. From the onset, the potter has a specific design and purpose for each piece of clay. Her designs are as varied as her creativity allows; yet each vessel has characteristics common to the potter's other creations.

Upon meeting Doug Bennett, most people would not identify him as someone who most assuredly would wield influence over others. Long-time Bennett assistant Steve Carter has described his head coach as "the humblest man I have ever met." Humility is defined, in part, by Webster as "not arrogant or prideful; showing deferential or submissive respect." Showing "deferential or submissive respect" does not exactly call to mind an aggressive "shaker and mover." Rather, one thinks of someone who is aware of the "otherness of people," one who understands that they are not to be used or manipulated for his purposes. A humble person treats others with dignity and respect. He understands that he is, like others, simply a created vessel, designed for a specific purpose not of his own choosing. Most appropriately, he is not as concerned about "making things happen" as he is about being the right type of vessel.

These vessels, jars of clay shaped by the potter, are personified such that they "understand" that the potter who made them has entrusted them with a treasure that is not of their own making or from their own resources. They are humble and yielded to the purpose of their creator: "Now we have this treasure in clay jars, so that this extraordinary power may be from God and not from us" (2 Corinthians 4:7).

In his devotional classic, *My Utmost for His Highest*, Oswald Chambers observes,"We always know when Jesus is at work because He produces in the commonplace something that is inspiring." Darlene English, a fellow 1974 graduate, describes Doug Bennett's influence in terms of his common, everyday demeanor and conduct: "He really had a great sense of humor and understood high school kids much more than the average adult. Coach B led by example, rather than lectures. He didn't demand respect from students; rather he earned their respect through his actions."

One simple habit of Doug Bennett accounts, to a large degree, for the source of his wisdom and humility. While I was playing football at Furman University, I accompanied the Swansea team to their preseason camp held at Winthrop University in Rock Hill before reporting for the start of Furman's workouts the next week. After a day filled with two practice sessions, meetings, and meals, the players and coaches retired to their dorm rooms. I was sharing a room with Coach Bennett. While I was preparing for lights out, I happened to catch a quick view of Coach on the other side of a desk with a tall built-in bookcase. On his bed, in boxer shorts and a T-shirt, Doug Bennett sat with his open Bible in his lap, reading a passage of scripture. I am sure he did not know I had seen him.

His mother had given him a New Testament when he was called up for duty in World War II. "Read your Bible daily and say your prayers every night..." she had told the eighteen-year-old. Apparently, he had taken her advice to heart and formed a habit over the years that had proven to be a source of strength and direction. It is a snapshot that is indelibly fixed in my mind.

In consideration of the spiritual impact of Doug Bennett at Swansea High School, one former student wrote, "By personal example he has taught three generations of Tigers that life really begins beyond the goalposts." Former player Terry Pound notes, "His friends remember him first and foremost as a person who provided a role model for them and for their children."

When asked to describe Doug Bennett in one word, five of his former assistant coaches replied, "Christian" or "Christ-like." Doug Bennett "walked the talk," and he did so without fanfare or false modesty. He was positive about life and consistent in his actions. As Bob Novinger, a former assistant, notes, "The positive Christian influence Coach Bennett had on his players and coaches cannot be measured."

ECHOES IN ETERNITY

"EVERYDAY LIFE MUST BE LIVED OUT AGAINST THE BACKDROP OF ETERNITY...."
TIM KIMMEL

In the coaching of any sport and at all levels of competition, there are "ME" coaches whose world revolves around themselves. While they may tell themselves that they are in coaching "for the kids," when it all boils down, it's all about themselves - it's "my team," "I'm in charge," and "My way or the highway." Some of these coaches, when they put a whistle around their neck, behave as though they have transformed into a deity - all-knowing, all-powerful, and unequivocally in control of their own little universe.

And then there are the "we" coaches. And if you ever had the privilege of playing for a "we" coach, especially if you ever had a "ME" coach, you understand the stark contrast. You appreciate how much more enjoyable it is to be on a team with a "we" coach at the helm.

One difference between these two types of coaches is that of their values. A "ME" coach is willing to live only for the present, what he can build for himself. The "ME" coach somehow convinces himself that his players cannot see through his selfish ambition and motivation. The "we" coach's focus, in contrast, is on how he might influence others for their good.

David Cutcliffe, head football coach at Duke University, was influenced by his own high school coach, the legendary George "Shorty" White. Coach White, one of the winningest high school football coaches in the state of Alabama, and indeed, in the country, coached in the first integrated game in Birmingham against Parker High School in 1969. His 1972 and 1973 teams at Banks High School won back-to-back state championships, two of his three state titles.

But White was concerned about more than winning football games. David White (no relation), author of a biography on Coach White, declares: "He's a man of character and discipline. He won a lot of football games, no doubt, but he did it the right way." Cutcliffe remembers: "You weren't around Coach White without being influenced by him. Everything mattered to him. But he communicated really well what mattered most."

When Cutcliffe became a head high school football coach in Alabama, he had a veteran coach share two principles of success in coaching in high school: "There's no bigger fool on earth than he who thinks he can fool a young person." and "Don't take winning and losing personally. It's not about you. You are their coach. It's about them."

Cutcliffe points out that because of the size of their squads, football coaches are uniquely positioned to have a far-reaching impact on a greater number of people:

> "You have to get the most out of the average athlete more than in any other sport. As a high school football coach you are teaching more people how

> to achieve, how to get the most out of their body, mind, and soul if you will. The power of influence of a high school coach can be so strong that at times, if things are not right in the family dynamic, that what he says actually becomes more gospel than what they are hearing elsewhere. I don't think that you can connect any better with young people at a very influential age than as a high school football coach."

> Cutcliffe says today that "the biggest thing I've carried from my era as a high school coach is to understand our purpose, why we are coaching. We are mentoring. We are going to influence these players for the rest of their lives."

* * * * * *

"He has planted eternity in the human heart." (Ecclesiastes 3:11)

The author of Ecclesiastes tells us that, as humans, we have a capacity for understanding that this life is not all there is: there is more. While being interviewed by the CBS news magazine *Sixty* Minutes, Tom Brady, quarterback of the NFL's New England Patriots at the time, made a profound observation about his life:

> "Why do I have three Super Bowl rings and still think there's something greater out there for me? I mean, maybe a lot of people out there would say, 'Hey, man, this is what it is.' I reached my goal, my dream, my life. I think, 'God, it's got to be more

> than this. I mean, this can't be what it's all cracked up to be....' I love playing football, and I love being the quarterback for this team. But at the same time, I think there are a lot of other parts of me that I'm trying to find."

When asked by the interviewer, "What's the answer?" Brady replied, "I wish I knew, I wish I knew."

Our actions in this life can have some impact or bearing on eternity. That awareness ascribes far more significance and value to what we choose to do and how we conduct ourselves. People in leadership positions have a responsibility to those whom they serve. "Leadership is not about being in charge, it's about taking care of the people in your charge," says Simon Sinek.

For thirty-six years, players and assistant coaches at Swansea High School were blessed to have had the opportunity and honor of competing with and for an ultimate "we" coach. Generations of athletes and students were the beneficiaries of his positive coaching and teaching. Doug Bennett had become a coach with the conviction that by conducting his life in this manner he might "make a difference." By choosing to be a "we" coach, indeed he did.

From my vantage point, Doug Bennett displayed strength, dignity, and humility during three significant moments in my life: the 1968 desegregation of Lexington County District Four schools, his intervention in my troubled life as an eighth grader, and once again, over forty years later, at my dad's funeral in December of 2012. Each incident evidenced my coach's awareness of the eternal as a "we" coach; each had a powerful impact in my life.

In these specific incidents and throughout his life, Doug Bennett displayed a goodness like that described by historian Stephen Ambrose:

> "The qualities of goodness in a man, I believe, include a broad sympathy for the human condition, that is, an awareness of human weakness and shortcomings and a willingness to be forgiving of them, a sense of responsibility toward others, a genuine modesty combined with a justified self-confidence, a sense of humor, and most of all a love of life and of people."[1]

In August of 1968, a court order mandated that the Lexington District Four schools be desegregated and that Swansea High School and the "separate but equal" Monroe Pinkney High School be consolidated into the previously whites-only facility on First Street. This educational merger produced considerable unrest as a majority of white families with school-aged children staunchly opposed the move. Very few white football players attended practices for a few weeks since their parents had pulled them out of class and they were ineligible to participate during the nine-day boycott.

Bennett's 1968 Tigers finished the season 1-9, the worst record of his career. The next year, the Tigers opened the season with four losses before winning the last six to finish 6-4. In 1970 as a freshman tight end on the junior varsity team, I traveled and dressed out with the varsity during the playoffs. I watched in amazement as Swansea High School, in its third season after a tumultuous desegregation, competed for the state championship. Even the heartbreaking loss to Blackville could not dampen the optimistic spirit that had emerged in a divided community.

No one was more equipped for these tense years than the highly skilled but unassuming World War II veteran. Doug Bennett, who had come to Swansea in 1954 to coach and teach, was made for the day of trouble. It is a tired cliché that "adversity builds character." More accurately, tough times reveal one's true character. Fortified with a humble Christian faith and strong convictions about racial equality and justice, Doug Bennett's character was refined by trial. He emerged from this crucible with his integrity intact and his moral principles nonnegotiable.

Throughout this ordeal he displayed a dignity and grace that appeared almost supernatural. What made such an impression on me was that he was fair with everybody. It didn't matter what their socioeconomic background or their race was. He treated every person with dignity and respect. In the process, he won the respect of the twelve-year-old manager of his '68 team and the admiration of hundreds more on both sides of this disturbing racial divide.

Another incident that opens a window into the nature of Doug Bennett's impact on me and countless others occurred when I was still in junior high. In the eighth grade, I was disciplined for a foolish violation. Ashamed of what I had done, I was even more shaken that I had deeply disappointed Coach Bennett, who only recently had taken on the dual responsibility of principal of the high school and junior high in addition to his coaching duties.

On the appointed day of reckoning, I was summoned to the principal's office to face the music for my offense. I watched nervously as the man I so admired reached into his desk and withdrew his disciplinary weapon of choice, a two-foot paddle that I'm sure had been built to Coach's exact specifications by E. F. Hoover, the school's Vo-Tech director. Finely sanded and stained with a deep rich walnut finish, the instrument had been drilled through several times with a three-eighths-inch bit to reduce drag and to render it aerodynamically efficient.

Before his first swing, Coach, - excuse me, Principal Bennett - told me how disappointed he was in me, and he expressed his concern that I never do anything that foolish and harmful again. Those words stung me far worse than any paddle ever could. Before he commenced, he uttered the dreaded "this hurts me more than it's going to hurt you" invocation. With one last glance at the paddle, I braced for the last full measure of discipline. Yet, with all due respect, I was skeptical that *his* pain would exceed *mine.*

Although he stood only a few inches above five feet tall and weighed less than a hundred and sixty pounds, Doug Bennett could "bring it." I don't recall how many licks I got, but they found their mark externally and more importantly, internally. Afterwards, there was something about his calm demeanor that I found oddly reassuring. It was over; it was time to move forward.

A third impactful event illustrating Coach Bennett's influence occurred during my dad's funeral on December 21, 2012. In what many may perceive as an odd twist of fate, the minister who presided over my dad's funeral as an ex-football player from Swansea High, a tough fullback from the 1969 team, Gene Rowell. Although I had not seen Reverend Rowell in nearly fifty years, a story from his days as a Swansea player came to mind:

I recalled that Reverend Rowell and another Tiger-turned-minister, Robert Jumper, masterminded a plot to request that I, as a manager, fetch them a "jock stretcher" before practice one day. Eager to please, I took a few quick steps from the equipment room door toward the storage room just before uncontrolled laughter pierced the pungent odor of a steamy locker room filled with high school boys. Doubled over in hilarity at their clever request, the future ministers conceded that if no jock stretcher were available, a "knee brace stretcher" would suffice.

In contrast to some of the fun times of locker room culture, in this sacred and yet everyday moment, as he had been at so many critical junctures in my life, Doug Bennett was there with his gracious wife, Jane. His respect, his reverence, and kind words helped my dad's sister, Sue Stanford - one of Coach's former girls' basketball players on his 1954 team - and me through a tough day as we received family and friends before the service. Reverend Rowell represented his former coach and teammates well. His carefully crafted words left no doubt in my mind about where my dad, a member of his congregation, would spend eternity.

When I read the obituary that my dad had composed in advance of this day, I marveled at how the same accomplished Army officer who carried the American flag in Eisenhower's inauguration, the man who would later serve as Lexington County's Civil Defense Director, (one of the first in the nation in the wake of the Cuban Missile Crisis), a former Airborne Ranger and paratrooper with the 101st Airborne Division, and retired Lieutenant Colonel U.S. Army Reserve could come to the end of his life virtually unknown by his son and his grandsons.

Sadly, my dad and I were never close emotionally. My sons missed out on having a grandad involved in their lives. And although Doug Bennett was a father-figure in my life, he would never be so presumptuous as to behave as though he was more of a father to me than my dad. That void could only be filled by the man whom Doug Bennett had come to honor - a fellow Christian, a US Army veteran like himself, and most of all, a fellow father. Coach's grace, humility, and respect were a quiet display of his inward depth.

I will probably go to my grave without accomplishing many of the amazing things my dad did. He was an Airborne Ranger! My boys would have loved his stories. Before whatever events or choices amputated his spirit, my dad was one of our nation's finest soldiers. And Coach Bennett was there that day to show his respect and offer his condolences.

I mistakenly thought that the last time Doug Bennett had coached me was in the East/West All-Star game in July of 1974 in Williams-Brice Stadium in Columbia. But with humility and respect he was honoring my dad on this day. He was still coaching me, forty years later, by his example. How could I do anything less than honor my dad as well?

* * * * * *

When you think of Douglas McDowell Bennett, remember the humble soldier who, along with his five brothers, proudly served his country in WWII. Remember the reticent but bold champion of justice and racial equality who, in his own mind, was just a coach trying to do the right thing without any fuss. Remember the caring teacher and professional educator who, like his medic brother in Europe, cared for many a wounded soul. Remember the man who, though he measured only a few inches above five feet, stood like a giant among his peers. But more than anything else, remember the humble Christian husband and father, this marvelous man whose life will one day "echo in eternity."

ENDNOTES

The Wonder Years

1. Nancy Sambets, "Circus Days in York: Bennett Brothers Circus",1.
2. Ibid., 2.
3. Ibid., 1.
4. Ibid., 1.
5. Ibid., 2.
6. footballencyclopedia.com, December 10, 2008.

Band of Brothers

1. Rick Atkinson, *An Army at Dawn: The War in North Africa,* (New York: Henry Holt and Company, 2004) 4.
2. Brian Curtis, *Fields of Battle,* (New York: Flatiron Books, 2016), 53.
3. Ibid., 8.
4. Ibid., 140.
5. Ernie Pyle, *Brave Men,* (New York: Gossett & Dunlap, 1954), 162.

Unintended Consequences

1. Skylar Rolstad, Fleet Football: Former Player Reflects on Old Erskine Team, Index-Journal .com, May 15, 2020,

https/www.indexjournal/sports/fleet-football-former player-reflects-on-old-erskine-team/article- a3b1-4042-0e87-52ab-9604-ac989-1a89-91.html.

2. Ibid.

Desegregation of Swansea High School and Lexington County District IV

1. William Bagwell, *School Desegregation in the Carolinas: Two Case Studies,* (Columbia: University of South Carolina Press, 1972), 5.
2. Stephen O'Neill, "Freedom of Choice, Grace and Style, and Other Misnomers in Greenville's Ordeal of School Desegregation," in *In Search of a Better South: Essays in Honor of Paul Gaston* (Montgomery: New South Books, 2015), May 22, 2015, 7.
3. Paul Wesley McNeil, "School Desegregation in South Carolina" PhD diss., (University of Kentucky, 1979), 3.
4. O'Neill, 6.
5. *Southern School News*, (July,1964), 6.
6. *Southern School News*, (November,1965), 1.
7. O'Neill, 5.
8. *Southern School News*, (November,1964), 1.
9. Ibid., 1.
10. *Southern School News,* (September,1963), 1.
11. "Interview with the Honorable Matthew J. Perry, Jr., "*South Carolina Political Collections Oral History Project,* (Columbia: University of South Carolina*),* 88.
12. O'Neill, 11.
13. Ibid., 8.
14. McNeill, 9.
15. Ibid., 9.

16. "Integration of College Athletics," *Encyclopedia of College Athletics,* 25.
17. Steven Travers, *One Night, Two Teams: Alabama vs. USC and the Games That Changed a Nation,* (Lanham: Taylor Trade Publishing, 2007), 115.

We Have a Dream

1. Charles H. Martin, "Integration of College Athletics, Encyclopedia of Alabama, September 2, 1968 http://encyclopediaofalabama.org/article/h-1968.
2. Dean Smith, John Kilgo and Sally Jenkins, *A Coach's Life: My Forty Years in College Basketball,* (New York; Random House, 2002), 2.
3. Martin, 2.

1974 State Championship

1. Mark Edmundson, *Why Football Matters* (New York: Penguin Books, 2014), 76-77.

Robert Maddox

*All quotations in this chapter are from a special limited souvenir edition of the *High School Sports Report, (Goose Creek: High School sports Report),* February 1995.

Echoes in Eternity

1. Stephen Ambrose, *Eisenhower: Soldier and President,* (New York: Simon & Schuster, 1990) 11.

SWANSEA HIGH SENIORS 1954-1989

Year by Fall Season

1954: 5-5

Paul Mack

Sherrell Jackson

Don Jeffcoat

* * * * * *

1955: 5-5

Reginald Jeffcoat

Fred Yon

Jimmy Pound

* * * * * *

1956: 10-0 District Champions

(*Ineligible for Playoffs due to Scheduling Error)

W.B. Adkins

C.L. Wise

Richard Lawson
Roger Rucker

* * * * * *

1957: 7-4 District Champion
J.W. Black
Bill Mack
Gaines Mason
Billy Wannamaker
James Wannamaker

* * * * * *

1958
Donnie Kirkland
Denzel Lawson
Steve Livingston
Larry Rucker
R.J. Rucker

* * * * * *

1959
Artie Lucas
Gene Ray Lloyd
Mickey Lowder
Jerry Mack
Eddie Spradley
Bruce Wannamaker
Marvin Williams

******

1960: 13-0 Class B State Champion

Clark Adkins
Johnny King
Alvin Chavis
Terry Pound
Arthur Chavis
Rollin Saylor
Davie Craft
Frank Hydrick
Larry Sturkie
Wayne Jumper

******

1961: 10-3 Class B State Championship Runner-up

Perry Adkins
Melvin Livingston
Ralph McGinnis
Troy Gunter
Benny Williams
Benny Shivers

******

1962: 9-1 Conference 5-B Runner-Up

Robbie Davis
Joe Phillips
Michael Fallaw
Phil Mack

Kary Hoffman
Larry Rucker
Charlie Jackson
Paul Lloyd

* * * * * *

1963: 6-5
Tommy Moore
Danny Woods
Martin Hutto
Tommy Craft
Tommy Wannamaker
Ernest Ellison
Sidney Livingston
Edward Reynolds
Johnny Lybrand
Kit Jackson
John Knight
Johnny Lybrand
Wayne Enlow

* * * * * *

1964: 2-9
Jody Pound
Tommy Williamson
Robert Ott
Gregg Riley
Eddie Jackson
Charles Rucker

Tommy Manuel
Leo Saylor

* * * * * *

1965: 9-2 Conference 5-B Champion
Tommy Dixon
Venson Williams
Dickie Martin
Warren Cope
Marshall Stabler
Tracy Chavis
Hampton Redmond
Paul Chavis
Lawrence Redmond

* * * * * *

1966: 5-6
Roddy Rucker
Ronald Bennett
Johnny Fogle
Tommy Goodwin
Buddy Wilson

* * * * * *

1967: 6-4
Larry Goff
Frankie Livingston
Curtis Goodwin

Steve Koon
Leonard "Skeebo" Smith
Tommy Bonds
Don Saylor
Robbie Lee Stabler
Fletcher Redmond
Glen Pound
Everette Berry

* * * * * *

1968: 1-9

Henry Dowd
Charlie Salley
John Gladden
Willie Wannamaker
Randy Jeffcoat
Nathaniel Williams
Michael McDaniels
Bill Wilson
Kevin Redd

* * * * * *

1969: 6-4

Gene Rowell
Robert Jumper
Joe Riley
Vernon Lee
Darbis Briggman

Samuel Colter
Jimmy Mack

* * * * * *

1970; 9-4 State Championship Runner-up

Jimmy Berry
Gene Redmond
John "Jimbo" Zeigler
Allen Jeffcoat
MacArthur Salley
Allen Lee
Tommy Williams

* * * * * *

1971: 2-8

Frankie Berry
Charles Pound
Hans Cheeks
Bruce Rucker
Michael Dixon
Stanley "Bobaby" Smith
Sammy Fogle
Tim Wilson
Tim Hart
Donnie Woolsey
Richard Lucas

* * * * * *

1972: 7-3

Jimmy Dibble

Charles Simmons

Lee Flake

Billy Smith

Gene Kyzer

Bubba Sturkie

David Rish

Bruce Taylor

Michael Salley

Willie Clay Williams

* * * * * *

1973: 8-2 Conference 5-A Runner-up

Elijah Edmond

Billy Mills

James Fields

Chris Sharpe

Jim Hutto

Brette Simmons

Carl Lybrand

Raymond Stoudemire

* * * * * *

1974: 11-3 Class A State Champion

Bobby Frederick

L.H. Peel

Clemon Furtick

Aaron Pinckney

Alton Harley
David Wayne Pinckney
Buddy Harley
Ricky Sturkie
Otis Lykes
Tommy Wilson

* * * * * *

1975: 14-0 Class A State Champion

Dennie Davis
Stevie Raulerson
Joe Davis
Lonnie Simmons
Walter Davis
David Streeter
Bernard Fields
Stanley Sutton
Elvin Jeffcoat
Ray Whitaker
Hozell Mills
Andy Williams
David Peel
Gregory Williams
Stanley Raulerson

* * * * * *

1976: 10-2 Conference 5-AA Champion

Charles Crum
Jimmy Smith

John Davis
Marty Wise
Stanley Sutton
Calvin Mack
Andra Sutton

* * * * * *

1977: 9-3 Conference 5-AA Champion
Johnny Huggins
Macy Washington
John Petrey
James Sutton
Roger Williams
Kurt Woodruff

* * * * * *

1978: 8-3 Conference 5-AA Champion
Bill Adkins
Wardell Mack
Mark English
Robert Maddox
Lee Etheridge
Johnny Raulerson
Kenneth Fields
Kenneth "Jimbo" Raulerson
Rhett Flake
John Riley
Terry Gaffney
Allen Rish

Yancy Heyward
Jerry Spires
Skip Jackson
Robert Taylor
Joseph Jupiter

* * * * * *

1979: 8-5 Lower State Runner-up
Charles Bookman
Faron Mangum
Mac Copeland
Jamie Matthews
Tommie Mack Granger
Tommy McIver
Eric Jeffcoat
Bernard Porterfield
Norman Lloyd
Michael Robinson
Reginald Davis
Dean Sturkie
Milton Fields
Joseph Wannamaker
Anthony Goodwin
Willie Washington
Ricky Lykes
John Sease
Jimmy Sharpe
Glenn Zeigler

* * * * * *

1980: 11-2 Class AA State Championship Runner-up

James Brown
David Myers
Silas Brown
David Rucker
Stevie Dibble
David Smith
Leroy Jackson
Ronnie Sturkie
Frankie Jumper
Troy Sturkie
Troy Jumper
Thomas Struckman
Alfred Mack
Andrew Walker
Barnell Mack
Matt Williams
Evan Mack
Laymond Zeigler

* * * * * *

1981: 11-1Conference 5-AA Champion

Charlie Brooks
Arthur Meyers
Clyde Dibble
Rusty Nance
Carson Dixon
Richard Pinkney
Greg Ellisor
Tommie Radford

Carlisle Fields
Paul Raulerson
Eddie Hamm
Andrew Riley
Bob Hawsey
Willie Riley
Kenny Hoffman
Lyndon Smith
Kipp Jackson
Prince Smith
Tyronne Jeffcoat
Willie Smith
Jamie Knight
Carlisle Sharpe
Brent Kohn
Curtis Wise
Alfonzo Lykes

* * * * * *

1982: 10-3 Lower-State Runner-up

David Colter
Gary Couillard
Tommy Dease
Adriano Filho
Sam Hallman
Franklin Hillis
Michael Lykes
Warren Lykes
Robert Peele
Elliot Richardson

Alvin Riley
Doug Riley
Sammy Smith
Greg Summers

* * * * * *

1983: 4-6
Gerold Ellsworth
Marcus Porterfield
Jesse Favor
Cecil Purvis
Rusty Gunter
Julius Riley
Michael Golson
Thomas Sharpe
Von Hall
Rodney Whiddon
Jonathan Hook
Lydell Zeigler
Andy Knight
Thomas Hampton

* * * * * *

1984: 4-6
Jackie Burns
James Padgett
Ronnie Dasher
Kenneth Riley
L.C. Jeffcoat

Billy Rucker
Wayne Johnson
Terry Zeigler
Dwayne Lykes

* * * * * *

1985: 7-3
Eugene Favor
Jon Hill
Victor Jeffcoat
Tony Rowell
Tommy Smith
Tyler Spinner
Marvin Sutton

* * * * * *

1986: 6-4
Lee Black
Greg Jeffcoat
Jerome Bonnette
Marvin Jeffcoat
Tommy Corley
Billy Johnson
Steven Hallman
Trent Prevatte
Donnell Isenhoward
Bryan Sharpe
Michael Jackson
Roslin Walker

******

1987: 4-6

Stephen Bolin
Wilson Lloyd
Henry Briggman
Fred Metz
Steven Bryan
Jim Rucker
Keith Gunter
James Spires
Peter Gunter
Stephen Sutton

******

1988: 4-7

Deaton Aiken
Ryan Mosier
Bill Berry
Rusty Sharpe
Bryan Corley
McGarrett Simmons
J.W. Jackson
Darryl Williams

******

1989: 3-8

Scott Asbill
Hamp Redmond

Barrett Black
Will Reynolds
Jason Lucas
Doug Robbins
David Jeffcoat
Kevin Simmons
Michael Jeffcoat
Tim Sulier
Travis Novinger
Willie Wannamaker

DOUG BENNETT IN ONE WORD

"Dedicated" - Scott Shull, student assistant trainer
"Humble: - Steve Carter, former assistant coach
"Excellence" - Diane Brady, student
"Christlike" - Susan Bennett, daughter
"Genuine" – Claudette Lucas, Student
"Inspirational" - Kurt Woodruff, former player
"Unselfish" - Jane Livingston, cheerleader
"Integrity" - Gene Redmond, former player
"Smiling" - Dennis Wilson, former player
"Trailblazer" – Joseph Jupiter, former player
"Soulful" – Dedra Fox Isenbarger, cheerleader
"Godly" - Bob Novinger, former assistant coach
"Leader" - Charlotte Knight Shull, student
"Kind" - Becky Jeffcoat, student
"Christian" - Donnie Woolsey, former player and assistant coach
"Exemplary" - Renee Bryant, student
"Servant" – Jane Ann Bennett Meredith, daughter and former player
"Persevering" - Randy Craft, former player
"Selfless" – Glenda Shannon Davis, student
"Spectacular" – Diann Jeffcoat Shepard
"Faithful" - Linda Flake, cheerleader
"Encourager" - Coralie Sharpe, student

"Patience" - Mary Corley, student
"Committed" - Robert Sharpe, nephew, former player
"Leadership" - Dedra Smith Isenbarger, cheerleader
"Inspiring" - Ricky Sturkie, former player
"Visionary" – Susan Lance Pittman, student
"Motivator" - Tammy Caudill, student and neighbor
"Consistent" - Angie Michelle Jones, former softball player
"Patriarch" – Donna Smith, student
"Noble" – Wanda Timmons Powell, student
"Legacy" - Paul Raulerson, former player
"Virtuous" – Fred Orr, former assistant coach
"Principled" – Margaret Livingston Levine, cheerleader
"Prayerful" - Tyler Spinner, former player
"Character" – Charlotte Knight Shull, student
"Committed" - Beth Cassidy Sadowski, former player
"Empathy" – Jane Livingston, cheerleader
"Indescribable" - Chad Meredith, son-in-law

DOUG BENNETT HONORS AND AWARDS

"Few persons have better exemplified the high ideals for which Erskine College stands nor the value of the Erskine athletic program. Doug Bennett brings honor to the Flying Fleet Hall-of-Fame."

Dick Haldeman, Public Relations Director,
Erskine College (1961-1995)

- Record of 265 wins, 140 losses, and 6 ties at Swansea High School
- Four District Championships
- Five Conference Championships
- Three State Runner-Ups - 1961, 1970, and 1980
- Southeastern Coach of the Year - representing eight states
- Columbia Area Coach of the Year
- State-Record Coach of the Year three consecutive years
- Head Coach and Assistant Coach in the SCACA All-Star Game
- Head Coach and Assistant Coach in the Shrine Bowl
- Swansea High School football stadium named in his honor
- Inducted into the South Carolina Athletic Coaches Association Hall of Fame

- Inducted into South Carolina Football Coaches Association Hall-of-Fame
- Inducted into the Erskine College Athletic Hall-of-Fame
- Inducted into York County (South Carolina) Sports Hall of Fame
- Received the Order of the Palmetto, the highest honor given to a private citizen of South Carolina
- Participant in Honor Flight Network that honors WWII veterans with a round-trip flight to Washington, DC, where ceremonies recognize veterans for their sacrifice and service to their country

Tragically, four members of the 1978-1979 class (pictured on the right) all left this world far too soon- the youngest 38 and the oldest 52.

Left to Right: Bill Adkins, Mark English

Lee Etheredge, Rhett Flake

LARRY RUCKER

One of the most devastating losses in Doug Bennett's career has nothing to do with a scoreboard. On November 12, 1966, Larry Rucker, a former Swansea player who went on to play end at the University of South Carolina, was the copilot of the Air Force Constellation radar plane that suddenly crashed into the Atlantic off the coast of Cape Cod. The twenty-five-year old Rucker, a member of the 961st Airborne Early Warning and Control Squadron, was one of nineteen men aboard. Fishermen in the area said they saw no parachutes as the plane plummeted into the fog-shrouded sea.

The Air Force immediately dispatched planes into the area. Coast Guard planes and surface craft, as well as other boats in the area including a Navy rescue ship, joined in the search for the missing plane. Debris found in the area was identified as parts of the missing plane. Rescue efforts, however, were hampered by blinding rain squalls. No signs of survivors - or bodies - were found.

To honor the memory of his former player, Doug Bennett and Swansea High School established the Larry Rucker Memorial Award, given each year to a member of the football team who demonstrates outstanding leadership and character.

MR. BENNETT GOES TO WASHINGTON

The Honor Flight Network is a nonprofit organization dedicated to providing veterans with honor and closure by transporting them to Washington, D.C., free-of-charge, to visit memorials dedicated to honor their sacrifices and those of friends. With 130 flight hubs in forty-five states across the country, the Honor Flight Network operates with a sense of urgency as approximately 640 World War II veterans die each day.

On September 5, 2009, Doug Bennett took advantage of the opportunity to make the flight to Washington. Arrangements for Coach Bennett's flight were made by Terry Pound, a member of his 1960 state championship team who served as the Columbia Operations Manager for the organization and coordinated all phases of the flights to and from Washington. With a departure from Columbia and arrival at Reagan Airport, the itinerary includes visits to the WWII Memorial, a tour of Washington, visits to the Korean, Vietnam, and Lincoln memorials before a trip to Arlington National Cemetery and the Tomb of the Unknown Soldier where veterans witness the Changing of the Guard. Hundreds of volunteers work together to ensure that these veterans receive rousing send-offs and receptions at each stop along the way.

ABOUT THE AUTHOR

An All-Conference and All State performer for Doug Bennett's Swansea (SC) Tigers as a tight end and linebacker, Brette Simmons signed a football scholarship with Furman University in 1974. At Furman, he was a two-time All-Conference selection at tight end; he was also named to the Southern Conference's All Academic teams in 1977 and 1978. Simmons graduated cum laude with a B.A in English and remained at Furman as a graduate assistant coach on Dick Sheridan's staff.

After serving for six years in campus ministry at the University of Tennessee, in 1987, Simmons rejoined Sheridan's staff at N. C. State where he served as a graduate assistant coach (1987-1988) and then as Recruiting Coordinator (1989-1992.) When Sheridan resigned for health reasons in 1993, he was named an assistant coach on new head coach Mike's O'Cain's staff 1993-1999.

Over the past twenty years Simmons has worked in sales and customer service. He currently lives in Lake Royale, North Carolina where he is pursuing a final career as a writer and public speaker. "Man in the Gap" is his first book.

Contact Brette: brettesimmons85@gmail.com;
@brette_simmons; Brette Simmons on Facebook/Messenger

CPSIA information can be obtained
at www.ICGtesting.com
Printed in the USA
LVHW081044120521
687195LV00015B/375/J

9 781641 116817